The Escapades of
Frank and Jesse James

The Escapades of Frank and Jesse James

by

CARL W. BREIHAN

A World of Books That Fill a Need

FREDERICK FELL PUBLISHERS, INC.

New York

For information address:
Frederick Fell Publishers, Inc.
386 Park Avenue South
New York, N.Y. 10016

Library of Congress Catalog Card No. 73-90513

Published simultaneously in Canada by
George J. McLeod, Limited, Toronto 2B, Ontario

Manufactured in the United States of America

International Standard Book Number 0-8119-0228-5

CONTENTS

DEDICATION

THIS BOOK IS DEDICATED TO THE MANY SINCERE AND FAITHFUL people who assisted in the work by sending me notes, photos, rare bits of information, incidents of little note, and by hundreds of other favors. I mention a few here, and if anyone has been missed, believe me, it is unintentional:

Charles Bragin, George Ullman, Wayne Walker, Kerry Ross Boren, Lester Fried, Wilbur Zink, Rick Lee Mach, Bill Pullen, Bob Mullen, Grif Lingenfelder, Tom Smith, Lulu May Courtright Hart, Julio Zagamini, Bill Green, Ed Bartholomew, Squire J. Winston-Coleman, Jr., Will Henry, Ed Gilson, Fred Hollander, Buford Jolly, Johnny Houska, Edward LeBlanc, Harold Preece, Gerry Vonder Haar, Fred Weber, Wayne Gard, Lauren Paine, Stacy Osgood, Luke Jones, Tom Pollard, Ron Costley, Jim Pope, Fr. Stanley, Bill Willard, Members of the Concord Lions Club, Mike Slay, C. T. Thomas, Charles Rosamond, Charles Mason, Leonard Saxon, Bill Stigers, Noah Rose, Helen Dortch Longstreet, Uncle Charlie Bell, A. L. Maxwell, Leonard Sanker, Joe Barbagallo, Lyle Bouck, Jr., Stella

James, Gary Williams, Lou Beuer, Gregg Gundlach, Jack Toohey, Frank Hellwig, Bob Frank, John Muir, Rick Huesling.

My thanks also to *Real West Magazine,* in which many of my articles appeared.

Carl W. Breihan
4939 Mattis Road
St. Louis, Missouri 63128

INTRODUCTION

1866–1882. A LONG TIME TO BE ALWAYS ON THE RUN FROM THE law. Not even Al Capone or John Dillinger in this century came close to this fantastic record. Yet two men of the last century made history for sixteen years moving over the Midwest with a black hand. They were Jesse and Frank James.

The full story of the private lives of Jesse and Frank James may never be known. There are too many gaps in time and place which prevent historians from piecing together all the facts. However, one man has come up with much new information on the subject, and he is the author of this book.

When asked to write an article on these two infamous outlaws of the West, I wondered what I could contribute to the history of the James boys that had not already been written. Much of the information we have today on Jesse and Frank James has been gleaned from John Edwards' work, *Noted Guerrillas,* first published in 1877. Then came books by Dacus, Buel, and Love, three great writers among many of that period. Nowadays they all trail a gent by the name of Breihan.

It was in the early 1950s that my hobby of collecting data on the James brothers turned into more or less of a science (taking much of my time). In the mid-50s I became close friends with the late William Samuel Lincoln, a cousin of our sixteenth President and friend of the Missouri James family. During our long friendship Mr. Lincoln had on one occasion given me an unpublished song written about Jesse and Frank James. We all recall:

> The dirty little coward
> Who shot Mr. Howard
> And laid poor Jesse in his grave.

But the following was lost to history over the years. Now, thanks to Mr. Lincoln, we can share a small piece of James history in this ballad published here for the first time:

> Oh, the people will forget a lot of names,
> But in every nook and corner they knew of Jesse James.
> The people used to read about him on a home-set night.
> When the wind blew down the chimney they would
> shake with fright.
>
> Oh, the people knew him all over the land.
> He was known from Seattle into Birmingham
> Clean across every state
> From Denver to the Golden Gate.
>
> Oh, Jesse said, "Some corn we need,"
> So he polished up his rifle.
> He put his trust in Steve his horse
> And galloped over to brother Frank's.
> To Frank he said, "We've got to get some money
> From the Platte City Bank."
>
> Oh, they rode into town at ten o'clock.
> The cashier of the bank got an awful shock.

Jesse kept him covered with his .44
While brother Frank took a half-million dollars or more.

Oh, Jesse was in his home alone.
His wife had left him there to clean some corn.
He was scrubbing in the kitchen
When at the front door someone started to bang.
In came four members of his outlaw gang.
Oh, Jesse turned to Bob Ford and said,
"Tonight we make a haul at ten.
We'll rob the Western Mail run."

Jesse reached up to take his rifle down,
And it was then a picture came tumbling down.
Jesse stooped to pick it up,
And Ford put a bullet through his head.
The news went around the country:
Jesse James was dead.

The next week on his tomb some verses did rhyme:
If you want to be a rounder, stay a single man,
For we all know Jesse would not have lost his life
If it hadn't been for that picture of his darling wife.

1957 R. L. Mack.

Although historically incorrect throughout, the song was sung for some time after Jesse's autistic demise.

And now, I suggest you grab your saddle horn and hold on—because Carl Breihan (he has this knack) is about to take you back to the days when a six-shooter was six times as handy as a single shot. You are about to RIDE with Frank and Jesse James!

—*Rick Lee Mack*

WHILE MANY THOUSANDS OF WORDS HAVE BEEN WRITTEN ABOUT the famous or infamous James boys, Frank and Jesse, we feel it is high time that a detailed accounting of the crimes in which they may have participated be told so that the reader may finally get a real appreciation of these escapades.

So many new events have taken place that it is difficult to uncover all of these incidents. There is one of which little is known—the attempted robbery of the First National Bank of Monticello, Wayne County, Kentucky, which occurred in 1876 or 1877. Even the history of the State of Kentucky does not contain the actual date. Anyway, shortly after the bank opened for business one day, the "James gang" rode into town, and one of the members of the gang sauntered into the bank. They were just about to pull their guns with obvious intentions when one of them spotted a group of armed men coming down the street. Thinking it was a posse out to capture them, he called to his partner, "Let's get out of here. We're surrounded!"

They bolted from the bank, mounted, and rode out of town in great haste. Actually, the "posse" was a group of duck hunters carrying shotguns, just returning from an early morning hunt.

An interesting note concerning Jesse refers to one day in a small Missouri town when he rode up to the watering trough, allowed his horse to drink, and then took a drink from the trough himself. Some bystanders snickered at this, and Jesse remarked, "Well, I'd rather drink after a horse than after some people I know. I can always trust a horse."

There seems to be an eternal mystery surrounding the robbery of the Bank of Columbia, Kentucky, sometimes referred to as the Kentucky Deposit Bank. Various descriptions identified the five strangers as Frank and Jesse James with Cole, Jim, and Bob Younger. Official evidence of the crime lies in an indictment for murder against John Warren (alias John James), John Younger (alias John Wilson), William Younger (alias William Wilson), Thomas Jenkins, and William Willoughby (alias Thomas Wilson) returned by the Grand Jury of Adair County on August 30, 1872. Sounds more like the "Wilson gang."

At any rate, at each term of the circuit court, bench warrants for the arrest of five men and summons of the witnesses were issued, but at the October term in 1877 the indictment was ordered filed away with leave to reinstate.

However, most official reports seem to agree that what happened was as follows: On the morning of April 29, 1872, five strangers rode up to the bank building. Three of them dismounted and entered. One report says that the five horsemen rode abreast down Burkesville Street, and at the intersection of Frazer Avenue two of them rode ahead, turned into Jefferson Alley where they dismounted, hitched their horses, and entered the bank.

April 29 was a nice spring day, and in agricultural Adair County the farmers were at work. Not many people were in the Bank of Columbia during the morning. At noon, while most of the business houses closed as usual, four men gathered in front of the fireplace in the bank room just off the square on Burkesville Street. They were R.

A. C. Martin, the cashier, who had come from Shelbyville to make his home in Columbia when the bank opened in 1866; James Garnett, lawyer and bank director; James Thomas Page, circuit clerk; and Thomas Claburn Winfrey, an Adair County lawyer.

While they talked, William H. Hudson, businessman, entered the bank. Mr. Hudson, who lived at the edge of town, had eaten his noon meal early, preparatory to this trip to town. A man representing himself as a cattle buyer had come to the Hudson home at about eleven o'clock and had accepted their invitation to eat lunch with them. After the meal, Mr. Hudson excused himself, saying he had business in town.

Outside the bank the robbers began firing and shooting at every movement they saw. Inside the bank, Mr. Hudson recognized one of the men as his late dinner guest. The men in the bank were caught unaware. Martin is said to have kept a pistol close at hand, but he had no opportunity to seize it. The robbers demanded that Martin open the safe, but he refused to do so. James Page told later that he was standing by Martin and one of the bandits held a gun on him. It was Mr. Page's belief that the man did not intend to kill Martin but thought to force him to open the safe by threatening to shoot Page.

Martin moved, and as the man swung the pistol around it fired and Martin was hit. Other reports have indicated that one robber, said to have been Jesse James, shot and killed Martin as the cashier reached for his gun.

In the confusion that followed, one of the robbers leveled his pistol at Garnett, who, as it fired, knocked the pistol up, receiving a slight wound on the back of his right hand. The wound, however, caused the amputation of his hand in later years. Hudson, who was a powerful man, then struggled with the robber and knocked him to the floor.

The four Columbia men managed to get out of the room. Page and Major Winfrey and the others escaped across the alley to an old tavern building on the corner, and they secured guns, but the fight was almost over by that time.

The bandits inside the bank scooped up all the ready cash they could find, and this amounted to somewhere between $1,500 and $4,000. The five men then rode out of town along Jamestown Street. Their use of the side roads showed that they had thoroughly planned their escape route, but they encountered an unexpected obstacle. Mr. William Conover with one of his farmhands was working in a field that lay along Glensfork. They had just entered the field and had closed the gate leading to another road.

One of the robbers ordered Conover to open the gate. The farmer, not accustomed to such rudeness, refused in no friendly terms. However, when the stranger leveled a gun at his head Conover turned to his helper and told him to open the gate. From that day on he was known as Open-the-gate Bill Conover.

A posse was quickly formed, led by James R. Hindman, who later became Lieutenant Governor of Kentucky. They lost the trail at the point where the robbers neared the Russell County line. The robbers then apparently worked their way north through Taylor and Marion counties to their hideout in Nelson County.

The body of Cashier Martin was taken to Shelbyville, Kentucky, for burial. Dr. Frank Winfrey, son of Major Winfrey, used to say that he once worked for Frank James in Kansas City. He said that Frank admitted privately that he had fired only to frighten Martin but that the man dodged into the line of fire. S. F. Coffey of Columbia told of meeting Frank James in 1901 when he admitted that he had been at Columbia and that an unfortunate thing had happened there.

Joe Williams, a small boy in 1872, stated that he was at Simon Spring when five mounted men came along and asked him the way to town. When he started to reply one of the men reached down and pulled him into the saddle with him, and the boy thus indicated the way into Columbia. Later Williams was a guard at Stillwater Prison when Cole Younger was a prisoner there. He identified himself to Younger, who then said he remembered him from that day in Columbia.

—Carl W. Breihan

Jesse James

Oh, he shot the banker dead
With a bullet in the head
And rode off with the gold—
This lad so cruel and bold.

The words were on all lips
How the guns hung from his hips,
And whenever he was near
His name rang loud and clear.

With the stages and the trains
He raised all kinds of Cain.
With ease he carried off the loot—
And, oh, how he could shoot!

They were always on his trail
But never landed him in jail.

Young Ford whom he clothed and fed
With one bullet shot him dead.

Of course he never knew,
As the legends grew and grew,
That some day TV and radio
Would make the outlaw glow.

—Carl W. Breihan

Cole Younger

Being an outlaw brought me fame.
    Cole Younger is the name!
It all began 'way back in '61
    When many lawless deeds were done.
Both sides fought with no holds barred,
Leaving Missouri scorched and scarred.

To settle down we tried our best,
    But never would they let us rest.
Ambushed by day, shot at by night,
    Always forced to renew the fight,
We took up arms against those who would
Destroy our home and livelihood.

"Those Younger boys, outlaws!" they cried,
As through the many towns we ride.

When banks and trains fell to bandit guns
The Jameses and Youngers were said to be the ones.
So we rode the lonely and forgotten trail
To clear our name, or forever fail.

—*Carl W. Breihan*

The Escapades of
Frank and Jesse James

CHAPTER 1

Frank and Jesse James
Out West

THE ACTIVITIES OF FRANK AND JESSE JAMES OUT WEST ARE difficult to trace, to say the least. Frequently they were using assumed names. They seldom remained in any one location more than a short period of time, and those with whom they stayed or those who actually knew their real names were hesitant about revealing any connection with the infamous James boys, for good reason. This hesitancy remained with these persons to the very last, and those who could have revealed the most revealed the least. Most of the information which can now be discovered comes from those who "heard it from" or "remembered father or grandfather saying so." But there are some official records, and there are bits and pieces of legitimate firsthand information, and from a complete compilation of these the following emerges.

The earliest mention of the James brothers out West comes from the lips of Robert Hereford. He was a Virginian who came West as a clerk employed with a trading company, traveling between far western forts. He arrived at Fort Bridger not long after Bridger erected it, and he engaged in hunting and trapping. During this period Hereford became acquainted with the entire region. He married a daughter of Uncle Jack Robinson, the Mountain Man, a half-breed. She was the daughter of Marook, one of Jack's two Indian wives. Marook was a sister to Jim Bridger's first wife, both being daughters of Chief Washakie of the Shoshones.

Hereford took sixty head of cattle into Montana in the 1860s, being among the first to do so. He owned and operated a trading post on the emigrant route, a large ranch in the Judith Basin of Montana, another on Henry's Fork southeast of Fort Bridger, and as county clerk he held other important offices also in Montana. In the mid-1860s he became an Indian interpreter, guide, and scout, later being appointed Indian Agent on the Wind River Reservation in Wyoming, headquarters at Fort Washakie.

Robert was the first to discover gold in Montana and, with his friend Louis Simmons, son-in-law of Kit Carson, he was also involved in the discovery of gold at Alder Gulch.

In the fall of 1873, after an extended stay in Montana, Hereford was returning to his ranch on Henry's Fork by way of Idaho City, Idaho, when he became acquainted with Frank and Jesse James. Both Frank and Jesse traveled with him to Fort Bridger, where they stayed for nearly a week in a cabin belonging to Uncle Jack Robinson at what was then known as Uncle Jack's Indian Camp, the Indians having settled around him in great number. Hereford extended an invitation to the Jameses to visit him at his ranch on Birch Creek near Henry's Fork, and they did so about a week later. Whether or not Hereford knew the identity of his two house guests at this time, he knew it by the time they left two days later.

Hereford was acquainted with a young man from southern

Utah by the name of Bill McCarty, who had bought some horses from Hereford at one time. Shortly afterward, Hereford had occasion to meet McCarty at Fort Washakie in Wyoming, under rather different circumstances. McCarty, it seems, had been arrested by Captain Noyes Baldwin, an army officer then living at South Pass City, for "annoying and molesting the Shoshone Indians so as to cause them to be angry, with possible retaliation against the populace." No other circumstances are on record to clarify this incident, but Hereford was called in to quiet the Indians and to aid in convicting McCarty. Nothing much came of it, however, and the matter was soon dropped. One assumes that McCarty was involved (with his two old friends from Brown's Hole, Jack Bennett and William Pidgeon) in selling firewater to the Indians.

A few months after the above incident, Bill McCarty, William Pidgeon, and Jack Bennett were caught peddling whiskey to the Indians at Fort Hall, and they ran off one jump ahead of local officers.

According to Hereford's information, Bill McCarty left his two companions shortly afterward and decided to go it alone. He drifted into Coeur d'Alene, Idaho, where he attempted to hold up a stage office but was caught in the act and barely escaped with his life. Despondent, on his way south he stopped at Lewiston, Idaho, to put in a few drinks at a local saloon.

While Frank and Jesse James were staying at Hereford's ranch in Utah, Hereford mentioned McCarty and, according to him, one of the Jameses remarked, "That's the same guy we met in a saloon in Lewiston just before we came here. He said his named was McCarty and that he had tried to hold up the stage office in Coeur d'Alene a few weeks back."

The James boys related that McCarty had been feeling sorry for himself because of his several recent failures, and Jesse, to cheer him up, told the young man that he was the famous Jesse

James—"And if you want some real action, instead of the small-time stuff, head for Missouri and look up Cole Younger. Tell him the Jameses sent you."

McCarty did just that, riding with the Youngers on several of their forays. Eventually he got into an argument with a man named O'Connor over the division of some of the loot. McCarty shot and killed him and was sent to prison for a short term. Upon his release, McCarty returned to his old home in Utah and organized his brothers, his son, and his nephews into a gang to rival that of the Youngers. With Butch Cassidy and Matt Warner he graduated from rustling into the big-time bank robbery as taught him by none other than Cole Younger and Frank and Jesse James. All of this accounts for a part of the activities of Frank and Jesse out West in the fall of 1873.

The Jameses next appeared in Baggs, Wyoming, and spent some time with the old Mountain Man, guide and scout, Jim Baker, at Baker's ranch on the Little Snake River. How or why Baker became acquainted with two men such as the James brothers is not easy to determine, but the fact remains that they were not only acquainted but were good friends.

Jim Baker had lived for many years in an old cabin built in 1834 by Uncle Jack Robinson on lower Henry's Fork (now Utah's oldest existing cabin), and his brother, John Baker, still owned one of the largest ranches along Henry's Fork, adjoining the property of Robert Hereford, Tom Welch, and others. In the fall of 1877, while the James boys were still his guests at Baggs, Jim Baker received word that his brother's Indian wife, Cora, had died. He immediately packed his gear and prepared to travel to Henry's Fork for the funeral in order to help his brother settle his business in his time of grief. Not wishing to leave Frank and Jesse behind, he invited them to come along.

On a bright day in November, 1877, Jim Baker and his two companions arrived at the ranch of Charles Crouse in Warren's Draw on Diamond Mountain, the southernmost boundary of

Brown's Hole. Crouse, an avid race horse fan, was in the process of trading horses that day; he owned some of the finest stock in the country, having gone as far as Kentucky to purchase them.

Trading horses with Crouse that day was a young man by the name of Cleiphas J. Dowd, aged twenty-one. Dowd had escaped from California earlier that same year after shooting his brother in an argument, shooting another man in a Sausalito saloon, and stealing his father's best racing horse. He had gone to work with James Warren on Diamond Mountain and had since acquired a sizable herd of horses and cattle of his own. One of his co-workers on the Warren ranch was thirteen-year-old Willard Erastus Christiansen, later better known as Matt Warner.

In September of 1877 young Dowd had slain a Mexican, Joe Herrera, who had attacked him with a knife. Dowd had drawn his weapon while lying on the ground and shooting the Mexican as he charged. Such a reputation had Dowd gained in this way with Crouse and others that he could not refrain from bragging to Jim Baker. The result was a contest between Dowd and Jesse. Frank was using the alias Charlie Frankoin, Jesse the name of Jim Wood. Dowd had no idea who they were at the time.

At first a bucket was suspended from a rope and allowed to swing back and forth. Jesse went first, emptying his gun and hitting the target easily. Dowd followed and did as well. Crouse decided they needed a harder target. So empty cartridges were set up along a pole fence, twenty for Jesse, twenty for Dowd.

Jesse again took first chance, taking careful aim and firing. There was no effort on his part to make a fast draw, but he shot deliberately and carefully. When he had emptied his gun, he told Dowd to take his shots while he reloaded, but Dowd declined. Jesse fired again, emptying his weapon once more, then a third time. When he had finished, he had not missed one shot in the eighteen, leaving two cartridges on the fence. He was pleased with himself and watched to see what young Dowd would do.

He was in for a surprise.

Dowd, who packed his gun in a specially designed belt waistband and never a holster, stepped forward. In a flash, the gun appeared in his hand, and the cartridges went flying in a roar of flame. After emptying his weapon, he turned and walked to where Jesse stood and held his hand out, palm upward. Jesse handed his own freshly loaded gun to the young man who whirled and fired as quickly as before. When he finished, not one cartridge was left on the fence. He had accomplished what appeared to be an impossible feat—twenty cartridges with only twelve shots.

What the men did not know was that Dowd had been scientifically trained in the art of handling and firing weapons. He was a graduate of the University of San Francisco at a time when the young men were being trained for a possible uprising and resumption of the Mexican War. He had merely used a well-known principle: "Every action causes a reaction." By shooting between the cartridges and not at them, he had been able to eliminate two and three at each shot. His feat won him the admiration of Jesse James.

The following morning, when they resumed their journey to Henry's Fork to attend the funeral of John Baker's wife, Dowd accompanied them.

After the funeral Cleophas Dowd returned to his cattle and horse interests in Little Hole, while Jim Baker, Frank, and Jesse James went into winter seclusion in Uncle Jack's cabin. Jim Baker wanted to remain near his brother John, until John felt like traveling, and then in the spring Jim hoped to take his brother back to the Little Snake River to live with him.

Not much is known about the activities of Frank and Jesse during that winter. There is a hint that they may have wintered in Brown's Hole or perhaps in Baggs, Wyoming, but they may have gone to California that winter, according to other accounts. Nevertheless, by the spring of 1878 they were back in Brown's Hole. Frank's wife bore a child on February 6, 1878. Whether or not he returned East at that time is uncertain, but he was back in Brown's Hole no later than May of that same year. He took up residence at Powder River, east of the Lost Cabin country in Wyoming. This was the habitual stomping ground of "Big Nose" George Parrott (Lathrope) and his gang.

Parrott owned a ranch on the Sweetwater River, but he didn't work at it. He used his ranching operations as a front for the more lucrative business of raiding emigrant trains and cattle and horse herds as they crossed the country. He had started as a member of several gangs, including "Doc" Bender's Powder Springs Gang and Mexican Joe Herrera's South Pass City Gang, but before long he operated his own small gang. At various times it was composed of as many as fifteen men but averaged usually about ten.

Big Nose George had killed at least one man previous to 1878, during a card game at South Pass City. Although the murdered man had been unarmed, for some reason Big Nose didn't go to trial, and his reputation was strengthened by his apparent brashness in the face of the law. His lieutenant was a hard case known as Dutch Charley Burris, a known stagecoach road agent from the Black Hills area of the Dakotas. Dutch Charley was a ruthless and merciless character, surpassed only by Big Nose George himself.

Frank James joined the Big Nose Parrott Gang on the Powder River, but Jesse was not present, perhaps because he may have returned East for a time. Or he may have been present under an assumed name which has gone undetected. There are those who believe that one Sim Wan, a member of the gang, was in reality Jesse James, but actually Wan was a Chinese from

Rock Springs, Wyoming. Perhaps there were two Sim Wans, but this seems unlikely. It is more probable that Jesse was not present at the time.

The gang consisted of Big Nose George, Dutch Charley Burris, Sim Wan, Jack Campbell, Tom Reed, Frank Towle, and a man known only as Sandy. Frank James constituted the eighth member of the gang; he used the name McKinney, was known as Mac, but used the aliases of Jim McKinney, Tom McKinney, and Al McKinney at various times during his stay with the gang. Frank was not the leader. That dubious honor belonged to Big Nose George. But Frank was a primary moving force of the bunch. He was the only one of the group to have practical experience in robbing trains, and he taught this art to his new-found friends.

Plans were laid to rob the Union Pacific Westbound Express Paycar #3 near Carbon, Wyoming, and Frank James was giving instructions on how it should be done. They waited for several days before starting, hoping to be joined by Joe Manuse. But Manuse didn't show up. Jack Campbell later explained that Manuse had gone over to Brown's Hole to kill a member of Mexican Joe Herrerra's gang for an alleged wrong. Frank grew impatient and urged them to set out without Manuse. However, Manuse must have returned in time to participate in the attempted robbery, for his name appears in the indictment brought against the Parrott gang.

They proceeded to a section toolhouse on the tracks at a place some miles west of Medicine Bow, broke into the place, and found picks and shovels. As they tried to pry loose a rail on the track, a train came into view. The men didn't have time to hide. Big Nose George was almost hit by the engine as it crossed the bridge where he was working. The train crew waved, thinking the men were merely a track crew working on the road bed.

The members of the gang were then able to loosen a joint of

the rails and tie a wire around it, which they had obtained by cutting the telegraph wire which ran to Rawlins. They had nearly completed this job when a small handcar came around the bend and through a cut, sending the outlaws scurrying out of sight, their work unfinished. The track crew noticed the loose rail and stopped to repair it. The foreman recognized the signs but didn't let on that anything was amiss. When they had finished, the track men again boarded the handcar and went pumping slowly away.

According to Big Nose George at a later date, Frank James wanted to open fire and kill the track crew because he suspected they would report that something was amiss when they reached the station down the line. But Big Nose and Frank Towle objected. However, weighing the evidence in the balance, it is just as probable that it was Big Nose who wished to do the killing and that it was Frank James who objected. Frank's knowledge of the business was more professional than that of his companions, and he knew the consequences of needless killing.

At any rate, the track crew reached the next station and reported the rail tampering by telegraph to Rawlins. Sheriff Jim Rankin organized a posse and set out, but not before notifying Sheriff N. K. Boswell at Laramie City. Boswell also formed a posse and commandeered a train, placing his men and horses on a flatcar and hastily departing for Carbon.

The two posses met at Percy. There was a dispute between Boswell and Rankin as to who should command the men, but Rankin won out. He divided the men into two groups and they set out for the Platte River, heading north and west, respectively.

On a hunch the two deputies, Henry "Tip" Vincent and Bob Widdowfield, elected to ride southward into Elk Mountain country. Vincent was a Union Pacific Railroad detective, and Widdowfield was a boss in the coal mines near Carbon. Both had been deputized by Sheriff Jim Rankin. At Rattlesnake Pass Widdowfield dismounted and remarked to Vincent, "It's hotter 'n hell around here, Tip. We'll have them before night."

At that very moment he was struck in the mouth by a rifle bullet fired by Parrott, the bullet ripping through the back of his head. Vincent whirled and fired in the direction from which the shot had come and attempted to ride out of the ambush, only to be brought down within three hundred feet with eleven slugs in his body, one through the heart.

The outlaws came out of their ambush and dragged the bodies into hastily prepared hiding places, then rode swiftly away.

Two days passed before Sheriff Rankin of Carbon County decided to search for the missing officers. When he and his party arrived at the ranch of John Foote, the rancher told them that both men had been there several days before and had set out early one morning in the direction of Rattlesnake Pass. Since Foote knew the country around his ranch, Rankin asked him to guide them to that location. As they entered the pass, Foote spotted a small brush shelter high on the mountainside. He pointed it out to Rankin.

"That wasn't there a few days ago," he said.

Rankin correctly surmised it had been constructed by the outlaws as a lookout and protection from the weather.

Entering the pass, which is in reality a canyon, the lawmen came to the place of ambush. It was mid-August and very hot, and the smell of death was evident. The bodies of the two slain officers had lain in the sun for two days. They were easily located by the stench and removed to the railroad, from which point they were taken to Rawlins for burial.

Sheriffs Rankin and Boswell sent out notices to every officer in the region, informing them of the murder of the two officers. Among lawmen who received the notices were Jeff Carr, Seth Bullock, Boone May, and W. H. H. Llewellyn. Seth Bullock identified one of the gang members as Jack Campbell, while Boone May was the first to recognize McKinney as Frank James. It was also Boone who identified Frank Towle.

When May first heard of the killings, he reported to Sheriff Boswell at Laramie, saying, "I know this man Towle. He held up a stage over near Deadwood while I was a driver there. He's my man. I know where he hangs out, so leave this one to me."

At the same time May told Boswell that McKinney was none other than Frank James. This was no surprise to Boswell, for he had at one time had Jesse James in jail but didn't know who Jesse was until after his release. Therefore he knew that both Frank and Jesse were operating in this area. Boone knew Frank James by sight because the Missouri outlaw had held up his stage north of Cheyenne some time back.

In October, 1878, Boone May appeared suddenly at Powder Springs on the outskirts of Brown's Hole and began asking questions about the whereabouts of Frank Towle. This was a dangerous thing to do, because every "resident" of Powder Springs was a member of one gang or another in the country. None of them appreciated unwarranted questions. But Boone May was fearless, and he somehow got his answer: Frank Towle was in Brown's Hole, working on the various enterprises of Tim Kinney, owner of the Circle K Ranch on Bitter Creek.

Boone May finally overtook his quarry somewhere in the Hole and dispatched him from ambush, just as Towle and his companions had dispatched the two officers on Elk Mountain. To show proof that he had "got his man," Boone cut off Towle's head and dumped it on the desk of the United States marshal at Cheyenne.

Had May only known it, when he killed Towle in Brown's Hole, he had been within grasping distance of Frank James, who was also working for the Circle K Outfit. At least he had been staying at the ranch as a guest.

Tim Kinney was an unusual character. To all appearances he

was a very respectable rancher, owning one of the largest outfits in southwestern Wyoming, the Circle K. By his own admission he had come into the region in 1868–69 as a very young man, as a gandy dancer for the Union Pacific Railroad. He also stated that he had been born in Ireland. He might have been the same Tom McKinney listed in the 1870 census of Wyoming under *Wyoming on the U.P.R.R.,* aged eighteen, born in Ireland. If so, why had he changed his name?

Kinney went into partnership with Duncan and Archy Blair, founders of Rock Springs, Wyoming, in the mercantile business shortly after arriving in Wyoming. Very soon after that, and at a remarkably young age, Kinney came into possession of a large herd of cattle which he ranged south of Rock Springs on Bitter Creek, near the northern lip of Brown's Hole.

This was, even at that time, the undisputed domain of the Tip Gault Gang, and Kinney certainly had some influence with that bunch or he could not have established such a ranching operation at that place. Such was the background of the man with whom Frank James was then living in that region, and Frank was soon joined by his brother Jesse.

Frank James might have taken the alias of McKinney, posing as a relative of Tim Kinney. But this can only be speculation. The only fact which emerges is that, in the late fall of 1878, Frank and Jesse James were living on the Circle K Ranch on Bitter Creek. But by December they were in Baggs, Wyoming.

Learning that Jim Baker was still over at Henry's Creek, helping his brother John to dispose of his property, Frank and Jesse passed back through Brown's Hole, stopping one night at Dowd's cabin in Little Hole. Fording the Green River at Little Hole, the two men crossed through the cedar hills of Dutch John Flat, forded the river again at Flaming Gorge, and rode up Henry's Fork to Baker's cabin. They found Baker at home, and there was nearly a foot of snow on the ground at that time.

It is assumed that they spent the winter of 1878–79 in the

cabin at Henry's Fork with Jim Baker. They were there in March, 1879, when the following incident took place.

March is the worst month in the year in Flaming Gorge country. The deep snows are heightened by cold, severe winds coming down from the mountains to the south and roaring off the Wyoming plains to the north. These are known locally as "ground blizzards." Many a man had lost his life in that region because of them. On such a night Frank and Jesse had stabled their horses in a small barn just east of the Baker cabin. Very little hay was being raised in the country, and on this occasion there was none in the barn for the horses. They broke loose from the barn during the cold night and wandered up Henry's Fork in search of food.

The following day Frank and Jesse decided to set out to retrieve their mounts, and Jim Baker volunteered to go along to show them the way. They bundled up heavily and began the long trudge up the valley. The weather was miserable, to say the least, and a high wind blew the snow into their faces with stinging force, clinging to their eyebrows and Jesse's mustache. The snow began to fall heavier and heavier. Soon they were unable to see more than a few feet in any direction.

Finally Baker saw a familiar landmark in some ledges to the south, and they scurried toward them and lay beneath an overhang most of the day, waiting for the storm to subside. After dumping more than six inches of snow upon the ground, the storm did lift somewhat. However, just as they started out again, the wind came up with renewed fury, and they were hopelessly entangled in the downfall along the creek. If they wandered away from the creek for more than a short distance, it took them an hour to find it again.

About two miles west of Baker's cabin on Henry's Fork was the ranch of his brother John and also the home of John's son-in-law, Dick Son.

"We'll have to wade the creek," said Baker. "We can find

John's cabin if we stick to the other side of the creek."

So the three men plunged into the icy waters and began the mile-long wade up the creek. Finally they could see the weak light of Dick Son's coal-oil lamp flickering in the window. They had made it to safety.

Dick Son answered Jim Baker's pounding and admitted the exhausted and nearly frozen men into his cabin. He lowered the oven door of his kitchen range and the men, on chairs, thrust their frozen feet into the oven. In no time life began to return to their frozen limbs, and Dick Son afterward remarked with a laugh that he had never heard grown men scream and dance more than those three did when their feet began to feel life once more.

The pain was nearly unbearable, and Dick Son's wife, a half-breed, daughter of John Baker, made them a poultice of wild tea leaves and rabbit brush to draw out the pain and swelling. Within a day or so all were well and ready to travel again.

Elijah ("Lije") Driscoll, who lived just west down the creek, had obliged by rounding up the stray horses and, as he had hay in his barn, he fed and kept them warm. Jesse, who owned a superb mount, was so grateful that he paid Driscoll forty dollars in gold, a sizable sum in those days.

Before passing from the subject, it should be remembered that John and Jim Baker and Lije Driscoll, in the 1870s, were involved in the same business as Frank and Jesse, having robbed a payroll near Rock Springs, Wyoming. They buried the loot in the buttes north of Henry's Fork until some time elapsed. Then they retrieved it and split it up among them.

In April, 1879, James Widdup moved to Burnt Fork, a small settlement at the confluence of Burnt Fork Creek and Henry's Fork, fifteen miles upstream from Baker's ranch. Shortly after moving there, Widdop traveled down the creek to borrow some harness from John Baker in order to do some spring plowing.

When he arrived at Baker's cabin, he noticed some horses tied up outside, but he thought nothing of it, except that someone must be visiting.

Knocking on the door, Widdup was surprised to see John Baker cautiously open the door only a crack, inquiring who was there.

"Hell, John," said Widdup. "You know who it is. Let me in."

When Widdup entered the cabin he saw two strangers in the room. John introduced him to the two men by the aliases they were using at the time. There was never any hint to Widdup as to the real identity of the visitors until Jim Baker arrived and soon left with the strangers to take them to his own cabin. John Baker then told Widdup that he had just been "jawing" with Frank and Jesse James.

John Baker died in 1895 and was buried on Henry's Fork near his old ranch. Jim Baker passed away in 1898 and was buried on the Little Snake River.

Frank and Jesse James left Henry's Fork in the mid-spring of 1879, going by way of Green River City. At this time, fifteen-year-old Tom Welch was helping his stepfather freight goods between Green River City and Lander, Wyoming. Young Welch was instructed to load goods onto the wagon from the Morris Mercantile while the stepfather went to the saloon on Railroad Avenue for a drink.

When Welch's stepfather came out of the saloon he told Tom, "You just watch down the street and you'll see something you won't ever forget."

Presently two men came out of the saloon and approached the wagon. Before they got there, Welch's stepfather said, "Tom, don't say anything to anybody, but them is the James boys."

Tom later recalled that he wasn't very much impressed because he didn't know the James boys from Adam's off ox, and "They was no different than you or me," he always said.

Frank and Jesse rode alongside the wagon as Welch and his stepfather proceeded onward to Rock Springs. Here they loaded additional supplies and Frank and Jesse asked to accompany them as far as South Pass City, where they would drop off. According to Welch, Jesse said he had "some business in South Pass City," after which they would have a long ride home.

The fact that Frank and Jesse James did visit in the vicinity of Brown's Hole is well known by the old-timers who saw them, knew them, or knew of their presence. The names of some of those who knew them and in later years spoke of it are as follows:

Charles Crouse, Cleophas J. Dowd, Jim and John Baker, Dick Son, George Widdop, Thomas Widdop, James Widdop, Tom Welch, James Rogers Lamb, George D. Solomon, Albert ("Speck") Welhouse, Boone May, N. K. Boswell, Jim Rawlins, M. F. Leech, Judge William A. Carter, Robert Hereford, George Hereford, George Finch, Elijah Driscoll, Clark Logan, Joe Davenport, Tom Davenport, Aaron Overholt, and many more. What stories they could have told!

Dutch Charley Burris (or Bates) was captured in Montana and brought back to Wyoming in the train by Sheriff Jim Rankin. When they arrived at Carbon, Dutch Charley was dragged from the train by an angry mob and taken to the station. Here telegrapher E. E. Calvin took down his confession. (Calvin later became president of the Union Pacific Railroad.)

Dutch Charley was taken out and made to stand on a barrel while a rope was placed around his neck and thrown over a telegraph-pole wire support. A sister-in-law of the murdered Bob Widdowfield was in the crowd that day. When someone asked Dutch Charley if he had anything to say before they hanged him, the woman stepped forward.

"No! The son-of-a-bitch has nothing to say!" and she kicked the barrel from beneath his feet.

Oddly enough, this act is what brought to mind the old saying, "He kicked the bucket." When a man was hanged and no other means was available, the executioners simply had him stand on a bucket, a noose around his neck. Then they simply kicked the bucket out from under him, sending him into eternity.

Dutch Charley strangled to death, and his body swayed in the breeze throughout the night. Coroner A. G. Edgerton arrived next morning from Rawlins and cut the body down.

Big Nose George was arrested in Montana in August, 1880, almost two years to the day after the attempted holdup and the murders. He was returned to Wyoming, also by Sheriff Rankin —ironically on the Union Pacific #3, the same train Parrott had tried to hold up. He was taken to Rawlins and put in jail, after giving his confession to M. F. Leech. Later Parrott was dragged from his cell and lynched from a telegraph pole by an angry mob. His body was buried in a barrel after much of his skin had been removed to fashion a pair of shoes and a doctor's medicine bag.

The following is an excerpt from a letter the author received from Mrs. A. J. Cooksley of Flying C Ranch, Ucross Mountain, Clearmont, Wyoming. It was dated March 27, 1971.

. . . But I must tell you what the old-timers of this area have said about Jesse. He spent at least a couple of winters in this area and had a Negro* who kept quite a string of horses ready for Jesse and his friends at a dug-out hide-out near the foot of the Big Horn Mountains. Jesse was known to be a gentleman. When ranchers had to leave their wives to go get supplies or hunt or look for cattle, etc., Jesse and one of his companions would see that these ladies were kept supplied with firewood, water, and the heavy chores taken care of. Many have said that even the murderers, thieves, and such of those that frequented the Hole-

*John Trammell.

in-the-Wall hide-out were always gentlemen in the presence of women and children of the local community. Of those who came in contact with Jesse, I have never heard them speak a harsh word about him. They only smiled and said what I have just related here.

John Trammell, 118 years old when he died, was born January 15, 1838, and his age has been verified by various means. John was a chief witness in the case of J. Frank Dalton, the man who claimed to be Jesse James and who claimed Trammell identified him as such. During my investigation of the exposé of J. Frank Dalton there came to light some amazing stories concerning Trammell, some true, others not. One of the most strange ones is related herewith.

In 1879 William F. ("Bear") Davis decided to settle with his family in the Goose Creek Valley of Wyoming. He had been a wagon-train captain and had gone back and forth across the western states from Independence, Missouri, to California and Oregon. He first used the Santa Fe Trail, then the Old Oregon Trail, and, lastly, the Bozeman Trail. In using the last he also worked a chain of forts, namely, Forts Phil Kearney, Reno, and C. F. Smith, and naturally he became familiar with the Goose Creek Valley and knew it was an ideal spot to settle.

After the danger from the Indians was over, Davis went to the Goose Creek Valley, and on June 11, 1879, he arrived at the old crossing on Little Goose Creek at the head of a train consisting of thirteen wagons. Three of the four mule teams and wagons belonged to the Davis family. The Little Goose Creek was running high at this time, and the wagon train had a lot of trouble in crossing.

The Davis wagon was the first to reach the creek and, as the water was out of its banks, it was likewise too much for the lead team and caused a commotion for a time until help arrived from the other side of the creek in the form of an old Negro called

"Nigger John" and whom Mr. Davis at once recognized as the man who had been a slave on his uncle Redmond Wilfley's plantation in Missouri. Mr. Davis had been born and raised only a few miles from the James home at Kearney, Missouri. Nigger John did not wish to be recognized by Mr. Davis, as he was in the employ of the James boys and their gang who, at the time, had some two hundred head of stolen horses in their possession near the old crossing on Little Goose Creek.

The wagon train crossed the creek and camped on the west bank just about opposite the present Big Horn Store. While the men of the wagon train were resting in camp that afternoon, Frank James and another man rode up and, naturally, Davis recognized Frank and talked awhile with him. Frank James advised Davis that his teams were in danger because the gang was moving east that night or the next morning and that some of the band had their eyes out for mule teams. Consequently the wagons were arranged in a circle, and the horses and mules were run inside. When darkness came on, Nigger John came to the camp and gave Davis the same warning.

There were five old log cabins standing in the Little Goose Valley when the family of Fred W. Hilman of Big Horn, Wyoming, moved there in 1879, and the largest one was on the Hilman homestead. This particular cabin boasted of a large fireplace that had a large mantel. Into this mantel the James boys had carved their names, along with the names of other outlaws who rode the trails in those days. Unfortunately this mantel has been lost. Its location as evidence would, of course, forever settle the question of whether the James boys resided briefly in that area.

The first irrigation ditch in or around Big Horn was named Nigger John Ditch and bears the name to this very day. It is also so recorded at the courthouse in Sheridan, and many people still use water from it during the summer. It was named after Jesse's cook, because old John used to sit hours on end watching the workmen building the ditch.

This story of the Nigger John Ditch brought forth other interesting material. Dalton's exploiters claimed that Trammell had identified the old faker as Jesse James, even stating that he himself had been cook for the James gang. I contacted John Trammell at the home of the Rev. James Ellis in Choctaw, Oklahoma, and he asked the minister to write the following letter to me, as John could not write. I had said nothing about the creek-crossing incident and had not mentioned the Nigger John Ditch.

July 25, 1955

Carl W. Breihan

My Friend:

Now sir: J. Frank Dalton was not Jesse James. Jesse told me that he had some relatives by that name. Jesse James went by some strange names when he did not want to be identified. He played a Rev. Jones in Mississippi, and his brother Frank took the part of a doctor.

Now, about the Negro cook named John, that's me. Where the James gang was on about June 11, 1879—Listen, Mister: If my mind serves me right we were near a little town in Wyoming. There was a big ditch near there, and I spent so much time along the ditch I believe they called it "The Nigger John Ditch." That has been a long time ago, but if my mind serves me right this is the information you are seeking.

Yours truly,
John Trammell

This letter proved two important points—that J. Frank Dalton was not Jesse James and that the Davis story is true in every respect. Trammell had no way in the world of knowing that I had learned of the creek crossing or of the ditch being named after him. In fact, John Trammell sent me another letter at a later date, and part of that letter read, "It sure surprised me how you found this out about the wagon train and Big Horn." Another old-timer, Archie Nash of Sheridan, Wyoming, has verified this story as well.

CHAPTER 2

The Liberty Bank Robbery
and Aftermath

IT HAS OFTEN BEEN DEBATED AS TO WHETHER JESSE AND
Frank James engineered the daring bank holdup which occurred on Friday, February 13, 1866. This was not the first
bank robbery in the country. During the Civil War, a band of
Confederates, escaping from a northern prison, robbed a bank
in Maryland en route homeward. However, it was the first
robbery by a band of organized outlaws.

Curious circumstances preceded the actual raid. On January
20, 1866, the sheriff of Harrison County attempted to execute
a warrant for the arrest of William Reynolds, at Pleasant Hill,
Missouri, who was under indictment for crimes allegedly committed during the Civil War. However, the sheriff was unable
to arrest Reynolds, as two ex-guerrillas, N. P. Hayes and
George Maddox, prevented his doing so. The sheriff swore in
a posse of citizens, and a quick fight resulted. Reynolds and
Hayes were killed, and Maddox was captured.

Numerous threats were received that guerrilla bands were

going to attack the town in an effort to liberate Maddox. These rumors persisted, and excitement reigned in Pleasant Hill until the news of the daring bank robbery at Liberty, Missouri, broke upon the town. The armed citizens then realized the threats had been a diversion, a "red herring" to keep attention from the neighboring towns.

On that eventful day, a band of armed men rode into Liberty from several directions, meeting in the square, where the leader deployed his men at strategic points. It was quite early in the morning, and no one paid any attention to the two men who entered the Clay County Savings Association. They confronted the cashier, Greenup Bird, who was alone in the bank except for his small son. Under threat of instant death to himself and his son, Bird was forced to open the vault, and the robbers stuffed two saddlebags with $58,000. (Even today, tourists may walk into the bank vault from which this money was taken.)

A young lad named George Wymore, who was accompanying Henry W. Haynes, a close friend of E. T. Estes of Kansas City, was on the way to William Jewell College. (Rev. Robert S. James, father of the James boys, had been one of the original trustees of this college.) Bird thrust his head out of a window as the outlaws prepared for flight and called out to Wymore, telling him of the robbery and asking to raise an alarm. The lad began to yell "Robbers! Robbers!" As he did so the bandits began firing and yelling with savage fury. Haynes quickly took shelter behind a tree, but young Wymore was not so fortunate. He was struck by four bullets and killed.

Several days after the robbery, the Wymore family received the following note:

We regret the death of your son and hope you will believe it was an accident as we had no cause to kill him and never really meant to do so. You have our deepest sympathy.

Jesse and Frank James

Now this note could have been sent by anyone to point suspicion in the direction of the Jameses, and it does not prove that they committed the robbery. On the other hand, one David Duncan, who owned a store at Cedarville, three miles from the James home, stated that he met them after the Liberty bank had been robbed. At first he said that Frank and Jesse James were in the gang. Later, he thought it best to say that he did not know for sure . . . which, of course, was safer for him.

A posse followed the trail of the outlaws as far as the Mt. Gileao Church, where the tracks showed that the party had divided into small groups or singles, so the pursuit ended.

The majority of the Clay County residents firmly believed that Jesse and Frank James were at Liberty during the robbery, or at least that they had instigated the affair. Friends of the Jameses stated that Jesse could not have been present, as he was still suffering from the lung wound he had received at the close of the war. Records show that Jesse lay in bed for nearly a year after receiving the wound, attended only by a Dr. Lankford, of Kansas City, who nursed him back to health. Jesse had been wounded in May of 1865; the robbery occurred in February of the following year. It is possible that he had been there, but it would have been dangerous and foolish for him to ride a horse in his condition. (The gaunt-looking robber at Lexington, October, 1866, seems likely to have been Jesse James.)

These facts are stated not in defense of Jesse, but only to bring all the available information to the reader, so that he may draw his own conclusions. The robbery of the Russellville, Kentucky, bank in March of 1868 was actually the first to be publicly attributed to the James gang.

Jim White and J. F. Edmunson were arrested in St. Joseph, shortly after the Liberty robbery, on suspicion, but they were released for lack of evidence. Many believed that these two, together with Bill Chiles, Ol Shepherd, Red Monkers, and Bud

Pence, positively were among the band. Others believed that Arch Clements, Dick Burns, and Andy Maguire also were in the group. It is known that Maguire spent money freely soon afterward and ran away to St. Louis with the daughter of Mr. Deering of Independence, Missouri. Maguire was captured at the old Seventh Street Depot in St. Louis and was returned to Liberty, where he was promptly jailed. In the same jail were several others suspected of being implicated in the same robbery. Shortly afterward all those suspected were taken from the jail by an angry mob and lynched.

Bud Pence had a brother named Don, who also had been a guerrilla under Quantrill. One day he learned that Stephen Major, a neighbor of the Jameses, had sold some cattle for a large sum, and he conveyed the news to Jesse. This was shortly after the Liberty affair, and Jesse and Frank James, with Don Pence, went one night to the Major home with intent to rob him. Mrs. Major knew who they were and was afraid that if she went upstairs to tell her husband they would come in and kill him. So her sister detained them, while Mr. Major jumped out of an upstairs window and ran in his stocking feet to the home of Mr. Benton, a neighbor. This saved his money . . . perhaps his life.

Another aftermath of the Liberty robbery was the arrest on June 10, 1866, of an ex-guerrilla named Joab Perry, who was lodged in the jail at Independence. On the 14th, a group of well-armed men galloped into town at midnight. They immediately rode to the jail and demanded Perry's release. Jailer Bugler refused to give up the prisoner, and a number of shots were fired into his home. Bugler was instantly killed; his young son was seriously wounded but recovered, to be later (of all things) accused of complicity in the train robbery at Glendale.

If anyone knew the identity of the raiders who failed in their purpose to release Perry, they said nothing. Everyone realized the desperate character of the Jameses and Youngers, and to have mentioned their suspicions might have brought about terrible reprisals.

Soon another robbery occurred, and at last the people of Missouri were beginning to wonder about the security of the country banks. On October 30, 1866, between noon and one o'clock, the banking house of Alexander Mitchell & Company, in Lexington, Missouri, was robbed of $2,011.50. The robbers were four in number, and to carry out their bold plan they had chosen the lunch hour, when no one was in the bank except J. L. Thomas, the clerk.

A few minutes before their entry, Thomas was standing in the doorway of the bank, when he noticed a couple of strange men approaching, in earnest conversation. Thinking they were coming into the bank, he stepped back, took his place at a desk, and was writing a letter when they entered. One of the men placed a $50 7–30 bond on the counter and asked what the "discount" was on it. Mr. Thomas did not like the laughing manner in which the request was made, and replied that the bank was not buying that kind of funds.

Just then the two other robbers entered. In an instant Mr. Thomas was covered by four deadly revolvers. They warned him that he would die if he did not obey orders to the letter. In the cash drawer, which was easily reached, they found $2,000 as well as $11.50 in silver. They then told Thomas that there was $100,000 in the bank, and that if he valued his life he had better tell them where it was. Thomas denied there was this much money in the bank. The bandits searched him for the vault key. He didn't have it, so they left. As they did so, they warned Thomas not to give the alarm under pain of death. Quickly they reached their horses, which had been tied in a nearby alley, and were soon out of sight.

Soon twelve well-armed citizens, including Jesse Hamlet, David and John Poole, James Cather, and Hedge Reynolds, started after the bandits and spent two days in a fruitless search. The trail led down to the road to Wellington. Dave and John Poole came upon the robbers eventually, after a sharp ride of several miles, and they fired. The Poole boys reported the party as being five men when they saw them, but they were unable to get close enough because of the fleetness of the outlaws' horses.

It was a bold robbery and one which stirred the countryside. Thomas described the men as all young and well under thirty years of age. The descriptions would easily fit both Frank and Jesse James, but there was some talk that the band might have been made up of Kansas "Redlegs," leftovers from the war.

The Younger brothers were loud in their assertions that they had nothing to do with these robberies. Nevertheless, they were friends of the Jameses, or were supposed to be, and their names were linked with those of Frank and Jesse as accomplices in these robberies as well as in many to follow. Suffice it to say, large amounts of reward money were offered for the capture of any of the Youngers, dead or alive.

The robbers struck their next blow in Savannah, Missouri, the seat of Andrew County, at the private banking concern of Judge William McLain. On March 2, 1867, six outlaws invaded the little banking office of Judge McLain. Some said only five robbers participated in the attempted holdup and declared they were: J. F. Edmunson, Jim White, Bill Chiles, Bid McDaniels, and a man named Pope. It was nearly high noon, and no one was in the bank except Judge McLain and his son. The bandits rode up and four of them dismounted, leaving their horses in charge of the other two. As the four entered the bank with drawn pistols, the judge looked earnestly over his spectacles and at once sized them up. He drew a heavy revolver from a desk drawer and began firing. His shots missed, however, and one of the bandits gunned him down.

Young McLain ran into the street and gave the alarm, which

brought many citizens to the rescue. The outlaws saw their position was becoming critical, so they all leaped upon their mounts and raced from town empty-handed. A posse of twenty-five went in pursuit of the bandits and trailed them for a great distance.

In the extreme northwest part of Missouri, the citizen squad actually located Chiles and White, but they were too timid to capture them, for it was apparent that there were many of their friends around. It also occurred to the posse that they were not in company with the sheriff or even a deputy, and they had located the two suspects far out of Andrew County.

Pope and McDaniels were arrested near St. Joseph, Missouri, but they were prepared with alibi witnesses and were released on March 19, after being held only one day.

Judge McLain's wound cost him the amputation of an arm. He lived to carry on his duties and to die a natural death.

The Hughes & Mason Bank at Richmond, Missouri, was open for business as usual on May 23, 1867, when a band of armed men led by Peyton (Payne) Jones entered. They robbed the cashier of $4,000 in gold coin.

Mayor Shaw, a brave and efficient officer, tried to intercept the raiders. He seized a revolver and ran across the street, at the same time trying to round up enough men to stem the attack. However, the moment he was discovered, three of the bandits rode swiftly upon him, and though the brave mayor fired away, his aim was bad and he fell to the street with four bullets in his body.

After robbing the Mason Bank, the bandits attacked the jail. Apparently this was done to liberate a number of prisoners who still strongly expressed their secessionist feelings. Jailer B. G. Griffin and his son refused to give up the prisoners, and a bitter fight started. The fifteen-year-old boy, Ben, Jr., had stationed himself behind a tree and was firing into the bandits' faces when he was surrounded and shot to death. Seeing the fate of his boy,

Griffin dashed to the side of his son, fighting desperately until he, too, died, with seven bullets in him.

By this time the citizens had gained enough courage to open fire on the bandits. However, the robbers rode unharmed out of town.

Richmond was in a virtual state of war. Business was suspended for several days while the jailer and his son were buried and warrants were issued for those who had been recognized: Peyton Jones, Dick Burns, Ike Flannery, John White, and Allen Parmer (who later became the brother-in-law of Jesse James). Why the name of Parmer was included is difficult to tell, because he was at that time in Kansas City working for J. E. Shawhan & Company. For some reason or other the names of the Youngers and the Jameses were again omitted from the list of recognized men.

Pursuit of the robbers became intense. Kansas City sent a squad of eighteen men after the robbers, and on the twenty-sixth, three days after the robbery, they learned that Peyton Jones was stopping at the house of one Evans, two miles west of Independence. Marshal Tom Mizery, who was in charge of the party determined to capture Jones, accepted the offer of a neighbor of the Evans family, a Dr. Noland, to send his daughter along as guide. That was a strange thing to do—sending a girl along on a raiding party.

The rain beat down furiously, and the night was pitch black, but the girl had no trouble locating the Evans house. As the posse closed in, Jones dashed into the yard firing a double-barreled shotgun. The buckshot instantly killed a posseman named B. H. Wilson and fatally wounded Dr. Noland's daughter. Without firing another shot, Jones escaped into the woods.

It was indeed a sad party that returned to Kansas City next day.

On the night following the attempt to capture Peyton Jones, a party of ten men from Richmond captured Dick Burns, and without any ceremony or loss of time they hanged him from the nearest tree. Andy Maguire was captured near Warrensburg several weeks later and was also hanged pronto. Indeed, the people of Richmond soon appeared to be the nemesis of the entire band. They refused to allow their anger to cool or to forget the terrible experience their town had gone through.

Tom Little, another suspect, was chased from cave to cave, over hills, into lonely places, until at last he boarded the *Fannie Lewis* at Jefferson City. When the boat arrived in St. Louis the police were at the wharf waiting for him, having been notified by the Richmond authorities. He was taken to Warrensburg for fear he would be lynched. There, he was soon promptly taken from the Warrensburg jail and hanged to the highest oak in town. The citizens remembered how he had robbed several of their best people and then ridiculed them when they tried to arrest him.

Jack Hines and Bill Hulse were also suspected of complicity in the Richmond robbery, and the hunt became so keen that they had to leave the country. The bitterest feelings prevailed, and wayside assassinations became so frequent as to put every man in jeopardy. Not until some of the most prominent men in the affected counties organized an effort for peace did this veritable vendetta come to a close.

Many persons said that Cole Younger was one of the band also and must be run down. However, this was not true, since Cole was in Texas at the time, preparing a home for his mother in an honest effort to remove her from the land which brought back haunted memories of the loss of her husband, the persecution of her children, and the destruction of all her earthly possessions.

Rare photo of Dr. Reuben Samuel, stepfather of the outlaw brothers, Frank and Jesse James (Thompson, Kansas City).

Mrs. Zerelda Samuel, mother of Frank and Jesse (W. A. Lloyd, Wichita Falls, Texas).

Mrs. Samuel, seated on the front porch of her home at Kearney, Mo. (Carl W. Breihan Collection).

A hitherto unknown photo of Jesse James, found in Frank James' album marked "Jesse James, My Brother" (Wilbur Zink Collection).

Jesse James in 1870, with his usual determined and thoughtful look (Carl W. Breihan Collection).

Jesse James at 24 (Carl W. Breihan Collection).

Jesse James in 1875 (Carl W. Breihan Collection).

Rare photo of Frank James at 33 (Carl W. Breihan Collection).

In 1870, Frank James looked like any young American man in his twenties (Carl W. Breihan Collection).

Jim Younger after capture, at the Earibault, Minn. jail in 1876. Jim first assumed the name Carter, but the ruse failed. Nonetheless, some writers have erroneously stated that one of the robbers was named Carter (Carl W. Breihan Collection).

Bob Younger as a young man on his father's farm at Lee's Summit, Mo. (Carl W. Breihan Collection).

Cole Younger, as he appeared during the Civil War (Carl W. Breihan Collection).

J. J. Schofield .45 calibre revolver found under the James home (R. L. Mack Collection).

The inside of this Schofield grip is insc... "Jesse James 1880" (R. L. Mack C... tion).

J. J. Schofield .45 broken open (R. L. Mack Collection).

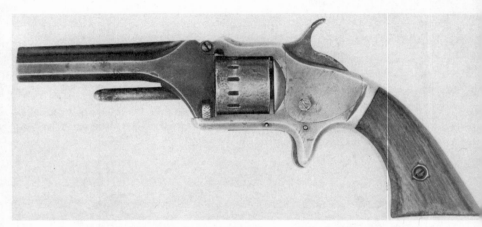

Rare photo of a hideout gun carried by Jesse James and given to the Armes family who lived near Ft. Dodge, Iowa. Manufactured by American Standard Tool Company, this 7-shot, .22 calibre revolver bears the numerals 272-1 (Carl W. Breihan Collection).

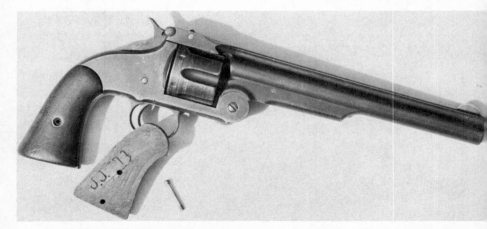

This S & W revolver is believed to have once been owned by Jesse James (property of Roy G. Jinks, Greene, New York).

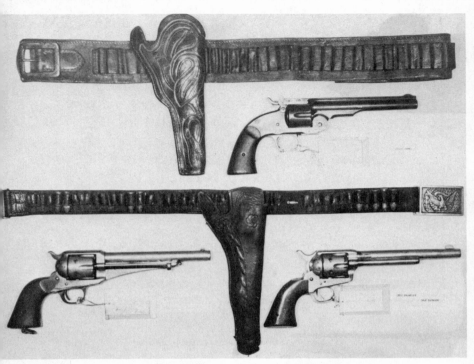

Three famous revolvers. Top: Jesse James' .45 Smith & Wesson Schofield, serial 366, given to the son of Governor Crittenden by Jesse's widow, for his kindness to the family. Left: Remington .44–.40 Frontier, serial 15116, the gun which Frank James surrendered to Governor Crittenden. Right: Cole Younger's Colt Frontier model, also presented to the Missouri governor (Carl W. Breihan Collection).

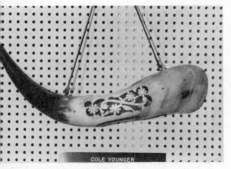

Cole Younger carved this horn while serving time in the Stillwater, Minn. Penitentiary (Gunfighters, R. R. Riss II Enterprise, New York).

Bowie Knife carried by Jesse James during the Civil War, made by Corsan-Denton-Burdekin & Company in the early 1860s (R. L. Mack Collection; photo by Rozelle).

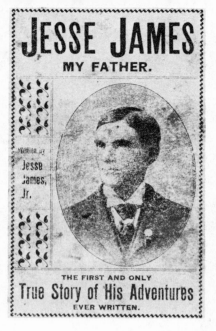

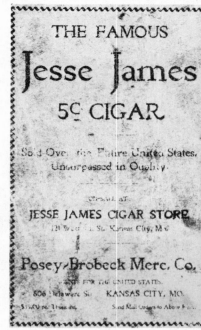

The cover of the book written by Jesse's son, Jesse Edwards James (Carl W. Breihan Collection).

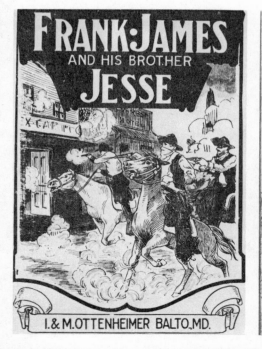

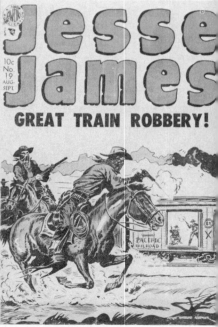

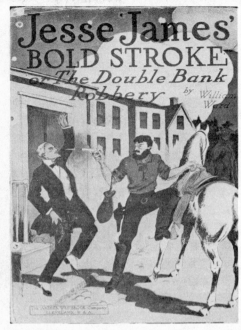

Six popular comic books and dime novels of the day. These "pulps" invariably depicted the James boys as heroes, and sold by the thousands prior to 1900. Now they're worth $10.00 to $15.00 each, if you can get their owners to part with them (all from the Carl W. Breihan Collection except *Frank James and His Brother Jesse,* Missouri Pacific Railroad).

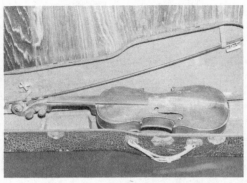

Frank James "fiddle" owned by E. Kelly (R. L. Mack Collection).

Close-up of Frank's "fiddle" engraved "Frank James—Kearney Mo. 1865" (R. L. Mack Collection).

Remington cap-and-ball revolver used by Jesse during the Civil War, and at Centra to slay Major Johnson (Carl W. Breihan Collection).

CHAPTER 3

The Russellville
Bank Robbery

MEMORIES OF THE EXCITEMENT CAUSED BY THE BOLD BANK robberies at Liberty, Savannah, and Richmond, Missouri, were still keen in the minds of many Missourians. This was especially true of the ex-Quantrillians who hoped that Jesse James would soon pull off another daring caper. But now nearly a year had passed, and by 1868 nothing new had happened to stir their blood.

That year was to bring about the trouble between Otto von Bismarck of Germany and Napoleon III of France—a disagreement that would lead to the defeat of France in 1870 by the armies of Count Helmuth von Moltke. The troubles between the bears and bulls of Wall Street did not concern the people in the quiet little villages and hamlets in the border states, but they did find interest in reading the stories of Buffalo Bill as they came from the prolific pen of Ned Buntline. The threatened impeachment of President Johnson created some interest, but only about as much as the fact that General U. S. Grant won the presidential election, carrying all but eight states.

Something new was in the making. The Missouri outlaws decided to extend their operations beyond the borders of the Show-Me state, and this first attack took place in Kentucky. The chosen target was the Southern Deposit Bank in Russellville, Kentucky. At the time this little Logan County village was a quiet, beautiful site. Its people were peaceful and decent, and it was a center of wealth.

Nothing exciting had ever happened in Russellville, and things moved in routine fashion. The citizens hardly noticed a well-dressed man, riding a superb mount, when he stopped before the private banking concern of Nimrod Long and George Norton. It was these same two men who had years earlier paid the bills for one struggling minister in the Baptist Church at Georgetown—yes, this minister was Robert James, the father of Jesse and Frank.

The stranger, who said his name was Colburn, stepped into the bank and asked Mr. Long to redeem a 7–30 note in the amount of $500. Mr. Long became suspicious when the stranger offered to sell the note at par when the interest coupons were still attached. Colburn said he was from Louisville, and Mr. Long, knowing very well that such a note was at a premium in that city, refused to buy it.

There are many versions of what occurred that March 20, 1868, when the robbers rode into town and raced up to the bank building, brandishing pistols and ordering people to stay inside. A great-grandson of Nimrod Long, president of the bank, said that eight men were involved; other reports say twelve, and some six. According to the grandson, Frank and Jesse James, Cole Younger, Jim White, George and Oliver Shepherd, John Jarrette, and Jim Younger spent a full week in Russellville, buying all the fast horses and guns in that small town, and looking over the situation.

At noon on the twentieth they robbed the bank. Mr. Long was at home eating lunch when he heard the shots. He jumped up from the table, exclaiming, "They are robbing the bank!"

Then he ran down the street and entered the bank at the side door, where his office was located. Jesse James met him in the hallway, and they scuffled. Jesse shot at him twice, but the bullets just grazed his head.

Jesse then returned to the front of the building, where the bank's cashier, Morton Barkley, had been tied by the other robbers, and he told them he had just killed the bank president. Several of the bandits were astride horses in front of the bank, and when Mr. Long ran out, shouting that bandits were robbing the bank, they took several shots at him but missed. The robbers scooped up $14,000 (failing to get $50,000 in the vaults) and made their getaway, dropping a hundred-dollar bill, which was later picked up by a Mrs. Grubbs and returned to Nimrod Long.

The robbers galloped out of Russellville along the Franklin Road, riding through an old covered bridge and disappearing into the wilderness.

One account states that Mr. Long was in the bank at the time Colburn and another man entered, placed a revolver at Long's temple and demanded the money. In a surprise move, Long wheeled around and leaped for a door leading into a rear room. Colburn (probably Cole Younger) did not fire. He seemed to be astonished and irked at the banker's unexpected effort to get away from the menace of the gun. When Long reached the back door, one of the bandits who was stationed there fired two shots at him, the bullets grazing his head. Long raced through the rear exit, yelling for help. Two of the mounted robbers fired at him but missed. The banker was able to round the corner at this point and make good his escape.

The first report sounds more reasonable, for it seems impossible that expert marksmen should fire at Long so many times and at such short range without killing him, yet both reports more or less agree.

Inside the bank, Colburn and his companion were busy keeping guard over the two clerks and stuffing money into the well-known grain sack. Outside, the other robbers were yelling for the two men inside to hurry up. A citizen named Owens had acquired an old six-shooter and was blazing away at the robbers. A volley from the bandits' guns quickly sent him scurrying. None of the shots had struck a target.

About twenty minutes after the bandits had dashed from town in the direction of Gallatin, a determined posse of some fifty hell-bent Kentuckians rode in pursuit of the gang. But it was a fruitless effort. The desperadoes were mounted on splendid horses; the townspeople were riding old farm plugs and buggy horses, with not one capable animal among the lot. Also, where the ex-Quantrillians could ride pell-mell through brush and thicket, these peaceful citizens of Kentucky were reluctant to go.

In Russellville the news of this daring attack on the town was spread far and wide. Names of all Missouri bandits were being uttered among the folks along the walks. Many of them had heard of Jim Younger and Frank James, because they had been with Quantrill in Kentucky in 1865 and had left a gory record. Jesse James and Cole Younger were but vague newspaper names to these hard-working people.

The weary posse returned to Russellville after tracking the bandits to the Mississippi River, where they had crossed and found sanctuary in the rugged hills of southeast Missouri.

There was much speculation about the identity of the raiders. Friends of the James boys declared it was impossible for Jesse to have been there. They stated that Jesse was at Chaplin in Nelson County, which is more than fifty miles from Russellville, when that town's bank was robbed. That nervy bandit wrote a letter to the Nashville *American,* in which he stated the facts which showed him to be at the Marshall House in Chaplin at the time of the robbery. However, the date that Mr. Marshall stated that Jesse was there did not agree with the date of the holdup. It was no great problem for Jesse James to ride more than fifty miles on horseback in six hours, and many times his alibis hinged on this fact. It is also noted that Jesse James was seen in Chaplin the day after the robbery.

As for Frank, friends said that he was still suffering from a hip wound suffered at Brandenburg when he was fired upon by law officers who thought he was a horse thief. But it was well known that he had sufficiently recovered so that he had no difficulty in riding a horse. He had made several recent trips on horseback from the Sayers' home in Nelson County to the home of his relatives in Logan County.

Some people were positive that Jesse and Frank were at the home of Mr. Thompson in San Luis Obispo County, California, at the time of the Russellville robbery, but they were mistaken, for they had not yet made their trip to California. Also, Jesse had been seen at the home of relatives in Logan County, just a dozen miles from Russellville.

Excuses in defense of the James boys were on the feeble side, but, since definite proof of their participation was lacking, no warrants were issued. Most residents of the area continued to believe that the James boys had been in the robber band, whether or not they were its ringleaders.

Mr. Nimrod Long employed the services of the famous Louisville detective "Yankee" Bligh in an effort to track down the robbers. Bligh had often remarked that it was his life's ambition to meet Jesse James, and that, if he should, he would be ready to die. One day Bligh met a man at the J. M. & I. Depot at 14th and Main Streets, Louisville, and had an interesting talk, afterward telling several friends about the fine gentleman he had met. Several days later he received a post card from Baltimore, which read:

> Dear Mr. Bligh: You have been quoted as saying on more than one occasion that if you could only meet Jesse James, you'd be content to lie down and die. Well, Mr. Bligh, you can now stretch out, lie down and die. The gentleman you met the other day in the R.R. depot of Louisville was yours,
>
> Sincerely,
Jesse Woodson James

Of course, this message disturbed detective Bligh, and he determined not to be denied. He had tracked the bandits but lost their trail at the edge of Nelson County. However, some of the residents had recognized some of the gang, and Bligh was furnished with some pretty good clues to follow. With another detective named William Gallagher and several Nelson County officers, he went to the home of George Shepherd.

At this time George W. Shepherd, Ol Shepherd, and several of the old guerrilla guard had their homes or hiding places in Nelson County. George was the same man who had taken Jesse James under his wing during the Civil War while fighting with Quantrill. He had married the widow of Dick Maddox, another famous Quantrill man. Dick Maddox had fought viciously at Lawrence and Centralia, and had participated in many desperate and bloody fights with Union troops in Missouri. He was killed by a Cherokee Indian in the spring of 1865. George Shepherd agreed to console the widow, and later he married her and settled in Chaplin some time before the Russellville raid.

While Ol Shepherd and several other old Missouri pals chose to escape into the wilderness regions of southeast Missouri, George Shepherd remained in Chaplin, never dreaming that Bligh suspected him of being one of the robbers. It was also known that horses provided from the Shepherd farm had enabled the outlaws to outrun the posse.

According to one report, the posse surrounded the house the day after the bank robbery and captured George Shepherd. He was taken to Russellville and put in jail. The grand jury of Logan County returned an indictment against him, and he was subsequently arraigned and tried in circuit court for aiding and abetting the bandits. He was found guilty and sentenced to three years in the state penitentiary at Frankfort. Later, Shepherd told newspapermen that he was not arrested at his Nelson County farm; that he eluded the posse, stating that he was chased for several hundred miles. He said that he was captured in a drugstore in a small Tennessee town before he could offer any resistance.

The name of George W. Shepherd had become well known during the Civil War when he rode with Quantrill's raiders. His name is also prominent because he is the man who is credited with engaging in a fight with Jesse James and his followers near Joplin, Missouri, resulting in the death of the outlaw and the severe wounding of Shepherd in the left leg. George was the son of James Shepherd, a prominent Jackson County farmer. He was born near Independence, Missouri, on January 17, 1842, on a farm which later was owned by the Staten family. He had two older brothers, John and James, and one younger brother, William.

In 1857 he went to Utah, where he joined the United States Army, at the time operating against the Mormons; his commander was General Albert Sidney Johnston. He returned home in 1859 and resumed farming operations with his brothers. He continued in this work on a farm a mile and a half from Independence until the start of the Civil War. He first fought as a regular Confederate recruit and participated in the battles of Wilson's Creek and Pea Ridge. Later, when the Confederate troops moved to Mississippi, George remained in Jackson

County, later joining Quantrill's command. His war record as a guerrilla would fill a book.

Oliver Shepherd, a cousin of George, was the only other suspected member of the Russellville robbers who came to a quick end. He was followed into Jackson County, Missouri, by the persistent Kentuckians, who wanted to arrest him. In order to do so they got a requisition from the governor of Kentucky and an executive order from the State of Missouri. But Ol was an old ex-guerrilla and would never surrender. The officers found him at his home near Lee's Summit and told him to surrender, but he refused. In the ensuing fight Ol received seven bullet wounds and died fighting to the last.

In the matter of George Shepherd, the Nashville, Tennessee *Banner* had this to say:

> The arrest of George Shepherd had been made first because he was by himself, the others of the gang having been traced to another part of the county. On gathering a posse to capture them, it was found that news of George Shepherd's arrest had gone ahead, and his cousin, Ol Shepherd, had immediately started for Missouri with one or two comrades. Inquiry easily developed information that Jesse James and Cole Younger went with him. It was then satisfactorily shown that Cole must have been the man who called himself Colburn at the bank. It was found also that Jesse James had been visiting in Logan County a few weeks before.

At that time the names of Jim Younger and Frank James were far better known in Kentucky than Cole and Jesse, because the latter two had not fought in that state with Quantrill. It was a natural thing, then, on finding that Jesse and Cole had gone with Ol Shepherd, for the detectives to claim that the other boys were in it too, especially as no trace of James or Younger could be found anywhere in Nelson County, where they had been stopping off and on for a year.

So the cry of "the Jameses and Youngers" was raised. More careful investigation developed the fact that on the day of the robbery Jesse James was at his hotel in Nelson County. He was slowly recovering from an old wound that would not heal, and this made it imprudent for him to ride on horseback on any rough journey. The romantic version of the raid is that it was undertaken to procure funds to send him on a sea voyage. Frank James had gone to California some months before.

Bligh followed the retreating raiders till he was satisfied of their destination, and then he sent word to the Jackson County, Missouri, authorities to look out for them. Ol Shepherd made a quick trip of it, and on arriving he was waited upon by a sheriff's posse. As they summoned him to surrender he broke for the brush and got about twenty bullets, which finished him.

The rest of the party were heard from a day or two later, and as better information by then had been obtained, Bligh and Gallagher went over with requisitions for Cole Younger, Jesse James, John Jarrette and Jim White, who were claimed to be the active participants with the Shepherds. However, the news of Ol Shepherd's death had given them warning to keep out of the way. The Younger residence was raided, but only the youngsters John and Bob were found at home. The balance of the band were never arrested.

Bligh still holds that Jesse James was accessory to the job, though he admits that Jesse was seventy-five miles away when it occurred.

Jesse James returned to Missouri right after the Russellville affair, riding from Chaplin, Nelson County, Kentucky, to Clay County, Missouri, where he was seen during the first part of April. It is no wonder that he and the men he led were able to escape the Kentucky lawmen. Jesse knew every trail across the swamps of southeastern Missouri, and every path in the rugged hills in the southern counties of Missouri. Moreover, in those early days after the Civil War the friends of the Jameses were numerous in the State of Missouri. It was through the advice of one of these friends, Dr. Joseph Wood of Kansas City, that Jesse decided to visit California. It was thought that the change of climate would be beneficial for his lung trouble.

In May of 1869 Jesse James left the home of his mother near Kearney for New York. On June 8 he booked passage on the steamship *Santiago de Cuba*, bound for Aspinwall, crossed the Isthmus of Panama, and there took a steamer for San Francisco. The spoils of the Russellville raid enabled him to take this trip for his health. Frank James at this time was hiding in the home of a respectable citizen in Nelson County, Kentucky. Even then, it was thought unsafe for him to remain in the States, and it was decided that he too should visit California.

One quiet evening, several weeks after the Russellville affair, Frank was driven north through Bloomfield, Fairfield, and on through Mt. Washington to Louisville. From there he boarded a train for St. Louis. There he registered at the Southern Hotel as "F. C. Markland, Kentucky." He notified his mother, Mrs. Samuel, at Kearney, that he decided to go west across the Rocky Mountains. Mrs. Samuel met her son at the home of a relative in Kansas City, where he remained for several days. Then he took passage for California, and arrived a few weeks before Jesse. From San Francisco Frank went to the home of his uncle Drury Woodson James in San Luis Obispo County, who, at the time, was the owner of a health spa called Paso Robles Hot Sulphur Springs. After spending some time at Paso Robles Frank went to the home of J. D. Thompson, an old acquaintance. He remained at the Laponsu Rancho for several months, until after the arrival of Jesse.

Jesse and Frank met at Paso Robles and in the autumn visited some of the Nevada mining districts. Their stay at the spa had done wonders for their health, and the boys were again anxious to be on the move.

Frank, grave, self-possessed, lithe of figure and graceful of manner, had a warm pressure of the hand and a winning glance of the eye for those whose friendship he desired. He was scholarly too, this rough fighter of the border, and he could speak German and Spanish fluently, as well as quote Shakespeare.

Jesse, smiling and warmhearted, made friends easily and was jovial and loved practical jokes. He was cautious, and his keen judgment prevented his social qualities from betraying him into conversational pitfalls.

Some rancher friends in the vicinity of Lake Tulare had been urging the James brothers to pay them a visit, and the accustomed exercise in the saddle, in a pure air, roused the craving for new excitement and fresh dangers. They also wished to look into the get-rich stories in the new mining areas. Bidding fond farewells to their relatives and friends in Southern California, the two James boys pressed forward to the new El Dorado. No one would ever have suspected them of being the most dangerous and most wanted outlaws in the world.

Striking back across the Sierra Nevada, they made their way to the mining camps in the Reese River country, and mixed anew in the wild life to which they were so accustomed. Here they met a few old acquaintances and also made a few new friends. But what could a mining camp offer in the way of excitement to these men who had ridden pell-mell over Missouri with Quantrill and made a regular business of bank robbery?

When some of the more adventurous of the Reese River miners followed a new strike on the other side of the Sonoma Mountains, Frank and Jesse joined in the fresh activities of a new mining camp. The town sprang up overnight. A main street was laid out, and saloons and eating places, dance halls and gambling dens, and noisy shouts and music and profanity made high noon in every one of the twenty-four hours of the day.

Neither Frank nor Jesse drank, but the thrill of the gambling tables appealed to them, as it did to most great desperadoes, and they soon became noted for iron nerve, high play, and clear judgment. Some of the disgruntled ruffians decided to rob the two men from Missouri by means of a friendly game, thinking it would be easy picking. Jesse and Frank and two friends were among thirty or forty men present.

Jesse's friend, sitting at the same table, had just called the hand of his rival, one of the conspirators.

"Three kings," said the gambler.

"Three aces," coolly replied the other, raking in his winnings, and added, "Friend, I discarded a king. When the cut was made for your deal, the bottom card was exposed, and it was a king. You got your third king from the bottom. Don't do it again."

"It's a damned lie!" shouted the red-faced gambler as his hand streaked for his gun.

The attention of all in that part of the room was now fixed upon the party. One gambler drew a pistol; the other a bowie knife. Jesse had taken in the whole situation in a glance. He knew that someone had to die following his friend's accusation.

Jesse's pistol roared and the gambler with the gun dropped dead. The gambler with the knife slashed at Jesse, but his aim was off a bit and Jesse's gun again roared, the heavy slug taking off half the top of the man's head.

The remaining conspirators now realized they were not playing with novices.

Frank and his companion had risen, and the strategic point of the four men was the door, their only possible retreat. More shots rang out, and more men hit the floor. Now the lamp was extinguished, and Jesse gave the word to rush for the door. When they were gone, the lamps were lighted again amid a scene of death, agony, and confusion. On the floor three men lay dead and five severely wounded. The place was a shambles, strewn with wreckage and bloodstained furniture.

The crowd that gathered determined to follow the four men

who were responsible for this outrage and to settle matters with them. A mile away they came upon the four Missourians taking the back trail for the Pacific Railroad. This would be an easy task, they thought.

"Don't attack us," warned Jesse. "We have fought before and will fight again."

At a given signal the four fired a volley into the group of followers. Four of them toppled to the ground. This was enough for the others. With a parting volley at the four outlaws, the mining camp men retreated and were content to do so.

The fight prompted the miners to call the place Battle Mountain. They certainly had fared badly in the melee, though one of their bullets inflicted a minor wound. When the four reached Winnemucca they were told of the horrible fight and were advised to skirt the area by all means. Here, Jesse and Frank James boarded an eastbound train and in due time were safe in their old haunts in Missouri.

CHAPTER 4

The Gallatin
Bank Robbery

MISSOURI OLD-TIMERS LOLLED LAZILY IN THEIR ROCKERS AS they puffed on their corncob pipes, wondering why things were so slow in Missouri during the year 1869. Many recalled that on May 10, that year, the last spike was driven at Promontory Point, Utah, an event that joined the Union and Central Pacific and signalized the completion of the first transcontinental American railroad.

These old codgers even tried to estimate the cost of the spikes of gold that were contributed by California and neighboring territories, as well as the value of the silver sledge which was provided for the ceremony. These things were all well and good, they agreed, but they were more concerned about things happening in Missouri and surrounding states.

The folks who followed the career of Jesse and Frank James were somewhat disappointed that no startling incident had occurred since the daring robbery of the Southern Deposit Bank at Russellville, Kentucky, in March of 1868. They thought a long time had elapsed since Jesse again decided to go into action. But in December they were in for another thrill.

It was December, 7, 1869, when two young men on spirited horses rode up to the door of the Daviess County Savings Bank in Gallatin, Missouri. One dismounted and, handing the bridle rein to the other, asked him to hold his horse for a minute. He then quickly entered the bank. A young man named James McDowell was in the bank on some business, and the cashier, John W. Sheets, was behind the counter.

The stranger, who had the appearance of a well-to-do stockman, took a $100 bill from his pocket and asked the cashier to change it. Sheets took the bill, walked back to the safe, took out a handful of bills, and was counting out the change when the stranger pulled out a navy revolver and shot the cashier through the heart, at the same time grabbing the money and stuffing it in his pocket. He fired a second shot immediately, which went through the cashier's brain. Before the startled McDowell could recover from his astonishment the deadly revolver was covering him, holding him at bay.

The robber went behind the counter, plundered the safe and till, and secured in all about $700 in currency. Thomas Lewis, the sixteen-year-old brother-in-law of Captain Sheets, ran into the bank and saw the outlaw pulling Sheets's body from under a counter.

Meanwhile one or two men who had come to the bank on business had been driven away by the confederate outside, and this, besides gunfire, had given alarm. The whole transaction occupied but a few minutes, but by the time the robber emerged from the bank a dozen townsmen had snatched up weapons and were converging on the bank.

The killer heard his comrade's warning cry and, rushing out into the street, saw the danger. Spooked by the shouts of the advancing crowd, the lead horse made a plunge just as Sheets's killer was about to mount.

The suddenness of the horse's movement threw the robber, who fell to the ground and was dragged about thirty feet head downward, with one heel caught in the stirrup. However, he succeeded in disengaging himself. For a second he lay prone, while the animal went racing off in the distance.

The crowd of citizens opened a lively fusillade, but the mounted bandit instantly rode back to his fallen comrade, who leaped up behind him, and together they raced out of town. Less than ten minutes had elapsed before the citizens were off in pursuit, and they must soon have overtaken the overloaded horse. It so happened, however, that about a mile southwest of town the fugitives met Daniel Smoot, riding an excellent saddle horse. Without a moment's hesitation they rode up to him, and with the muzzle of a revolver an inch from his nose told him to dismount. Of course he took to the brush with great alacrity, and the two robbers were once more thoroughly equipped. They seemed to have little fear of capture after obtaining Smoot's horse.

Between Gallatin and Kidder they talked with several people, boasting of what they had done. Nearing Kidder, they met the Rev. Helm, a Methodist minister and pressed him into service by means of their weapons, forcing him guide them around so as to avoid the town. On leaving him, one of them told the Rev. Helm that he was Bill Anderson's brother and that he had killed S. Cox, if he hadn't made a mistake in the man. He claimed that this was an act of vengeance for the death of his brother Bill. As Bloody Bill Anderson had been killed by a volley from ambush, it is probable that the robber was framing a tale based on some fact of the old guerrilla warfare that would tend to show that the raid on the bank was not made for plunder alone. This was undoubtedly the object he had in mind.

The pursuing posse followed hot upon the heels of the fugitives. About six miles south of Kidder, the pair took to the woods, going toward the Missouri River, and with the approach of night made their escape.

The horse that had nearly disabled one of the outlaws in front of the bank was found by the sheriff of Daviess County. The escaping robbers were traced across the river into Clay County, and the abandoned horse was identified as the property of a young man named James, whose mother and stepfather lived about four miles from Centreville, Clay County (now Kearney), Missouri, near the Cameron branch of the Hannibal and St. Joe Railroad. Reports stated that the James boys were dangerous killers, having had a lot of experience with Quantrill's raiders during the Civil War. The most careful inquiry was made in order to leave no question as to the identity of the robbers, and most people did not doubt that Jesse and Frank James had been the pair. Later on, of course, Jesse claimed that he had sold the recovered horse to Jim Anderson some time before the robbery.

On hearing that they were accused of the Gallatin crime, Jesse and Frank boldly rode into Kearney and denied the charge. However, they were careful not to ride into Gallatin, for there a warrant had been sworn out for Jesse's arrest. The boys' display of wrath and injured innocence was convincing to most of the residents.

As soon as it was definitely ascertained who the men were and where they lived, two of the citizens of Gallatin, thoroughly armed and mounted, rode away to Liberty, Clay County, where they called on Captain John S. Thomason, former sheriff of the county and an ex-officer who had served well in the regular Confederate Army. Thomason felt that for the honor of Clay County he should lead the expedition against the raiders and return them to Gallatin for just punishment. The captain, accompanied by his son Oscar and the two men from Gallatin, started at once for the Samuel residence, some twenty miles from Liberty.

Approaching the residence of Dr. Samuel, stepfather of the

James boys, some strategy was necessary. The men from Gallatin watched the house from the side next to the woods, while the captain and his son dismounted at the gate in front of the house and walked very deliberately up to the door. Before reaching it, however, a little Negro boy ran past them and on to the stable. Just as he got there the door opened suddenly and out dashed the two robbers on splendid horses, with pistols drawn, and took a lot of fence at a swift gallop. The Gallatin party from the fence above opened fire on sight. The ex-sheriff and his son followed suit, as did the James brothers, but no one was hit. Then the chase began.

Thomason's horse, a fine animal, was the only mount to clear the fence, and so while the balance of the pursuers used the gate, the captain found himself some distance from his men. Thomason was riding like the wind, and he gained upon the brothers, as well mounted as they were. Several shots were exchanged, but the speed was too great for accuracy. Carried on by the heat of the chase, Mr. Thomason soon found himself far in advance of the supporting column, and, in fact, hotly pursuing two desperadoes with nothing but his empty revolver.

Just what happened will probably never be known, as there were no witnesses but the principals, who chose to remain silent about it. A short time afterward, Mr. Thomason came back to Dr. Samuel's house on foot, having evidently made a forced march through the brush. The horse he had been riding was later found, shot dead. He borrowed another horse and started for Centreville. He had hardly been gone ten minutes when the two James boys returned to the house and when they heard from their mother that the captain had had the nerve to come back there, they went after him, vowing to kill him. They missed him, however.

Thomason reached Liberty about ten o'clock that night and found the town in considerable excitement over the report that he had been killed. His posse, having lost track of him, had returned before him and circulated that report. Thomason's story about the affair was that he found he could not hit the boys from a running horse, and so he dismounted to get one well-aimed shot. The boys later said that when they found only one man close to them, they turned on him and killed his horse, whereupon he plunged into a thicket. They were willing enough to let him get away, but they had no idea that he would have the gall to go to their house for a fresh horse.

Of course the whole country turned out to catch the Jameses, without success. The robbery was perhaps the most remarkable of all that were committed by the Missouri bandits, partly because only two men were engaged in it, and partly because of the utter wantonness of the murder.

Jesse was so furious about the borrowed horse that he wrote Thomason a letter threatening to kill him if the animal was not returned at once, though he said that he was reluctant to do such a thing since the ex-sheriff had been a soldier in the Confederacy. The captain promptly returned the horse, although he made a claim that he ought to be paid for the horse he had lost. Ironically enough, years later, after the death of Captain Thomason, Jesse James met Oscar Thomason on a Texas street, and actually paid him $125 for the animal he had killed.

In the Thursday, January 20, 1870, issue of the Lexington *Register,* the following item appeared:

REWARD OFFERED

A reward of three thousand dollars is offered for the apprehension and delivery to the Sheriff of Daviess County of the bodies of the murderers of John W. Sheets, cashier of the Gallatin bank. These murderers are believed to be Jesse and Frank James of Clay County, Mo., and are described as follows: Jesse—about 6 feet in height, rather slender build, thin visage, hair and complexion rather light and sandy. Frank—about 5 feet 8 or 10 inches tall, heavy build, full in face and hair and complexion same as Jesse.

These descriptions were inaccurate. Frank was the taller of the two.

Mrs. Frank A. Fitterer of Gallatin wrote the author in March of 1952:

I am writing at the request of my father [Thomas Lewis], now ninety-nine years of age. He feels he is too nervous to write and has asked me to take down, word for word, his statement. The story follows:

Capt. John Sheets was killed by the James boys at 12:00 o'clock noon on Dec. 7, 1869. I was just across the street—18 years old at the time.

James McDowell ran by and said, "Sheets has been killed." Capt. Sheets was my brother-in-law.

I forgot the shooting and ran into the bank where he had been killed. There was a man in there, pulling the body from under the counter, where it had fallen after he was shot. While I was in the bank, this man had gone back into the alley. As he attempted to mount, his horse threw him and jerked loose in front of the bank. I heard the crowd holler, "Catch him!"

I darted out the door. The crowd was behind the bank. This man had gotten up on his feet, he saw me, and drew a revolver. I rushed toward him, he pointed the gun at me and drove me back. I backed away and watched until I got out of sight around a corner of the bank building.

I then ran across the street to the Post Office, and Chris Gillihan handed a revolver across the counter. I reached for it, but E. Barnum grabbed it.

We both ran back to the door of the Post Office. The two men were trying to get on one horse. They left town, both on this one horse.

Two or three citizens after them on horses got close enough to shoot, but their guns were rusty or failed to operate, and the robbers got away.

They went South and met Preacher Helm, told him that if he

did not take them to a certain red barn, near Kidder, a small town, they'd kill him.

Now Preacher Helm didn't know anything about this red barn, but luckily for him he struck it just right, and they released him unharmed.

Thomas Lewis

The raiding band of outlaws went into seclusion after the Gallatin robbery, spending another eighteen months in Texas and Mexico. They had a well-defined policy of action by which they were guided in their social activities as well as in their dangerous adventures. Secret communications were kept up when the band was divided, and each one was always on the alert for special opportunities in the practice of their peculiar profession. Jesse and Frank visited Mexico at one time during the lull in their activities and nearly met with disaster at Matamoros. While attending a public fandango, they were unable to execute the graceful steps of the Mexican young bloods, but they tried. Their gestures were so amusing to the audience that soon the Mexicans began to mimic the Jameses and to poke fun at them.

This was too much for Frank, and he simply downed the Mexican who was laughing the loudest. A large, raw-boned Mexican reached out and struck Frank full in the face, knocking him into a group of onlookers. Jesse brought up his revolver and shot the Mexican through the head.

Jesse and Frank rushed for the door, but it was blocked by a dozen belligerent Mexicans. They shot their way through, killing four of the Mexicans. The others struck with stilettos, stabbing Jesse in the right arm and Frank in the shoulder.

Putting spurs to their mounts, they raced for the Rio Grande. They stopped at Concepcion, Texas, where they remained under the care of a doctor for nearly three months.

Returning north, the young outlaws avoided Missouri and

holed up at the home of their uncle, Major George B. Hite, who lived within three miles of Russellville, Kentucky.

After a long period of idleness, plotting, and recuperating, the reorganized band, consisting of the two James boys, Cole and Jim Younger, Clell Miller, Jim White, and one other (possibly Jim Koughman) decided to rob the Corydon County treasurer's office at Corydon, Iowa. The frightened clerk was unable to open the time-lock safe. When he finally convinced the outlaws that he was telling the truth, they walked down the street toward the Ocobock Brothers Bank.

It was June 3, 1871, when three of the outlaws entered the bank, while the remaining four stood guard outside. At noon, the bank cashier was confronted by three revolvers aimed at his head. All alone in the bank, the poor cashier willingly gave up the keys to the safe, and the robbers took all its contents—$40,000. It was one of the largest hauls they had made up to that time.

After putting their haul in a grain sack, the three emerged from the bank after binding the cashier, something new in the technique of the James band. Apparently this was done so that the group might attend a meeting being held in the town square.

The entire party masked themselves with bandanas and rode over to the meeting, which appeared to be a political one of some sort. The crowd was being addressed by Henry Clay Dean, when Jesse James interrupted the speaker and asked for the privilege of saying a few words. In his usual drawling manner, Jesse said, "You-all been having your fun and we ours. We've just been down to the bank and robbed it of every dollar in the till. If you'll go down there you'll find the cashier tied and gagged, and then, if you want any of us, just come down and take us. Thank you for your kind attention."

At the conclusion of this strange speech the seven outlaws set up a wild yell, lifted their hats and sped southward. The crowd at first thought it was just a trick to break up the meeting, but they soon learned the truth. After discovering the robbery there were hasty preparations for pursuit, and a posse of a dozen resolute men, headed by the sheriff, dashed off in haste after the bandits.

On the second day the outlaws were overtaken in Daviess County, Missouri, and a fight ensued, but the citizens were forced to give way without doing any damage. Others joined in the chase, however, and the trail was followed into Clay County and then into Jackson, where it was lost.

The Kansas City detectives continued to search for the perpetrators of the robbery, and two months later they arrested Clell Miller in Clay County and took him back to Iowa. He was tried at Corydon in November, 1872, the court proceedings lasting from Monday, November 10, until the Friday following, when, owing to insufficient evidence, he was released. The mask he had worn had saved him.

As usual, the Jameses and Youngers presented alibis, naming many persons in their home counties, who, they swore, could testify to their presence in Missouri when the Iowa bank was robbed.

It is interesting to note that the Osceola *Republican* gave an account of the Corydon affair, as well as descriptions of several of the raiders. One was described as about twenty-five years old, wearing false whiskers, height about five feet eight inches, no necktie, dark barred muslin coat, barred pants, black slouch hat, and linen coat. This, of course, was probably Jesse James. Frank James's height was six feet or over, although after the Gallatin Bank robbery the Lexington *Register* had given the James boys' description in reverse.

CHAPTER 5

Jesse James'
First Train Robbery

TRAIN ROBBERY WAS UNHEARD OF IN THIS COUNTRY UNTIL the night of October 6, 1866, when an Adams Express car was boarded and robbed. The train had been boarded in the dark forest a few miles outside Seymour, Indiana, by two masked men who crept along the tops of the cars until they reached the car which held the safe. Carefully swinging down, they ripped through the door and blackjacked the messenger in charge. They then shoved the great safe across the floor of the car, tumbled it out through the door, rifled the small express safe of $16,000, and pulled the bell cord.

It was eventually proven that the Reno brothers—John, Frank, Simeon, and William—had been responsible for that first train robbery. John was later taken to the Missouri State Penitentiary for holding up the county clerk at Gallatin, and his three brothers were hanged by a lynch mob on December 12, 1868 at New Albany, Indiana.

Apparently the fate of the Reno brothers did not bother the

James boys or the Younger brothers. No doubt they considered themselves smarter in the art of robbery than most outlaws; they would not make the mistakes of other badmen. It was with this idea in mind and looking for new opportunities that Frank James and Jim Younger left their hideout in Jackson County, and made a trip to the northwest, going through Omaha and as far west as Cheyenne, where they remained for some time.

Both the Youngers and the Jameses had relatives in California, and it was thought that information concerning gold shipments over the Union Pacific Railroad from San Francisco could be obtained easily. An uncle of Jim Younger owned a large general store there, while Frank's uncle, Drury Woodson James, operated the Paso Robles Hot Sulphur Springs in San Luis Obispo County.

Back in Missouri other members of the gang were growing restless awaiting the return of Jim Younger and Frank James. The winter of 1872–73 had been a severe one, and when May rolled around the bandits became restless.

Jesse James decided that the five members left in hiding in Jackson County should go into action. With Cole and Bob Younger, Clell Miller, Bill Chadwell (alias Bill Stiles) and himself, the five would ride to Ste. Genevieve, Missouri, and plunder the bank. On the May 1, 1873, the five left Jackson County and stopped at a country place a few miles south of Springfield. From there they went to Bismarck, on the Iron Mountain Railroad, remaining there but a day. From that point they rode through Ste. Genevieve County and, on the morning of May 27, they appeared in the town, three entering from the south and two from the north, shortly after nine o'clock.

As three of them entered the bank they found no one inside except the cashier, O. D. Harris, and a son of State Senator Firman A. Rozier, the president of the bank. The robbers leveled their pistols and ordered him to open the safe. Rozier began to speak but was cut short.

"You keep still, you damned little rat, if you don't want to die!"

"For what?"

"Not another word."

Driven by a sudden and overpowering urge, young Rozier leapt down the steps near the landing and raced from the building. The two bandits who stood guard outside fired three times at the fleeing boy, one bullet passing through his coat. Mr. Harris accepted the more sensible alternative and opened the safe door, allowing the outlaws to remove all the funds then in the bank, amounting to about $4,000. The money, much of which was silver, was thrown into a sack and, mounting their horses, the bandits rode away.

On the way from town the money sack fell to the ground, spilling silver all over the place. They were compelled to return to scoop up what money they could before making a hasty departure. A posse was quickly organized but, as in previous cases, the "brave citizens" were induced to return home after the bandits had fired a few volleys in their direction. The robbers were really fit to be tied when they learned how faulty their timing had been. At the time of the raid the bank was winding up its business and, to facilitate this, the capital and funds had been deposited with the Merchants Bank in St. Louis, and all the deposits had been withdrawn except for the small amount needed to carry on the daily business of the bank.

When the five outlaws reached Jackson County from Ste. Genevieve, they found Frank James and Jim Younger waiting. A new campaign was planned. Hitherto they had plundered the banks but they were now about to commence another line of business. Plundering a railway train was something entirely new. The public mind had not become accustomed to accounts of the arrest of railway trains and the robbery of the passengers by a band of armed outlaws. The Missouri bandits decided to offer the thrill-seeking public something to gasp over.

The first suggestion was to rob a train on the Hannibal & St. Joe Railroad or some other road in Missouri. But this idea was rejected after due deliberation. The plan for going into Iowa was suggested and met with favor, for it had been learned by Jim Younger and Frank James that a fortune in gold would be shipped over the Union Pacific Railroad, reaching Omaha on the morning of July 21. The plans for the raid were laid before the gang separated. On the fourteenth of the month the bandits met at the house of a friend in Clay County, and the final arrangements were made; a place of rendezvous was designated, and the gang then separated in pairs. As usual, Frank and Jesse James took the same route, Cole Younger and his brothers another, and Chadwell and Miller still another. It has been claimed that two of the robbers were outlaws named Bob Moore and Comanche Tony, but this has never been substantiated.

The bandits leisurely pursued their journey, and on July 20 they were near the line of the Chicago, Rock Island and Pacific Railroad, some eighty miles east of Council Bluffs, Iowa. On the afternoon of the thirty-first it was agreed to wreck the evening passenger train. The spot selected for this purpose was about a mile or so west of Adair, a small town in Adair County, where there was a sharp curve in the road which obscured the rails sixty yards in advance of the engine. The outlaws tied their horses some distance from the tracks out of sight from the train and, procuring a spike bar, loosened one of the rails. To this loose rail they tied a rope leading several yards out into the grass, where they concealed themselves. The passenger train consisted of seven coaches, including the two sleepers, and was due at the point of ambush at 8:30 P.M.

As the cumbersome train puffed up the incline Engineer John Rafferty spied the rope from his cab. He understood the situation and threw his engine into reverse, but the distance was so short, while the momentum of the train was so great, that the engine plunged through the break in the tracks, crashed into the ditch, and toppled over on its side. By some miracle the cars remained upright. Rafferty, trapped in the engine, was scalded to death by the steam, and in the coaches men, women, and children screamed in fright.

From the wrecked engine Dennis Foley, the fireman, got up and staggered forward, screaming in agony, his oil-soaked overalls in flames. Rolling desperately in the high grass, Foley was able to extinguish the flames, but he was badly burned. It was an heroic effort on the part of this young man in his twenties. Engineer Rafferty, the real hero of the disaster, a man who refused to leap to safety from his post, was about thirty-five years old, married, and the father of one child.

Undismayed with the results of their plan, the robbers quickly boarded the cars, two of them entering the express car, while the others forced the excited and demoralized passengers to deliver up all their money and valuables. The express messenger, John Burgesse, was forced to open the safe and give the bandits what money he had, but the amount was small—around $3,000. This was a bitter disappointment to the raiders, for they expected to find not less than $50,000 in gold in the safe. The express messenger told them that the heavy shipment of gold was scheduled to pass on the following train, and therefore Jesse's first train robbery was a failure—it was twelve hours too soon! When Conductor William A. Smith walked toward the express car the bandits fired into the air, chasing him back into the coaches.

The entire booty taken in the holdup amounted to about $26,000 and, with this in the sack, the seven robbers waved their hats and shouted farewell to their victims, leapt onto their horses, and galloped away to the south.

Some years ago Mrs. John F. Rafferty said this about the robbery: "My husband is the son of the engineer who was killed. He heard it from his mother. He says it is best you should bring it out that his father could have saved his life and jumped. He was a hero, but is usually not given credit for sticking to his post at the cost of his life."

It is most fitting that at this time due recognition be given to this courageous engineer who gave his life while trying to protect the passengers and property assigned to him. I, for one, shall make it a point always to talk about his deed.

The excitement over the outrage was great, and hundreds of brave men volunteered to track down the desperadoes. The trail led straight through Missouri and to the Missouri River, where there was unmistakable evidence that the outlaws swam the stream with their horses. Following the tracks on the other side, the band was tracked into Jackson County, where, as usual, every trace of them disappeared. A party of detectives went to Monegraw Springs in search of the outlaws and found two of the Younger brothers, who promptly disarmed the possemen and compelled them to have coffee with them.

Bob Younger told the officers this before allowing them to depart: "You know that my brother Cole was accused of being in the band that robbed the Iowa railroad train which occurred July 21, 1873. At that time, my brothers and I were all down at the bottom at Monegraw Springs in St. Clair County, Missouri. The robbery was committed on Monday, and Sunday we attended preaching. This we could prove by a great many people of Greenton Valley, Lafayette County, Missouri, and Reverend Mr. Smith, who was here in this very same hotel at the time on a visit."

On the day after the robbery five of those believed to have been the bandits ate dinner at the home of a farmer named Stuckeye, in Ringgold County. He described the men as follows:

1. Seemed to be the leader; five feet seven or eight inches tall, light hair, blue eyes, heavy sandy whiskers, broad shoulders, short nose a little turned up; high, broad forehead; looked to be

well educated, not used to work; age thirty-six to forty.

2. Tall and lithe, with light complexion, high forehead, light brown hair, long, light whiskers almost sandy, long, slender hands that certainly had not done much hard work, nose a prominent Roman. He was very polite and talked little. Looked thirty-six years old.

3. Slender, five feet nine or ten inches tall, hair cut short and of light brown color, straight nose, uncouth and sarcastic in speech, brown eyes, and wearing a hard, dissipated countenance. Middle-aged, and wore dark clothes.

4. Dark complexion, dark hair, clean-shaven, five feet eight inches tall, heavy-set, straight, black eyes, straight nose, good-looking but appeared dissipated. Middle-aged, and wore light pants, hat, and vest, and dark coat.

5. Five feet ten inches tall, large, broad shoulders, straight, blue eyes, reddish whiskers, Roman nose. Middle-aged, and very pleasant in appearance.

These descriptions fit those of Frank and Jesse James, Clell Miller, Jim and Bob Younger. What happened to the other two men remained a moot question. It was definitely known that the seven outlaws were together when they rode through Missouri.

Others also wanted to get into the act. The *Kansas City Times* received communications supposedly implicating other people, but nothing much came of this. The most prominent accusation was that of Jack Bishop, when he wrote to the paper naming Ike Flannery as one of the band.

After the Adair train robbery the outlaws enjoyed a long period of inactivity, and were not heard from again until the early part of 1874.

Of all the holdups and robberies attributed to the James-Younger band of outlaws there is still some material evidence of their connection with some of the crimes. The bank buildings robbed at Liberty, Missouri, and Russellville, Kentucky, are still standing; the old iron safe in Ste. Genevieve could tell an interesting story, and in Northfield there is on display a piece of the scalp from the head of one of the robbers. Several revolvers dropped in a hasty getaway after the bank robbery at Huntington, West Virginia, are resting comfortably in a museum.

The only bit of such evidence connected with the Adair train robbery is a gold signet ring which had been tossed away by the robbers in the Nodaway River bottom as they rode away from the train wreck. It belongs to Elmer Johnson of Greenfield, Iowa, and has been in his family for three generations.

It seems that Elmer's father, then about ten, was returning home with his father, John Johnson. As they rode across an unfarmed area in their wagon young Johnson spied something on the ground. It was a bunch of cheap rings. Mr. Johnson gave each of his children one of the rings and turned the rest over to the postmaster. Elmer Johnson is very proud of this souvenir from the first train robbery west of the Mississippi, and justly so.

At Adair, Iowa, on Wednesday and Thursday, July 21–22, 1954, the train robbery was reenacted in a gigantic celebration. Many old-timers declared the crowds which thronged Adair during the festivities were the largest ever to attend a celebration there. One feature of the activities was the unveiling of the marker at the robbery site. The marker is not in memory of the outlaw band, but a monument commemorating the first train robbery west of the Mississippi River. It stands some twenty-five miles northwest of Greenfield, a few miles west of Adair on Highway 6, on a cutoff lane which leads to a knoll. Thereon are mounted three markers, one an old engine wheel and a section of a century-old track, the other a plaque which reads: "The Adair Train Robbery, World's First Robbery of a Moving Train—Committed Here on July 21, 1873, by the notorious Jesse James and his Gang of Outlaws." The present Rock Island tracks run just a short distance beyond the markers.

CHAPTER 6

The Gads Hill
Train Robbery

ON JANUARY 31, 1874, AT 9:30 A.M., THE ST. LOUIS AND Texas express train, with a large number of passengers, the mails, and valuable express freight, departed from the Plum Street depot in St. Louis, bound for Texas, via the St. Louis, Iron Mountain and Southern Railroad. C. A. Alford was the conductor in charge of the train when it departed and when the event which we are about to describe occurred.

Gads Hill, a name rich in historical associations, was a lonely wayside station on the railroad, situated in the northeast corner of Wayne County, Missouri, about seven miles from Piedmont, which was the nearest telegraph station. January 31 was a dreary winter day; cold gray clouds veiled the sky, and no ray of sunlight filtered through the wintry pall.

The passengers had not yet had time to become acquainted with one another. It was no relief to look out the windows of the coaches. The landscape was cold, dreary, and forbidding. The winds came blowing from the north with a chill that made the passengers wish they had stayed home. Iron Mountain, Pilot Knob, and Shepherd's Mountain, and the beautiful Arcadia Valley, all decked out in their winter beauty, failed to appeal to the passengers. They were anything but merry, and with the coming of nightfall, their prospects of having their spirits lifted were slim indeed.

It was now 5:30 P.M. and the train was approaching the little station of Gads Hill, an area named after Sir John Falstaff who defeated the Buckramite host in a section with the same name. As the train drew near the station, the engineer saw the red flag displayed and signaled the brakeman to stop the train.

Had the engineer been aware of what had occurred that afternoon he might have sped by, even though the train was greatly slowed down by the steep climb. He did not know that at 3:30 that afternoon a band of seven heavily armed horsemen had arrived at the station, taken the agent into custody, and secured the blacksmith and some of the citizens, as well as several passengers awaiting the incoming train.

One was Dr. Rock, a member of the state legislature from Wayne County. The prisoners were confined to the small station house, under guard of one of the robbers. It was fortunate, however, that the engineer was unaware of all this, for one of the robbers had opened the end of the switch, so that if the train had tried to pass the station it would have been derailed. The bandits had also set the signal flag on the track, then waited for their quarry.

As the train slowed to a halt, Alford was ready to step upon the little platform. The robbers did not show themselves until the cars were at the station. When Alford stepped to the platform he was instantly confronted by the yawning muzzle of a heavy revolver and greeted by the bandits.

"Give me your money and your watch and be quick about it," he was ordered.

Alford surrendered his wallet, containing fifty dollars, and a fine gold watch. He was then shoved into the station house with the other prisoners.

While this was going on, one of the robbers had covered the engineer with his revolver and compelled him to leave his cab. Meanwhile, part of the band occupied the platforms of the passenger coaches, while two of them went through the train and commanded the passengers to give up their money. Seeing the guns, the defenseless passengers could do nothing but obey.

John H. Morley, chief engineer of the St. Louis, Iron Mountain & Southern Railroad, was among the passengers, and he too was forced to turn over his valuables. The bandits made a clean sweep, taking all the money and jewelry available. After stripping the passengers, the robbers went to the express car, broke open the safe, and removed the contents. The mail bags were next cut open and their contents rifled. The total amounted to about $10,000.

Before they left, one of the bandits stepped up to Alford. "Since you are the conductor of this damned train, you'll probably need your watch," he said, and gave the astonished conductor back his gold watch. They also released the engineer and told him to head for Piedmont.

Several amusing events—or at least afterward they were considered so—occurred during the train holdup. As the robbers passed through the cars, relieving the passengers of their possessions, they asked the name of each of the men. One of the victims, a man named Newell, asked, "What do you want to know that for?"

"Damn you, out with your name, and ask questions later."

"Well, my name is Newell, and here's my money, and now I would like to know why you want to know my name."

"You're a cool one," said the robber. "I'll tell you why. That damned Allan Pinkerton is on this train, or was supposed to be, and we want to get him. That is why we picked this train."

During the entire holdup the bandits displayed their hatred

for Allan Pinkerton, and it was fortunate for him that he was not on that train. This incident led many to believe that the leaders of the band were Jesse and Frank James. They nursed a deep hatred for the Pinkerton detective; the very mention of his name threw them into a rage.

The leader of the band handed the conductor an envelope, saying, "This contains an exact account of the robbery. We prefer this to be published in the newspapers rather than the grossly exaggerated accounts that usually appear after one of our jobs."

Oddly enough, the papers carried the item:

The most daring on record—the southbound train on the Iron Mountain Railroad was robbed here this evening by seven heavily armed men, and robbed of ————dollars. The robbers arrived at the station some time before the arrival of the train, and arrested the station agent and put him under guard, then threw the train on the switch. The robbers were all large men, none of them under six feet tall. They were all masked and started in a southerly direction after they had robbed the train. They were all mounted on fine blooded horses. There is a hell of an excitement in this part of the country.

The citizens were released, and the robbers mounted their horses and rode away in the gathering darkness. Gads Hill was then in the midst of a wilderness country, with few settlements, so it was impossible to organize a posse. At Piedmont, the news was quickly telegraphed to St. Louis, Missouri, and Little Rock, Arkansas. The citizens of that vicinity were aroused and before midnight a well-armed posse of a dozen men rode into the hills.

Pursuit was hopeless, however, for the robbers were sixty miles away when dawn broke, and their horses were vastly superior to those of the possemen. On the morning after the robbery, the bandits called on a widow named Cook, a mile from Carpentersville, on the Current River, to prepare breakfast for them. Mrs. Cook later stated that only five men came to her home and that each was armed with a pair of revolvers and a repeating rifle.

The robbers left the home of Mrs. Cook and later stopped at the residence of Mr. Mason, a state legislator, who was away at Jefferson City, and demanded food. They remained there all night, and in the morning proceeded westward. It must be mentioned that the posse did stick to the trail for a while. During the day after Mrs. Cook had served the robbers breakfast, the posse arrived at her home, having tracked the bandits sixty miles. But there they lost the trail and returned empty-handed to Piedmont.

As a result of the Gads Hill robbery, the famous Pinkerton Detective Agency was engaged by the railroad trust to track down the outlaws in Missouri. Allan Pinkerton assigned John W. Whicher, one of his shrewdest operatives, to capture Frank and Jesse James.

Clues gathered by the detectives from Mrs. Cook and Mrs. Mason quickly led them to believe that the two Jameses, the Younger brothers, and perhaps George Shepherd and several Texas gunmen had taken part in the Gads Hill robbery.

Intense investigation went into the case, for many reasons. Rewards were offered by Governor Woodson of Missouri and Governor Baxter of Arkansas, as well by the railroads, and the Pinkerton Agency longed to claim fame as the destroyer of the James gang.

While all this was going on, the James boys were living in the vicinity of Kearney, Clay County, near their mother's home. On March 9 Jesse even had the nerve to spend a portion of the day in Kearney, and to have several horses shod at a local blacksmith's.

On Wednesday, March 10, 1874, J. W. Whicher arrived from Kansas City and took up a room at Liberty. Whicher was a daring and vigorous young man, twenty-six years old and recently married to a beautiful young woman from Iowa City, Iowa. Apparently Allan Pinkerton and young Whicher were unaware of the ingenuity of the Jameses, their line of communication, or that they had many friends in Clay County and elsewhere.

Whicher's next step was to call on Mr. Adkins, president of the Clay County Savings Association Bank, and to make known to him his purpose in the neighborhood. Adkins was unable to supply the detective with all the information he desired, so he referred him to Colonel O. P. Moss, ex-sheriff of Clay County.

Colonel Moss tried in earnest to persuade Whicher to abandon his reckless course of action. He told him that the James boys could not be caught unaware, and that his presence probably was already known to them. But to no avail. Whicher had obtained what he regarded as positive evidence that the James boys had planned the Gads Hill affair, and nothing could divert him from his determined path. Apparently Whicher did not know the meaning of the word fear, or he would have waited for help in his quest to capture the James boys. He had determined to go that very evening to the Samuel house. Disguised as a farm laborer, with an old carpet bag swung on a stick, Whicher took the evening train for Kearney, and there made inquiries for work on a farm. He did not remain at the station very long, and set out for the Samuel place.

But Whicher's fate had already been determined by those whom he hoped to capture and bring to trial.

The very day that Whicher arrived in Liberty, a man named Jim Latche saw him visit with Mr. Adkins, and from there traced him to the home of Colonel Moss. He at once came to the conclusion that this man must be looking for the James boys. Latche had ridden with the Jameses in one of their raids and was now staying with them near Kearney. He happened to be in Liberty when Whicher arrived. When Latche saw the detective disguise himself as a farmhand he felt certain of his guess. He hastily gave a report to Jesse of what he had heard and observed.

When Whicher arrived in Kearney the Jameses knew of it, suspected what he was after, and were ready for him. It was in the evening when Jim Anderson, Jesse James, and Bradley Collins were waiting at the roadside, about a half mile from the Samuel house. Whicher soon came along. He was carrying the carpet bag, dressed as a farmhand. Jesse James came out of their concealment alone and met Whicher in the road.

"Good evening, sir," said Whicher.

"Where in hell are you going?" James demanded.

"Well, that's a rude response. I'm looking for farm work. Do you know of anyone needing a hand?"

"No, not much, don't want any. Old Pinkerton has already given you a job as long as you live, I reckon."

With that Jesse laughed a cold, hard laugh that meant only one thing. The detective was helpless, as he had been under the guns of Jesse's companions the moment Jesse stepped into the road.

"Who do you take me to be?" asked Whicher. "What do I know of Pinkerton and his work? I am a stranger in this country and want something to do. I don't see why you should keep that pistol pointed at me. I don't know you, and have never done you any harm."

"Oh, damn you, you would like bring in the James boys, wouldn't you? A real sneak, you are!"

"I don't understand you, sir," replied Whicher. "I am not a sneak. I know nothing of the James boys. If you cannot be more polite, I must bid you good evening."

"You'll die instantly if you take another step."

Whicher now realized that his chances of escape were very slim indeed. He knew that the man before him was Jesse James, and he made up his mind to sell his life dearly. He wanted desperately to reach for his pistol, but Jesse James had him at a disadvantage.

"Well," said Whicher, "you certainly have made a mistake. I know nothing of the men you speak of. Let me go now. I must find a stopping place for tonight."

Jesse James laughed outright.

"What were you doing in Liberty today? Why did you go to the bank to talk with Adkins, and why did you talk to Colonel Moss? Where are the clothes you wore into town? Plotting to capture the James boys, eh?"

Jim Anderson and Bill Fox, who had also joined those men in hiding, came forward, pistols in hand. Whicher now saw that his case was hopeless—that the outlaws had known of his plan all along. He had underestimated the Jameses and now would pay with his life for the mistake.

"Young man, we want no more from you," said Jesse. "Boys, I don't think it best that we do the job here. For certain reasons I think it should be done across the field tonight."

All this time Whicher stood still. He knew what they meant. He decided to watch for any incident that might be in his favor. But none arrived. He had already been tried and convicted by a court from which he could not appeal. He knew the sentence would be carried out tonight.

"Boys, take his weapons," ordered Jesse James.

Whicher thrust his hand into his coat, but it was too late. Fox and Anderson sprang upon him, while Jesse placed the muzzle of his pistol against the detective's head. In an instant the outlaws had relieved him of his Smith & Wesson revolver. Whicher felt he had been betrayed either by Adkins or Moss. He was never to learn the real truth.

Whicher was bound securely, and a gag was placed in his mouth so that he could not call for help. The outlaws put him on a horse, his legs bound under the animal's belly, and his arms tied to the saddle horn, and he knew that he had fallen into the hands of Jesse James, Bradley Collins, and Jim Anderson.

About 3:00 A.M. on the morning of March 11, the drowsy ferryman at Blue Mills, on the Missouri River, was roused by the shouts of men on the north side, who signified their desire to cross the river.

"Hurry up, man," cried Jesse, "we are after horse thieves and must get across quick."

Thus appealed to, the ferryman lost no time in getting his boat across the river. When the outlaws came down to the ferry, one of them said, "We have caught one thief, and if you want to keep your head on your shoulders you had better get us across the river fast."

The ferryman saw that one of the men was bound and gagged. It was poor Whicher, and he was unable to help himself. The winds sighed sadly as the strange group moved off on the Independence Road. They rode away in the darkness, and just how or who carried out the murder of Whicher will never be known.

The next morning an early traveler on the road from Independence to Blue Mills, halfway between the towns, in a lonely place, came upon Whicher's body, a bullet hole through the heart and one through the head.

CHAPTER 7

The Corinth
Bank Robbery

EVENTS WERE HAPPENING FAST IN MISSOURI DURING THE
year 1874. Incidents occurred which gave the ex-Quantrillians
much to discuss and much to guess about as well. Many believed the James and Younger brothers were innocent in most
part for the crimes laid at their doorsteps. However, the Pinkerton Detective Agency thought otherwise when they sent John
Whicher to Missouri to apprehend the boys. Whicher had been
in Clay County only a short while when he was murdered,
presumably by Jesse James.

Soon afterward Jesse got married to his cousin, Zerelda
Mims, at the home of her sister, Mrs. W. B. Brander, at Kearney, Missouri. The Rev. William James, Jesse's uncle, offi-
ciated.

Again the headlines blazed when John Younger was slain in
a fight with officers, in March of that year, near Osceola, Missouri, in St. Clair County. When the fight was over Jim
Younger escaped with only a slight wound, Deputy Sheriff Ed

Daniels was dead, and Pinkerton operator Captain Louis J. Lull was wounded so severely that he, too, soon died.

The year 1874 appeared to be a good year for letter-writing too. From various hideouts Cole Younger emulated the letter-writing of Jesse James, bombarding the newspaper editors with his alibis. Just prior to several daring robberies which were to occur that December, a typical letter from Cole was published in the *Missouri Review* of Pleasant Hill, Missouri, November 26, 1874. It is written by Cole Younger to his brother-in-law, Lycurgus Jones, of Cass County.

Dear Curg:

You may use this letter in your own way. I will give you the outline and sketch of my whereabouts and actions at the time of certain robberies with which I am charged. At the time of certain bank robberies, I was gathering cattle in Ellis County, Texas, cattle that I had bought from Pleas Taylor and Rector. This can be proven by both of them, also by Sheriff Barkley and fifty other respectable men of that county. I brought the cattle to Kansas that fall and remained in St. Clair County until February. I then went to Arkansas and returned to St. Clair County about the first of May. I went to Kansas where our cattle were, in Woodson County, at Colonel Ridge's. During the summer I was either at St. Clair, Jackson, or Kansas, but as there was no robbery committed that summer, it makes no difference where I was then.

The gate at the fairgrounds in Kansas City was robbed that fall. I was in Jackson County at the time. I left R. P. Rose's that morning, went down Independence Road, stopped at Dr. Noland's and got some pills. Brother John was with me. I went through Independence, from there to Ace Webb's. There I took dinner and then went to Dr. L. W. Twiman's, stayed there until after supper, then went to Silas Hudspeth's and stayed all night. This was the day the gate receipts were robbed at Kansas City.

We crossed the river at Blue Mills, and went along the other side. Our business there was to see E. P. West. He was not at home, but the family will remember we were there. We crossed the bridge and stayed in the city all night, and the next morning we rode through the city. I met several of my friends, among them Bob Hudspeth.

We then returned to the Six-Mile country by the way of Independence. At Big Blue we met James Chiles and had a long talk with him. I saw several friends who were standing near the gate, and they all said they did not know any of the party that did the robbing. Neither John nor I were accused of the crime for several days after.*

My name never would have been used in connection with this affair, had not Jesse James, for some cause best known to himself, published in the *Kansas City Times* a letter stating that John, myself, and he were accused of the robbery. Where he got his authority I don't know, but one thing I do know, that he had none from me. We were not on good terms at the time, and have not been for several years. From that time on, my name and John's have been connected with the James brothers, although John had not seen either of them for eighteen months before his death.

And as for A. C. McCoy, John never saw him in his life. I knew McCoy during the war, and have not seen him since, notwithstanding the Appleton City papers say he has been with us in that county for two years. Now if any respectable man in that county will say he ever saw A. C. McCoy with me or John, I will say no more; or if any respectable man will say that he ever saw anyone with us who suited the description of A. C. McCoy, then I will be silent and never more plead innocent.

McCoy is 48 or 49 years old, six feet, dark hair and blue eyes, and low forehead.

Poor John, he was hunted and shot down like a wild beast, and never was there a boy more innocent. But there is a day coming when the secrets of all hearts will be laid open before that All-Seeing Eye, and every act of our lives will be scrutinized; then will his skirts be found white as the driven snow, while those of his accusers will be doubly dark.

I will now come to the Ste. Genevieve robbery. At that time I was in St. Clair County, Missouri. I do not remember the date,

*Author's note: It has been definitely established that Jesse and Frank were the only ones involved in the fairgrounds holdup.

but Mr. Murphy, one of our neighbors, was sick about that time, and I sat up with him regularly, where I met some of the neighbors every day. Dr. L. Lewis was his physician.

As to the Iowa train robbery, I have forgotten the day, I was also in St. Clair County, Missouri, at that time, and had the pleasure of attending preaching the evening previous to the robbery, at Monegaw Springs. There were about a hundred persons there who will testify in any court that I and John were there. I will give you the names of some of them: Simeon C. Bruce, John S. Wilson, James Van Allen, Rev. Mr. Smith and lady. Helvin Fickle and lady, of Greeton Valley, were attending the Springs at that time, and either of them will testify to the above, for John and I sat in front of Mr. Smith while he was preaching, and had the pleasure of his company for a few moments, together with his lady and Mr. and Mrs. Fickle after service. They live in Greenton Valley, Lafayette County, Missouri, and their evidence would be taken in the Court of Heaven.

As there was no other robbery committed until January, I will come to that time. About the last of December, 1873, I arrived at Carroll Parish, Louisiana. I stayed there until the 8th of February, 1874. I and brother stayed at William Dickerson's near Floyd. Dickerson was Master of a Masonic Lodge, and during the time the Shreveport stage and the Hot Springs stage was robbed, also the Gads Hill robbery. Now if the Governor or anyone else wants to satisfy himself in regard to the above, he can write to the Masonic Fraternity, Floyd, Carroll Parish, Louisiana. I hope the leading journals will investigate the matter, and then if they find I have misrepresented anything, they can show me up to the world as being guilty, and if they find it as I have stated, they surely would have no objections to state the facts as they are.

You can appeal to the Governor in your own language, and if he will send men to investigate the above, and is not satisfied of my innocence, then he can offer the reward for Thomas Coleman Younger, and if he finds me innocent, he can make a statement to that effect.

I write this hurriedly, and I suppose I have given outlines enough. I want you to take pains and write a long letter for me and sign my name in full.

Thomas Coleman Younger

I should like to state at this point that I checked with the Masonic Order in New Orleans and at Baton Rouge, and was informed of the authenticity of the lodge at Floyd. I was also in contact with persons there who stated they recalled Cole Younger as having been there. One man said that Cole had carried him about on his shoulders when he was a little boy at Floyd.

But not all the documents supporting the Younger brothers' claims that they were falsely accused of crimes emanated from Cole's pen. There is an ample supply of affidavits garnered by the brothers to support their alibis. Among those affidavits which particularly bear out the defense in Cole's letter to the *Missouri Review* is one signed by William Dickerson, Master of the Masonic Lodge at Floyd, Louisiana. It reads in part:

> On the 5th of December, A.D. 1873, the Younger brothers arrived at my home in Carroll Parish, Louisiana, and remained there until the 8th day of February, A.D. 1874, during which time Cole Younger was engaged in writing the history of Quantrill and his own life. While he was at my house I asked Cole if he was a Mason, to which he replied in the negative.

Another important affidavit in support of Cole's alibis ran something like this:

> I hereby certify that I attended Mr. Murphy of St. Clair County, Missouri, during his sickness in November, 1872, and that on the day of the Ste. Genevieve Bank robbery I saw at the house of Mr. Murphy, in the County of St. Clair, Thomas Coleman Younger, generally called Cole Younger, and that he could not possibly have had any hand in the said bank robbery, as he was sitting up and nursing Mr. Murphy during his sickness.
>
> *L. L. Lewis, M.D.*
> Treasurer and Collector of St. Clair County.

The startling robberies at Muncie, Kansas, and at Corinth, Mississippi, occurred at nearly the same time, thus giving contemporary writers a problem in placing what robbers at what location. Many said that Cole Younger had been at Corinth; others placed him with Jesse at Muncie. The fact that Jesse and Cole were not very friendly at this time would more likely indicate that Cole probably was at Corinth, since he was in the vicinity at the time, although no indictments implicating Cole in the Corinth affair were issued by the authorities.

In the early part of November, 1874, four men who claimed to be cattle dealers from Kentucky made their way through Tennessee. Their destination was Corinth, Mississippi, just a few miles south of the Tennessee state line. The target at Corinth, county seat of Alcorn County, was the Tishomingo Savings Bank. The four men stayed for a while in McNairy County, Tennessee, riding into Corinth about the first of December. Prior to this, several members of the band had visited Corinth, no doubt to familiarize themselves with the lay of the land. Now they took lodging at a boardinghouse and made their plans.

The bank was on Fillmore Street, away from the heavy commercial district, and that made the task easier. They told the owner of the roominghouse that they were resting a few days before returning to Kentucky and that they wanted to exchange their gold for paper money. The men called at the bank each day to negotiate the sale of their gold, but in reality were furthering their plans to rob it.

They managed to fool Alonzo H. Taylor, the bank president, with their talk of gold and paper money. The holdup appeared to be an easy operation, for Taylor had no assistant and the bank was off the beaten path. Finally, the bandits decided they would rob the bank on Monday, December 7, during the noon-hour lull. On that day they were observed studying a map while they were eating an early lunch at Bill Goings's restaurant. They then quietly left.

Three of the bandits rode up to the bank building, where they met their companion. They gave him the horses to hold and entered the bank, where they met a Negro and Mr. Taylor, the former having left his horse near the door and gone in to make a deposit. While two of the robbers engaged Mr. Taylor in conversation, telling him they had decided to sell their gold, the third man slyly locked the door and pulled the curtain down over the glass panel.

The two who had been talking to Mr. Taylor informed him that the real object of their visit was to get hold of all the money and everything else of value in the bank. They said they meant business and were not to be trifled with, and threatened to kill him if he didn't do as he was told. In the meantime the man who had locked the front door pointed a pistol at the terrified Negro.

Taylor tried to dissuade the men from their purpose, but they commanded him, on pain of death, to open the safe, which had a combination lock. Taylor replied that he did not believe they would kill him, and one of them said, "Damn you, you ain't afraid," and drew a knife, while his companion leveled a pistol at Taylor's head. The bandit with the knife rushed at Mr. Taylor and cut him on the forehead.

"Now unlock the safe, or die!"

Taylor unlocked the safe, and the bandits removed the contents and tossed them into a seamless bag. They headed at once for the exit. Their companion, who had been left outside, commenced firing his pistol as the men emerged. They mounted their horses and dashed down the street, the man who had acted as guard firing at every person in sight. A man who chanced to come around the corner as the robber sprinted past was fired at, but the bullet missed him and killed a dog nearby.

The robbers rode rapidly away with their stolen valuables, which amounted to about $8,000 in bonds, $6,000 in currency, twelve gold watches, and $25,000 worth of diamonds. They raced up the Charleston Road some distance, then turned north toward the Tennessee River, twenty miles away.

The bandits had spent about fifteen minutes in the bank and were not bothered by passersby, who believed the bank president was out to lunch. Dr. A. J. Borroum was standing in front of his home on the outskirts of town when the raiders rode by.

One of the band lifted the white bag aloft and said, "Here goes your Corinth bank!"

The sheriff's posse pursued the robbers vigorously for a time, but when one of the robbers turned and killed an officer's horse, the chase slackened. Near Glen, Mississippi, the trail was lost, and near that point a logger named Bud Patrick found some papers the bandits had discarded. These papers were returned to Mr. Taylor.

Who were these bold robbers? It was anybody's guess, and the wires and gossip lines buzzed with suggestions as to their identity. The mayor of Corinth wired the following descriptions to the Chief of Police at Memphis on the evening of December 7.

Bank robbed at this place this evening, two thousand dollars reward for them. The following is a description of the robbers:

One is a large, red-complexioned man, weight 190 pounds, 6 feet high, broad, square shoulders, heavy set, about 35 years of age, said he was 42 years of age; short, sandy hair and short red whiskers all over his face, as if he had not shaved for several days. He gave his name as J. C. White; said he was formerly from Kentucky, and was just off from a horse expedition. It is believed he is a Kentuckian.

The other man is about 6 feet high, auburn or dark sandy hair, and gave his name as Ed Mason, said that he was 22 years of age, and looked about that age, has a large scar on his left wrist on the inside of the wrist. He says that it was a burn—though it may have been a shot or a burn—large blue eyes and thin red beard, said that he was from Central Kentucky, and has the appearance and accent of a Kentuckian.

The third man gave his name as Lewis, said he was a Kentuckian, tall, spare-made man, long dark hair, reaches to his shoulders, about 140 pounds, black whiskers all over his face, a good set of teeth, about 35 years of age.

One man gave his name as Castle; said he was a Kentuckian, straight as an Indian, about 6 feet high, square shoulders, fair skin, red complexioned, round face, large, full blue eyes, about 23 years of age, has a sandy beard several weeks old.

They pretended to be horse and cattle traders, and said that for several years they had been trading horses and cattle in Kansas, Texas, etc. They are said to have a drove of horses on the cane on White River in Arkansas. Look out for them on the Memphis and Charleston railroad tonight. I think they will make for Arkansas.

J. P. Collier, Mayor

Alonzo Taylor, the bank president, hired private detectives, but none of the loot was ever recovered, and the bandits were never identified. About a year later a man named White was arrested in Forrest City, Arkansas, and questioned about the Corinth affair. The reason for his arrest was never divulged, but he was not the Mr. White who had been at Corinth.

This question has been raised: Was the "J. C. White" at Corinth Cole Younger? The description of the robber who was large, red-complexioned, square-shouldered, heavy-set, about thirty-five years old, certainly does fit Cole's description. Of course, many writers place Cole at the Muncie robbery as well, but it seems improbable that his ill feelings toward Jesse could have been smoothed out by then—at least, not according to Cole's letter of November 26, 1874.

We also know that the name "White" was not alien to Cole. Jim and John White had been accused of being members of the band that robbed the bank at Richmond, Missouri, and also that Cole Younger hated Jim White for some reason. It is conceivable that he would take such an alias, partly, perhaps, to throw suspicion on another. It could be, too, that Cole, weary of inaction at Floyd, Louisiana, and in need of money, concocted the idea to rob the Corinth bank. Who the other three men were we never will know.

The James-Younger band had no permanent members, very few regular riders. It was very largely a succession of groups of men who were of necessity itinerant and who were seldom together for any length of time.

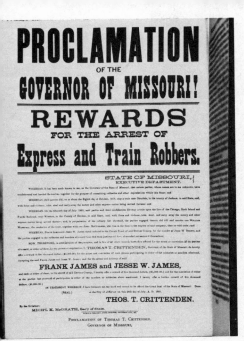

Governor Crittenden's reward proclamation (Carl W. Breihan Collection).

Winston robbery reward poster (Carl W. Breihan Collection).

Warrant, issued by the State of Missouri, for the arrest of Jesse James (Carl W. Breihan Collection).

State of Kansas warrant for the arrest of Jesse James. Many people claimed no such warrants were issued (Carl W. Breihan Collection).

REWARD

$15,000 REWARD
FRANK JAMES
DEAD or ALIVE

$25,000 REWARD FOR JESSE JAMES
$5000 Reward for any Known Member of the James Band
SIGNED
ST. LOUIS MIDLAND RAILROAD

Frank James reward poster (Union Pacific Railroad Museum Collection).

Jesse James reward poster
(Carl W. Breihan Collection).

$5,000 REWARD

JESSE JAMES
For Train Robbery

Notify AUTHORITIES
LIBERTY, MISSOURI

few of Jesse James' possessions still in the family: the boots and spurs he wore the [da]y he was killed, his wallet and one of his revolvers (Carl W. Breihan Collection).

[Th]e home at Kearney where Jesse James was born. Frank was born in a cabin near [thi]s one, but it was destroyed and the family moved here (Carl W. Breihan Collection).

In this little cabin near Noel, Missouri, Jesse and his bride Zee spent the first few days of their honeymoon (Carl W. Breihan Collection).

Bat Masterson (The Kansas State Historical Society, Topeka).

Respectfuly.
Tho. Howard
No 1318 Lafayette.
St. Joseph
Mo

Jesse James as he appeared in 1882, in a likeness drawn from his corpse, eyes opened, above the signature of Thos. Howard (Carl W. Breihan Collection).

Guerilla Tom Hunt, accused of being involved in the Glasgow Stage Robbery and identified as Jesse James; he was later released from prison when it became known that he had not been with Jesse at the time and was certainly not the outlaw (Charles Rosamond Collection).

Rare photo of Sam Hildebrand, noted guerrilla in the Bonne Terre—Farmington, Missouri area. Hildebrand sometimes rode with Quantrill's men (Carl W. Breihan Collection).

Pacific Express, westbound at Granite Canyon, Wyoming, 1911. It was this type rain which Big Nose Parrott tried to hold up near Carbon, Wyoming (Union Pacific lroad).

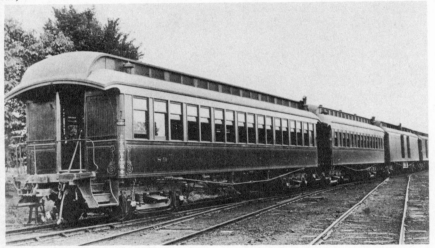

The old wooden passenger coaches which were in use from 1870–1880 (Missouri Pacific Railroad).

This type of train was typical of those besieged by outlaws (Missouri Pacific Railroad).

From Kansas City

AND THE

Southeast.

Notwithstanding the fact that this fast service originates from Chicago, special attention has been given to the connections from and via Kansas City. Additional first class Pullman Sleeper will run from Kansas City to San Francisco, leaving Kansas City 9:30 a. m., connecting at Cheyenne with "The Fast Mail."

Trains will continue to leave Kansas City same as at present, and close connections will be made at Cheyenne, Wyo., with the fast trains from Chicago and Omaha.

NOTE—Your special attention is called to the fast time and through service from Chicago, Omaha, and Kansas City to San Francisco and Los Angeles.

Condensed Time Schedule.

			No. 1 Overland Limited	Day of the week	No. 3 Fast Mail	Day of the week
Lv.	Chicago	(C. & N. W. Ry.) Central Time	6.00 p. m.	Sunday	10.45 p. m.	Sunday
Ar.	Council Bluffs	"	7.40 a. m.	Monday	2.55 "	Monday
Lv.	Omaha	(Union Pacific) "	7.55 "	"	3.20 "	"
		"	8.10 "	"	3.30 "	"
	Fremont	"	9.25 "	"	5.08 "	"
	Kearney	"	1.25 p. m.	"	9.15 "	"
Ar.	Denver	Mountain Time		"	7.50 a. m.	Tuesday
	Cheyenne	"	9.55 p. m.	"	6.30 "	"
Lv.	Kansas City	Central Time	7.30 p. m.	Sunday	9.30 a. m.	Monday
	Topeka	"	9.40 "	"	11.20 "	"
	Salina	"	1.25 a. m.	Monday	2.55 p. m.	"
Ar.	Ellis	"	5.10 "	"	6.30 "	"
	Denver	Mountain Time	2.25 p. m.	"	3.35 a. m.	Tuesday
	Cheyenne	"	10.00 p. m.	"	6.20 "	"
Lv.	Cheyenne	Mountain Time	10.10 p. m.	Monday	6.45 a. m.	Tuesday
Ar.	Green River	"	7.55 a. m.	Tuesday	7.00 p. m.	"
	Ogden	"	1.40 p. m.	"	7.45 a. m.	Wednesday
	Salt Lake City	"	3.10 "	"	9.15 "	"
Lv.	Ogden	(Cent. Pac. Co.) Pacific Time	1.15 "	"	1.00 "	"
Ar.	Sacramento	"	4.50 "	Wednesday	5.50 "	Thursday
	San Francisco	"	8.45 "	"	9.45 "	"
	Los Angeles	"	10.00 a. m.	Thursday	7.30 "	Friday

An early railroad timetable (Union Pacific Railroad).

Portrait of Big Nose George Parrott. Parrott, whose real name was George Lathrope, was lynched at Rawlins, Wyoming, on March 22, 1881, after an attempted train hold-up and several murders, and was said to have once been a member of the original Butch Cassidy bunch (Union Pacific Railroad).

Rawlins, Wyoming, 1879—the town where Big Nose George Parrott was lynched (Union Pacific Railroad).

Rawlins, Wyoming—the original hotel and eating house, later a club for railroad employees (Union Pacific Railroad).

(Union Pacific Railroad)

TRIAL JUDGE AND LAWYERS IN FRANK JAMES CASE.

S. GOODMAN,
Trial Judge.

WM. D. HAMILTON,
For the State.

J. H. SHANKLIN,
For the State.

F. HICKLIN,
the State.

H. C. McDOUGAL,
For the State.

WM. H. WALLACE,
For the State.

N P. JOHNSON,
the Defense.

JOHN F. PHILIPS,
For the Defense.

JAMES H. SLOVER,
For the Defense.

T. GARNER,
the Defense.

J. W. ALEXANDER,
For the Defense.

WM. M. RUSH,
For the Defense.

(Carl W. Breihan Collection)

THE JUDGE.

The Judge, October 21, 1882, satirizes the surrender of Frank James (St. Louis Public Library).

Marker showing the place where Whiskey-Head Bill Ryan was arrested (Carl W. Breihan Collection).

The grave of Frank James and his wife at the Hill Park Cemetary, Independence, Missouri (Carl W. Breihan Collection).

"The Jesse James Stove"—Freighted in by wagon from the Union Pacific Railroad (Carter Station, near Fort Bridger) to Henry's Fork in the late 1860s or early '70s, this stove first belonged to John Baker and was later acquired by his son-in-law, Dick Son. Frank and Jesse and Jim Baker thawed their frozen feet in its oven in the winter of 1878–79 (Kerry Ross Boren Collection).

Frank James, with dog; identity of others unknown (Carl W. Breihan Collection).

CHAPTER 8

The Bombing

of Castle James

ALLAN PINKERTON WAS FURIOUS. THE STATIC ELECTRICITY
literally flew from the carpet of his plush Chicago office as he
paced back and forth across the room, taking some of his
vengeance out on a battered cigar.

Pinkerton brooded over the death of Whicher, a young man
whom he regarded as more than just an employee. This incident, coupled with the death of two other officers, Captain Lull
and Edward Daniels, on March 17, 1874, in a fight with John
and Jim Younger near Osceola just about unnerved the famous
man-hunter. Pinkerton had learned about Jesse James's wedding. He knew the situation in Missouri, that Jesse was being
protected by the people in the country; but he was a bulldog of
a man and was convinced that his man, Whicher, had been
murdered by the James boys. The famous detective was determined to capture the bandit; he felt that his reputation was at
stake.

If Jesse's charmed life depended on the help he received from his neighbors, then Pinkerton knew that the way to bring him down was to convince the people of Clay County that Jesse and Frank were nothing better than common thieves and murderers. He spent almost a year at this task, pulling the strings from Chicago, and by the end of 1874 there were many neighbors around the Samuel farm who felt that the James boys had overstretched their natural sympathy for their troubles during the war.

About the first part of 1875, Pinkerton commenced a campaign against the bandits which was meant to clinch the case against them. The most elaborate and careful preparations were made, in utmost secrecy.

William Pinkerton, brother of Allan, arrived in Kansas City to direct the campaign to bring Jesse to bay, and to tie together all the data collected by spies in the vicinity of "Castle James," as the Pinkertons called the James-Samuel house.

Many of the respectable citizens of Clay County had grown weary of the presence in their midst of outlaws and had agreed to assist the Pinkertons. With these people, William Pinkerton had arranged for a system of cipher codes to be used when transmitting messages back and forth. Those in the neighborhood of Kearney were watching and noting every incident in the vicinity of the Samuel home, and daily sending their news to Pinkerton at Kansas City.

It was known to some of the immediate neighbors of Dr. Samuel that Frank and Jesse were at home. They had been seen now and then at the Kearney railroad station, three miles from their homestead. Other neighbors, casually passing the farm, had seen the boys about in the barnyard. All this had been faithfully reported to the Pinkertons at Kansas City.

At last the opportune time for striking a decisive blow seemed to have arrived. Dispatches in code were sent to Chicago for reinforcements, and special orders were given. The Kansas City division of the officers was held in readiness to cooperate with the force from the east. The zealous citizens of Clay County also received final instructions as to their part in ridding the county of the dangerous outlaws.

Extraordinary precautions had been taken to maintain profound secrecy as to the movements and purposes of the detectives. No strange men had been seen loitering about Kearney. Everything that could possibly be done to allay suspicion on the part of the outlaws had been done.

On the afternoon of January 24, several small bands of men arrived in Clay County and filtered into Liberty long after nightfall. Late on the evening of the twenty-fifth, a special train came up from Kearney with a detachment of Pinkerton agents from Kansas City. They were met by citizens well acquainted with the locality and were led to a rendezvous.

Late that night the detectives surrounded the Samuel house. Two men approached from the rear, carrying turpentine balls for lighting up the house. When they attempted to open the shutters, they awoke an old Negro servant, who spread the alarm. Dr. and Mrs. Samuel and the young children stumbled about in the dark. A turpentine ball was thrown into the kitchen, and a fire started to rage. Mrs. Samuel quickly recovered her presence of mind and began to give directions and personally to exert herself in subduing the flames. She was permitted only a moment or so to engage in this task. There was a sudden crash, and a great iron ball wrapped in flaming kerosene-saturated rags struck the floor. Dr. Samuel thought it was another turpentine ball and attempted to kick it into the fireplace, to no avail. The thirty-three-pound makeshift iron grenade-bomb rocked the place with a terrific explosion. A piece of the grenade struck Mrs. Samuel's right arm below the elbow and her hand dangled helplessly at her side as she fought the flames.

Another piece of the bomb struck nine-year-old Archie Samuel in the chest and nearly went through him. He died within a few hours. (On January 28 young Archie Samuel was laid to rest in the Kearney cemetery, Clergyman Thomas H. Graves officiating. Mrs. Samuel was too grief-stricken to attend the funeral; besides, she was in great pain because of her injured arm.)

Despite claims that Jesse and Frank were not in the house when the bomb exploded, contemporary records definitely establish that not only were the James boys in the small upper room of the Samuel home, but also that Clell Miller and Dora and Bill Fox followed the Jameses out through the window. This room was not above the original cabin but was part of the added-on structure which formed more contemporary living quarters. Some will say there was not room enough for all these persons when they view the present section; they are right—the original added-on section was removed to the Columbian Exposition Grounds in Chicago, and the present section was added to the old cabin in 1890.

To further substantiate the fact that the outlaws were there, Jack Ladd, a member of the attacking forces, was wounded by them as they escaped, and he later died in Chicago. Ladd had been Pinkerton's lookout on the Dan Askew farm, next to the James place, for nearly two years, so as to report on the movements of the James boys in that area. Since no member of the Samuel family had fired a weapon, how then would Ladd have been so seriously wounded if the outlaws had not been in the area?

Reporters and officials who visited the Samuel home the day following the bombing found evidence that a desperate fight had taken place on the premises and that somebody had been hurt, for blood was evident on the grounds. The number of shots fired was said to be from four to twenty. Seven holes appeared in the fence at the northeast corner of the yard, besides the marks of bullets on the fence separating the yard from the house lot, showing that they had been fired from the icehouse. Numerous footprints were found at the rear of the ice-house as well as at the rear of the barn. The detectives had attacked in three squads—one from behind the icehouse, one from behind the barn, and one against the kitchen at the north-west corner.

The detectives retreated across the wheatfield west of the barn, leaving an easy trail, plainly showing they were in a great hurry to leave the locality. Drops of blood were found near the stable as well as in the pasture lot south of the house. Hoof-prints, made by horses in great haste, were seen leading from the barn. It must also be noted that Jesse's favorite horse was found roaming loose on the Samuel farm the next day after the bombing, graphic evidence that the outlaw left in a great hurry on another animal or riding double with a companion. Jesse James would never have left his horse behind unless absolutely necessary.

In the case of Archie Samuel, the verdict at the inquest read: "We, the jury, find that the deceased, Archie Peyton Samuel, came to his death as a result of the explosion from a torpedo thrown through the window of the Samuel residence, by person or persons unknown."

This verdict should also be conclusive proof that the vicious object thrown into the kitchen by the detectives was a bomb and not simply a railroad pot flare, as some writers would have us believe.

The Pinkertons claimed that Jesse and Frank had been in the house when they attacked; others said they left the place early that evening. However, contemporary reports indicate a fierce battle had taken place in the yard and bullet holes were found in the fence and pools of blood were discovered near the stable. Moreover, Jack Ladd, a Pinkerton spy, had been acting under cover at the Askew farm, next to that of the Samuels, and it is known that he was wounded in the affray and died later in Chicago. The governor of Missouri sent his adjutant-general to get a report of the bombing; his report substantiates facts as given. The following report of the adjutant-general of the State of Missouri, which official report appeared in the *Liberty Advance* issue of February 11, 1875, should also end this argument.

To His Excellency, Chas. H. Hardin
Governor of Missouri

Dear Sir:

In pursuance of instructions received from you on Friday, I proceeded without delay to Clay County, to ascertain as far as possible the facts relating to the recent outrage perpetrated in said county upon the family of Dr. Samuel, the stepfather of the notorious James brothers. Dr. Samuel resides about 2½ miles east of Kearney, a small town 9 miles north of Liberty . . . On the night of Jan. 26th, between 12 and 2 o'clock, the residence of Dr. Samuel was approached by a party of men . . . The party approached the rear and west portion of the building and set fire to the weatherboarding of the kitchen in three or four places, and threw into the window thereof a hand grenade.

This instrument was composed of cast and wrought or malleable iron, strongly secured together and covered with a wrapping saturated with turpentine or oil. As it passed through the window and as also it lay upon the floor it made a very brilliant light, alarming the family who supposed the kitchen to be on fire and rushed in to extinguish the flames. Dr. Samuel . . . mistook it for a turpentine ball and attempted to kick it into the fireplace . . . It then exploded with a report which was heard a distance of two or three miles. The part composed of cast iron broke into fragments and flew out with great force. One of the fragments shattered the right arm below the elbow of Mrs. Samuel, the mother of the James brothers, to an extent which made amputation necessary. Another entered the body of her little son, Archie, wounding him mortally and causing his death in about four hours.

Dr. Samuel succeeded in putting out the fire in the weatherboarding and aroused the surrounding neighbors with a cry of murder . . . Four pistol reports were heard by the neighbors . . . but . . . the parties perpetrating the outrage had disappeared.

On Monday, January 26, about half-past seven o'clock in the evening, an engine with only a caboose attached came down the road from the north and stopped in the woods about two miles north of Kearney. Several unknown men then got out of the caboose, which then continued south in the direction of Kansas City. About two or three o'clock in the morning, Tuesday, the same or a similar engine and caboose came from the direction of Kansas City and stopped for a considerable time at the place where the unknown men had been left.

The tracks of persons who were stationed behind the house and of those who set fire and threw the grenade into the kitchen, made by boots of superior quality, quite different from· those usually worn by the farmers . . . in the surrounding country. In following the trail of the parties on their retreat, a pistol was found which is now in my possession . . . This pistol has marks upon it which . . . are identically such as are known to be on the pistols of a well-known band of detectives.

The parties who perpetrated the outrage doubtless approached the house under the belief that the James brothers were there . . . on discovering that they had murdered an innocent lad and mutilated his mother, they deemed it prudent to retire and leave as little evidence . . . as possible. There are no details concerning the signs of the struggle which took place near the barn and elsewhere on the premises. . . .

> Respectfully,
> *G. C. Bingham, Adjt. General*

The wrath of the community and of the whole state over this atrocity forced the withdrawal of Pinkerton detectives from the area. No thoroughly satisfactory explanation has ever been given by representatives of the firm, or by any other law enforcement agents, for this clumsily executed attack.

The effect of the raid on the home of Mrs. Samuel, the mother of Jesse and Frank James, was to create a diversion in favor of the boys. The tragedy of that event was of such a horrible nature that public sentiment set in strongly against any further attempt to capture the Jameses by force.

Widespread sympathy for the James family stemmed from the Pinkerton attack on their home. Men of prominence and political influence publicly expressed the opinion that the crimes of which Jesse and Frank were being accused were an aftermath of the Civil War's bitter passions and that, if amnesty for their acts during the war should be granted to them and their former guerrilla companions, a climate of reconciliation between the Jameses and the representatives of the law could be established.

These views and opinions in respect to the Jameses and Youngers assumed a formal shape in the early part of March, 1875, by the introduction in the Missouri House of Representatives, by General Jeff Jones of Callaway County, of a bill, or preambles and resolution, offering amnesty for all past offenses to: Jesse W. James, Thomas Coleman Younger, Frank James, Robert Younger, and James Younger. This to be done on condition that they should return to their homes and quietly submit to such proceedings as might be instituted against them for acts alleged to have been committed by them since the war.

The preambles and resolution offered by General Jones received the approval of Attorney-General John A. Hockaday, and of many other lawyers of note. General Jones supported the measure with great zeal and eloquence and ability. Its rhetoric was preserved for posterity, even though it is not in the statutes of Missouri, for it failed. In part, it reads:

> Whereas, such discrimination (against ex-Confederates) evinces a want of manly generosity and statesmanship on the part of the party imposing, and of courage and manhood on the part of the party submitting tamely thereto; and
> Whereas, under the outlawry pronounced against Jesse W.

James, Frank James, Coleman Younger, Robert Younger, and others, who gallantly periled their lives and their all in defense of their properties and principles, they are of necessity made desperate. Driven as they are from the fields of honest industry, from their friends, their families, their home and their country, they can know no law but the law of self-preservation, nor can have no respect for and feel allegiance to a government which forces them to the very acts it professes to deprecate, and then offers a bounty for their apprehension, and arms foreign mercenaries with power to capture and kill them; and,

Whereas, believing these men too brave to be mean, too generous to be revengeful, and too gallant and honorable to betray a friend or break a promise; and believing further that most, if not all the offenses with which they are charged have been committed by others, and perhaps by those pretending to hunt them, or by their confederates; that their names are and have been used to divert suspicion from and thereby relieve the actual perpetrators; that the return of these men to their homes and friends would have the effect of greatly lessening crime in our state by turning public attention to the real criminals, and that common justice, sound policy, and true statesmanship alike demand that amnesty should be extended to all alike of both parties for all acts done or charged to have been done during the war; therefore, be it Resolved:

That the Governor of the state be, and he is hereby requested to issue a proclamation notifying the said Jesse W. James, Frank James, Coleman Younger, Robert Younger, and James Younger, and others, that full and complete amnesty and pardon will be granted them for acts charged or committed by them during the late Civil War, and inviting them peaceably to return to their respective homes in this state and there quietly to remain, submitting themselves to such proceedings as may be instituted against them by the courts for all offenses charged to have been committed since the war, promising and guaranteeing to them and each of them full protection and a fair trial therein, and that full protection shall be given them from the time of their entrance into the state, and this notice thereof under said proclamation and invitation. . . .

The above bill was introduced about the first of March, 1875, and was referred to the Committee on Criminal Jurisprudence, of which its author was a leading member. The bill was fully discussed in committee and finally, through the influence of its author, a majority of the committee agreed to make a favorable report on the measure to the House of Representatives. Some time toward the close of the twenty-eighth General Assembly, the bill came up for its third reading in the House. General Jones made an earnest speech in advocacy of the measure.

One member aroused a strong opposition to the measure from the very side of the House from which General Jones had hoped to obtain assistance in carrying it through. The member simply read a portion of a message transmitted by Governor Silas Woodson to the 27th General Assembly denouncing these same outlaws; and the Democratic Legislature of Missouri refused to pass the bill.

This curious bit of proposed legislation, though it did not become law, did arouse much interest. The Jameses themselves apparently wished to see it pass, and they communicated with Missouri's Governor Hardin and Attorney-General Hockaday about it.

No doubt a deciding factor in the minds of the legislators who voted against the proposed amnesty bill was the cold-blooded murder of Daniel H. Askew on Monday, April 12, 1875. All through the war the Jameses had considered Askew a Union spy, but up to the time of the bombing he had not been molested by the outlaws. After that time, however, Askew, a Radical, was held in contempt by the James family and their friends. Also, Jesse believed that Askew had been a member of the Pinkerton band which attacked his mother's home in January.

The incident occurred while this bill was being considered, and many felt that it also had an ill effect on its passage, besides the words of Governor Woodson.

Among those who had expressed strong disapproval of the conduct of the James boys was Daniel H. Askew, a rich farmer of Clay County, whose property was near the home of the James boys. The outspoken opinion of Askew had disturbed the Jameses and their friends, and when the night raid was made in January on the James home they at once suspected that Askew had been partly instrumental in bringing it about. This belief was bolstered by the fact that friends of the Jameses had found some blankets and other evidence of the late presence of men among Mr. Askew's haystacks. Also, the conspicuous absence of the Askew farmhand, Jack Ladd, added fuel to this fire of suspicion.

On the night of April 12, 1875, Daniel Askew went with a bucket to a spring some distance from his home and returned to the house with the water. He had set the bucket on a bench and was standing on his back porch. He hadn't yet entered the house. Just in the rear of the house, and within ten paces of the edge of the porch on which Askew was standing, there was a pile of firewood reaching to the height of five or six feet. Behind this protection the assassins found a convenient hiding place. Whoever they may have been, they had hitched their horses and walked through the field to their place of concealment.

Suddenly a shot rang out, followed by two more, and Mr. Askew fell dead upon the floor. Three bullets had crashed through his head.

The three men raced from their hiding place, mounted their horses, rode by the house of Henry Sears, and summoned him to the door. Later Sears stated that he saw three men in the road who told him they had just killed Dan Askew, and if anyone asked about it to say that detectives had done it. Shortly after, Jesse and Frank James and Clell Miller met a farmer on the road and told him that Askew had been killed because of the Pinkerton detectives harassing them and their families.

The jury at the inquest said: "We, the jury, find that Daniel

H. Askew came to his death by a gunshot wound from the hands of unknown person or persons."

The James boys were accused of this crime, but only by gossip. From one quarter came the report that Askew was killed by Jesse on account of a heated dispute his mother had with Askew regarding a line fence. In Kansas City some years ago this author talked with a person who said this was true, yet it was surely an inopportune moment to commit such a murder. However, Jesse was known to be high-strung and impulsive. In his anger he could have forgotten the amnesty bill for a moment and killed Askew. No one will ever know.

Jesse and Frank and their relatives retorted that their enemies had killed Askew in order to defeat the amnesty bill then pending in the legislature. Whatever might have been the motive, or whoever might have been the killers, the shooting did have the effect of renewing strong feeling against Jesse and Frank, and the defeat of the amnesty bill followed.

The Jameses and the Youngers remained outcasts, and every hand was turned against them.

CHAPTER 9

The Huntington
Bank Robbery

IT WAS 1875. MOST MISSOURIANS, ESPECIALLY THE old-timers, were struggling for a livelihood due to the great panic of 1873 . . . the Black Friday when the great Jay Cooke & Co., who had invested heavily in the construction of the Northern Pacific Railway, suspended operations on September 18. Some of the better-read citizens recalled that Congress had passed a law providing for the resumption of government specie payments that year; a law which would take effect on January 1, 1879. Others, reading the newspapers of the day, commented on the fact that a man named Alexander Graham Bell had invented some kind of a talking machine. In the discussions, one old gentleman from Osceola recalled that the first message was sent from 109 Court Street in Boston, and that the words were: "Mr. Watson, please come here, I want you."

Of course, these facts were interesting but not important to the average Missourian who longed to read of the exploits of the Jameses and the Youngers. They were still slapping their thighs with glee as they recalled the daring robbery of the train on its eastbound trip on the Kansas Pacific at Muncie, Kansas.

Early in December of 1874 three horsemen were seen heading north near the southern bridge which spanned the Kansas River at Kansas City. At some point between Kansas City and Muncie, a distance of eight miles, the three were joined by two others, and about the middle of the afternoon of December 13 the five riders reached Muncie, where they donned masks and closed in on the station.

The station agent, John Purtee, was robbed of twenty dollars, then the section hands were compelled to place several T-rails across the railway track. The station agent was forced to flag down the engineer, Robert C. Murphy, who immediately brought his engine to a halt. Conductor J. O. Brinkerhoff, when confronted by an armed robber, leaped from the rear of the train and scurried up the track. He knew that a fast-approaching freight train would crash into the stalled passenger train if it were not stopped. Although the bullets that whizzed past his head urged him to stop, he was able to convince the bandit of his real purpose in running, and so a tragic accident was averted.

Over $25,000 in currency and gold dust had been obtained by the daring robbers, and, while a posse jogged after the train robbers, they turned back soon after crossing the state line into Jackson County, Missouri. Five horsemen crossed the southern bridge at full speed.

Seth Jones, whittling away on a corncob, recalled with dismay that two days after the Muncie robbery William "Bud" McDaniels was arrested as one of the train robbers. Bud had hired a horse and buggy in Kansas City so as to take his girl for a ride. She wasn't at home when he arrived and, much provoked, he drank to excess and soon was driving through the streets in a reckless manner. He was arrested and searched. He had over $1,000 in his pockets, two revolvers, and some jewelry, which he said he had bought to give to his girl. Further investigation identified the jewelry as that taken from passengers on the train at Muncie. Others stated they had seen Bud in town that day. It was a clear case, so he was taken to Lawrence, Kansas, to await trial.

Good news hit the papers for the ex-Quantrillians when they read that on Sunday, June 27, 1875, Bud McDaniels walked out of the Lawrence jail with another prisoner. But the good news turned to gloom later on when they read that pursuit was kept up all night, and that at 3:00 P.M. on Monday afternoon three farmers discovered McDaniels and Dunn, the other prisoner, about seven miles west of Lawrence. After exchanging shots, the escaped prisoners abandoned their horses and took to the brush.

The news soon spread, and with it the number of pursuers increased until the prisoners were surrounded.

Bierman, a German farmer, shot McDaniels with a squirrel rifle, the ball striking him in the lower bowel. On Tuesday morning the wounded McDaniels appeared at the home of a colored man and asked for food and water. The sheriff was called and the prisoner was brought into the city. The wound was a bad one. That evening, at seven o'clock, Bud McDaniels died.

Other things, too, were happening in 1875, and the friends and admirers of Jesse and Frank James noted that in June of that year Frank married Annie Ralston at Independence, Missouri, against the wishes of her family. The couple went to Nashville, Tennessee, where Jesse and his wife, Zee, were living. On August 31, 1875, at 606 Boscobel Street, Zee gave birth to a son. The boy was named Jesse Edwards James, after Jesse's friend, Major John Newman Edwards, the fiery ex-adjutant to General Jo Shelby.

The month before, Cole Younger had turned up in Nashville with Tom Webb, alias Tom Keen. During a short stay in Cin-

cinnati, Cole made the acquaintance of the sharp, black-eyed Tom Webb. This man had spent many years in Kentucky and West Virginia, being at all times a suspicious character, and it was he who proposed the robbery of the bank at Huntington, West Virginia. Cole Younger and Frank James considered the proposition and, meeting Tomlinson McDaniels, a brother of Bud, at Petersburg, they laid the scheme before him, and then the four decided to raid the bank. Cole wanted Jesse to join them in the Huntington robbery, but Jesse refused to leave his family.

On Monday, September 6, 1875, the well-armed and mounted quartet rode into Huntington, each man wearing a long linen duster over a heavy winter coat. They made directly for the bank, where two of them dismounted, leaving the other pair to clear the streets of people. The latter two then opened a fusillade with their pistols, driving everyone indoors, while their companions entered the bank with pistols drawn.

John H. Russell, the president of the bank, was at lunch at the time of the robbery, and inside the bank was only the cashier, R. T. Oney. Both robbers leaped over the counter and grabbed a revolver that Oney was trying to get hold of. They told him to put up his hands and ordered him to open the vault. He told the outlaws the safe was open, but they ordered him to get the key for the inner drawer. He refused.

"If you do not get the key and open the drawer, we'll kill you!" said one of the men.

"All right, then, do that, and you'll never get the money," responded the brave but foolish cashier.

Oney saw that the men meant business, so he produced the key and opened the money drawer. He handed out two packages, and told them that was all, but he was seen to push back a package. They ordered him to hand them that package also, which he did. Oney later stated that the bandits seemed very disappointed that there was no more money in the vault.

"Any of this money yours?" asked one of the robbers.

"Yes, I have a balance of seven dollars in the bank," Oney replied.

"Well, we don't want this little scrape to cost you anything," said the big robber, and counted out his seven dollars. They also told him that he was the coolest man they had ever come across.

By that time, the firing had subsided in the street, and the bandits in the bank decided it was time to leave. At that very moment a colored messenger named Jim came into the bank with the mail. The bandits asked him if there was any money in the packages and he said he did not know.

"All right, then, stand there in the corner and you won't get hurt," he was told.

After a thorough search the robbers took Oney and Jim and marched them across the street to where their horses were. Russell, in the company of Ben Davis, was cautiously turning the corner at that time. As soon as Oney found only one of the robbers was pointing his pistol at him, he yelled and tried to jump to safety. The robbers meanwhile mounted their horses and dashed from town.

By this time Russell had aroused Sheriff Smith and a general alarm was given. Russell was mounted on his fleet gray horse, armed with a shotgun, and in short order he and the sheriff were in swift pursuit of the bandits. Soon others followed—among them the Rev. Gibson, J. Emmens, A. Pollard, F. Donnell, W. Stuart, T. Noble, and J. Elkins. The sheriff and Russell came so close to the bandits that they saw them drop a money sack. It contained thirty dollars in nickels and a $5,000 deposit certificate. A man who was taken by the robbers and compelled to go with them later said the pursuers were so close that the robbers debated whether to wait for them and kill them. Two were in favor of doing so, and the other two said it would do no good, so they continued on.

While the pursuit was in progress, urgent telegrams were sent to Catlettsburg and all the stations between there and Louisa; also to Charleston, Barboursville and other strategic points. George F. Miller organized a party from Barboursville and started after the outlaws, to try and head them off, but got behind them. The posse from Huntington followed them to the Big Sandy River and then returned—but Russell, A. Pollard, W. Stuart, Donnell, and Buffington rode twenty miles into Kentucky to Cracker's Neck and did not return to Huntington until Tuesday night, with Miller even then continuing the pursuit.

When he returned to the bank, Russell and Oney determined that nearly $20,000 in valuables and currency had been taken. The loss of the money, however, did not stop the bank from doing business, for Erskine Miller, a stockholder, arrived the next day with a supply of currency, and other funds were sent in from Charleston.

The chase went on, and on Saturday evening the following telegram was received in Huntington:

Willard, Ky., Sept. 10, 1875

To John H. Russell, President, Huntington Bank

We are at West Liberty. Have fifteen fresh men and horses after the parties. Think they will overhaul them. They have gone toward Cumberland Gap. Will stay until we hear.

G. F. Miller

On Monday morning Miller and several of his men returned to Huntington, bringing with them the gray mare which had been ridden by one of the bandits. He had left it on the road with a man to take care of and hired another mount. He rode this horse about twenty miles, then bought another for a hundred dollars.

On Friday Oney received a letter from the chief of police of

Louisville, Kentucky, enclosing a photograph and a description of the man he suspected of being the leader of the robber band. Oney recognized it at once. The picture was taken to Mr. Crump's home, where the bandits had stayed the Saturday night prior to the holdup. They were not advised as to the identity of the man in the photograph but were simply asked if they had ever seen the man in the picture.

Without hesitation Mr. Crump and his son stated, "Yes, he is one of the men who stayed here Saturday night."

The photograph was that of one of the Younger brothers, men who were known to be associated with the James gang and who also had been accused of various robberies since the Civil War.

Daily reports from the pursuers were sent, showing just where the bandits were last seen, and which way they were going, calling on the people to look out for them. And the people turned out. Two brothers named Dillon, becoming very much interested in the reports about the bandits, concluded that the robbers would approach their place. Each procured an old army musket which they loaded with slugs and then kept a sharp lookout for the outlaws.

On the night of the fourteenth, the brothers saw four figures, discernible in the moonlight, moving through the woods on foot about fifty yards south. Near the road they stopped to and talk for a moment. Then two of them came down the road, while the other pair headed toward the brothers. This was the moment. They were tall men, wearing linen dusters and armed with pistols, whose handles protruded from the front of their coats. Two against two, without any odds, provided the first shots were accurate. . . . But what if those muskets missed? The Dillon boys perhaps never thought of this. As the bandits approached, the brothers commanded, "Halt! Throw up your hands!" Instead of obeying, the bandits drew their pistols, and four shots blazed. The outlaws ran off, but one of them moved in a manner that plainly showed he had been wounded.

On the following morning the two brothers returned to the spot, and were rewarded by the sight of bloodstains on the ground. Following the trail into a cornfield for a distance of two hundred yards, they found a man with a gaping wound in his side. The brothers carried him to their house and, placing him upon the bed, sent for a doctor. The wounded bandit, with the fever on his brow, cried out in his delirium for "Bud."

Then as the hand of death lifted the veil of unconsciousness the robber cried out, "Yes, I am dying. Where are my friends?"

He was asked his name and those of his companions, but he answered, "I'll never betray a friend."

On the body of the outlaw there was found only a seal ring and two photographs. One was of a man who proved to be Bob Ricketts, who later said that Tom (or Thompson or Tomlinson) was the only person who had his picture. The other was of a woman who was known to be a sweetheart of McDaniels. This woman received, some days later, a piece of black crepe enclosed in a letter. The seal ring was identified as one McDaniels had worn.

On the day after the robber's death, September 19, three men came to the house where the body lay and asked to view the remains. It so happened that only Mrs. Dillon and some women friends were present at the time. They became frightened, believing that the three were the surviving bandits of the Huntington raid. Mrs. Dillon, therefore, refused the request by saying that the remains were in the coffin which had already been permanently sealed.

One man spoke in a firm voice, saying, "Madam, we are sorry that circumstances require us to appear rude; we came to see the dead body, and therefore we ask you again to show us the body."

Mrs. Dillon, frightened, conducted the three strangers into another room where the coffin rested on two chairs. A screw-

driver lay on the window sill, and with this the lid was readily
removed from the coffin. The trio looked long and sorrowfully
at the dead man's face. The largest man betrayed great emotion
as tears streamed down his cheeks. After a speechless gaze of
many minutes, the three men asked if the person who did the
killing was about. Informed that he was not, they courteously
bade Mrs. Dillon good-bye and left.

Oney, the Huntington bank cashier, had been to Pine Hill the
second day before this occurrence, and had fully identified the
wounded man as one of the two who had entered the bank and
forced him to give up the money. He returned by way of Louisville, and while there, received the following dispatch, which
was published in the *Courier-Journal:*

Louisville, Ky., Sept. 20

Robt. T. Oney:

The other three entered the house and had the coffin opened;
said he did not look like he looked before. One of them was
crying. They asked for me and then went into the cornfield. I
was at the house about five minutes after they left. I look for a
desperate attack today.

W. R. Dillon

There was no attack, of course. The three survivors remained
hidden for a time, two of them eventually escaping, while the
third was wounded and captured in Fentress County, Tennessee. He had about $4,000 in his clothes. He was identified as one
of the men who wore a long duster at Huntington. He was taken
back and tried for his part in the crime, and was sentenced to
fourteen years in the state prison at Moundsville, booked as
Thomas J. Webb (alias Jack Keen), Prisoner #457, received
12–8–75.

In justice to Cole Younger and Frank James, the following

suspicions concerning the identity of the other two robbers are given, for it is my intention not to draw inference unsupported by reasonable conclusions. Regardless of the information which led to introducing Cole Younger and Frank James as plotting with Jack Keen in the robbery of the bank, it is not certain that either of them were at Huntington. It is claimed that Clell Miller was one of the party, while the name of the fourth man is in dispute. Some hold that it was Cole Younger, because Cole was commonly called "Bud" by his comrades, and they think that McDaniels' delirious inquiries as to whether Bud was captured referred to Cole or Bud Younger. Others say that McDaniels, being out of his head, was raving about his brother. The matter never was settled. The following is a description of the robbers, published a few days after the raid. One fits the description of Frank James and one could have been that of Cole Younger:

1. Heavy set man, at least six feet tall, weight two hundred pounds, tolerably dark hair, with reddish whiskers and moustache, red complexion, black hat, long linen duster and blue overalls, gold ring on little finger.

2. Tall, slim man, in height about six feet, one hundred and fifty pounds, delicate-looking, light hair and sandy whiskers, high forehead, long nose, gold buttons on shirt, left little finger had a ring, long duster and blue overalls.

3. Tall, slim man, about six feet high, weight one hundred and sixty-five pounds, short, black whiskers and black hair, slim face, black hat, long duster, blue overalls, suit of black twilled cloth with stripes, fine boots, two gold rings on little left finger; had two collars washed with "London" printed on the bands.

4. Heavy set man, about five feet ten inches tall, weight one hundred and eighty pounds, very stout, square-looking man, brown hair, round red face, patch of red whiskers on his chin, light-colored hat, linen duster, gray striped coat and vest, pants similar, but not like coat and vest, red drilling overalls, fine boots, gold ring with flowers cut on it on his left little finger.

On March 11, 1876, a man named Keeney was arrested at Sedalia, Missouri, on suspicion of having had a hand in the Huntington raid. He had received a large sum of money by express from a brother living near Huntington. He gave no satisfactory explanation to the authorities, but in the absence of positive evidence of any connection with the robbery, he was released after two weeks.

Detective Bligh of Louisville at first boasted that Jesse James was captured when Keen was arrested. Statements subsequently made by the convicted robber left no doubt that Frank James had been with him and probably Cole Younger. Regardless of the details, the deed was undoubtedly committed by members of the organization of which the James boys were the most noted leaders. At any rate, the leaders of the Huntington raid escaped, carrying the bulk of the bank's funds with them.

Wagon train loaded with supplies for construction crews in Echo Canyon, Utah (Union Pacific Railroad).

The St. James Hotel, Selma, Alabama, where Frank and Jesse stayed before the Muscle Shoals Robbery (R.A. Rosenberg).

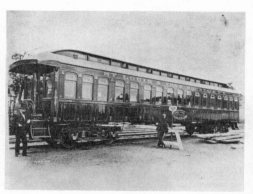

St. Louis & Iron Mountain Coach, 1870 (Missouri Pacific Railroad).

The type of train held up at Adair, Iowa (Carl W. Breihan Collection).

Empire City, at Short Creek diggings (Wayne Walker Collection).

Three rare pieces of history: The James Boys Rocks, found in the 1890s on the Kansas-Nebraska border. Left to Right: "Jesse James 1881"; "Sept. 25, 1881 the James Boys of Missouri"; "Frank James" (R.L. Mack Collection).

The Bank of Columbia, Kentucky, also known as the Kentucky Deposit Bank, robbed by a band of outlaws in April, 1872 (Carl W. Breihan Collection).

The Old Southern Bank, Russellville, Kentucky, robbed by the James Gang in 1868, still houses the vault from which the money was taken (Carl W. Breihan Collection).

This safe, in the Ocobock Bros. Bank, Corydon, Iowa, was robbed by Jesse James on June 3, 1871. It is now in the Wayne County Museum (Carl W. Breihan Collection).

Front Street, Dodge City, Kansas. It was here that Jesse James' brief meeting with Bat Masterson took place (The Kansas State Historical Society, Topeka).

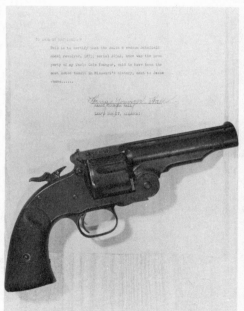

Cole Younger's revolver (Carl W. Breihan Collection).

The John Baker cabin, in which his son-in-law, Dick Son, lived when Frank and Jesse James and Jim Baker were lost in the snowstorm during the winter of 1877–78, and in which they thawed their frozen feet in the oven of the cookstove (Kerry Ross Boren Collection).

James Baker.

John Baker, brother of mountain man Jim Baker. John Baker owned a ranch on Henry's Fork in what is now Sweetwater County, Wyoming. Frank and Jesse James visited Baker at his ranch and attended the funeral of his wife, Cora (a squaw) in 1877 (Kerry Ross Boren Collection).

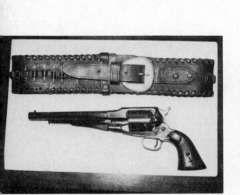

Top: Frank James' .22 cal. shell belt. The buckle is hand made and the shells in the belt loops are originals. Bottom: .44 cal. C&B Remington, found under the home where Jesse James was murdered. It was discovered when the house was moved in 1939. Note the "X" on grip (R.L. Mack Collection).

Cummins rode into Galena and heard rumors of the impending bank raid at Empire City (Wayne Walker Collection).

The Liberty Bank Building, Liberty, Missouri, robbed in 1866 by a band of outlaws (Carl W. Breihan Collection).

The James-Younger Gang crossed this bridge when entering the town of Northfield, Minnesota in 1876, prior to the famous bank raid (Carl W. Breihan Collection).

These two revolvers were dropped by the fleeing bandits after the Huntington, West Virginia bank robbery (Carl W. Breihan Collection).

Gallatin, Missouri bank (Carl W. Breihan Collection).

The house in which Jesse James was born, alleged to have been destroyed by a bomb in 1875 (Pinkerton's National Detective Agency, Inc.).

Jesse James II or Jr. (Bell, Kansas City, Missouri).

Wedding photo of Robert Franklin James, son of Frank James, December 26, 1901; taken at F.W. Guerin Studios, St. Louis, Missouri (Carl W. Breihan Collection).

Wedding photo of Mae James, wife of Robert, December 26, 1901; taken at F.W. Guerin Studios, St. Louis, Missouri (Carl W. Breihan Collection).

These two stones, one face down and one leaning, were carved by hand by Jesse James to place on the graves of his twin sons who died in infancy in Humphrees County, Tennessee. The other stone in this small family cemetery bears the date "April 30, 1847" (Carl W. Breihan Collection).

The James Home after the bomb blast (Carl W. Breihan Collection).

Henry Washington Younger, the father of the Younger Brothers (Carl W. Breihan Collection).

Uncle Jack's Cabin at Linwood, Utah (ca. 1900). In this, Utah's oldest existing cabin (1834), Frank and Jesse James spent the winter of 1877–78 with Jim Baker, the mountain man who had lived in the cabin intermittently for some forty years (Kerry Ross Boren Collection).

Frank and Jesse attended this school near the homestead at Kearney, Missouri. Jesse went only as far as the 5th grade; Frank graduated. This building has now been made into a residence (Carl W. Breihan Collection).

Mrs. Samuel (seated) and Mary James at the James homestead (Carl W. Breihan Collection).

A very rare photo of Bill Ryan, the first member of the James band to be brought to justice by a court of law.

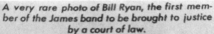

Bill Ryan (Rosamond Collection).

The back of this arch in Northfield, Minnesota reads: "This stone arch marks the starting point of the famous James-Younger raid on the Northfield Bank in 1876." (R.L. Mack Collection)

CHAPTER 10

The Rocky Cut
Train Holdup

IT WAS JULY, 1876. THE WORLD WAS IN FLUX. THE UNITED States was straining at the seams, bursting with growth and progress, crouched on the threshold of the twentieth century. All this seemed of little interest to the ex-Quantrillians and ex-Confederate soldiers of Missouri, as they waited patiently for word that the Jameses and the Youngers had added another coup to their growing record of bank and train robberies.

It had been almost a year since the fantastic holdup of the Huntington (West Virginia) bank, and the main news now in the local papers covered the Custer battle in far off Montana Territory. But the Missouri backwoodsmen and farmers were not well acquainted with Custer, Terry, and Crook, the famous men who were carrying out the Sioux campaign.

The general mercantile store at Liberty, Missouri, boasted of having one copy of a newspaper which carried an account of the Custer battle, taken from the Bismarck (Dakota Territory)

Tribune. This paper gave the cracker-barrel historians a chance to mull over the matter, and to discuss the pros and cons of Custer's inexplicable movements preceding the battle with the Sioux on the Little Big Horn. Most of them agreed it was an awful way for Custer and his troops to come to an end; some of the older Confederate soldiers just shook their heads in puzzlement.

On the morning of July 8, 1876, the wires buzzed with news that stirred these Missourians into excited action and conversation. Word had come to Liberty and the entire nation that another train had been robbed by the James gang. This time it was the Missouri-Pacific railroad train that had been stopped and robbed.

The robbers had picked a lonely spot for their handiwork— a place called Rocky Cut, at the Lamine bridge, near Otterville, Missouri. The date was July 7, 1876.

This robbery, however, had a different aspect to it, inasmuch as the whole story, including the names of the robbers, the details of their plan, and the route of their escape were soon to be revealed. In no other robbery was this accomplished except after the Northfield Raid, which was soon to follow on September 7, two months after the Rocky Cut affair. The identity of the Northfield raiders was ascertained in a positive-proof manner, for in that all but two of the gang, Jesse and Frank James, were killed or captured. In subsequent years I was able to prove beyond a doubt that the two men who escaped from Northfield were the James boys.

Bud McDaniels, a member of the James gang, who had been shot and killed after the Muncie (Kansas) train robbery, needed replacement. Jesse made the mistake of taking along Hobbs Kerry, inexperienced and much too talkative, who was soon captured after the Rocky Cut affair and persuaded to confess. Although the Jameses went to the trouble of sending denials to various newspapers, they kept carefully out of sight and there is no particular reason to doubt the essential truth of Kerry's story.

Kerry stated that Cole Younger, Clell Miller, Charlie Pitts (a Missourian, whose real name was Sam Wells), and he rode to the vicinity of California, Missouri, where, a few miles outside the town, they met the James brothers, Bill Chadwell (alias Bill Stiles), and Bob Younger. There was no mention of Jim Younger's being present. Kerry later insisted there had been twelve men in the group (and that would have been a rather large number for Jesse to use in a train robbery) but he was unable to name the other four. This led some people to believe that Kerry's story, told under duress, was simply not the truth. Kerry said the whole idea had originated with the James boys, for he had heard Cole Younger remark, "You fellows suggested this caper."

Kerry went on to say that the gang stayed in or near California July 5 and 6 because of a heavy rain, and that on the seventh most of the group met two miles east of the Lamine bridge about two in the afternoon. Miller and Kerry were staying in an unidentified house all day and did not reach the rendezvous until about six P.M.

On July 1, 1876, eight rough-looking and well-armed men converged upon a small farmhouse in southwest Missouri, in the lead-mining district. These men were Frank and Jesse James, Cole and Bob Younger, Clell Miller, Charlie Pitts, Bill Chadwell, and Hobbs Kerry.

The policy of the bandits was to conceal their presence, even from friends, just before a robbery, so as to make the crime such a thorough surprise that after its commission people would be too badly confused for an immediate and intelligent pursuit.

The old tactics of the outlaws were to be put into practice at the robbery of the Missouri-Pacific train, one of the most daring and successful holdups ever made by the band.

Three or four of the robbers went quietly down to the bridge. Here they found the watchman, an old Swiss immigrant, Henry Chateau, sitting by the pump house, smoking a corncob pipe. Entirely unsuspecting and rather lonely, Chateau was glad to see his visitors. Watching the bridge across the Lamine River was a dull and lonely job, and he would have welcomed any company.

The strangers chatted amicably. When one of them asked Chateau what his job was, the watchman explained that all he did was watch the bridge. "I show a white light for passing trains if all is well, and a red light if there is any danger," he said.

"What time is it?" asked the biggest of the bandits, probably Cole Younger.

"Ten minutes after nine . . . it's about time," remarked one of his companions.

Of course, this meant nothing to the watchman at the time, and his suspicions were not aroused.

One robber rose, asking for a drink of water. Chateau stepped into the pump house to get it and suddenly found himself a prisoner, with a cocked revolver at his head, while the remainder of the group donned masks of various types. It is strange that the group allowed the watchman to see their faces in the first place, unless they believed he would bolt and give an alarm if he saw a group of masked men approaching him.

The frightened watchman was blindfolded and was taken back to Rocky Cut, a few miles east of Otterville. Signal lanterns in hand, Chateau presented a dejected figure.

"You ain't gonna hurt me, are you?"

"What do we want to hurt you for? All we want is the money," and so saying, the bandit pushed a wicked-looking revolver into the poor man's face.

While their captive was held under guard, the gang piled ties on the track. There was no switch spur there and no way of being sure that the engineer might not take alarm and try to run past the robbers. One of the bandits loosened a rail to make certain the train would not get by them.

All but two of the gang went down to the tracks, leaving Miller and Kerry with the horses. As the sound of the approaching train came nearer, the leader of the gang lighted the red lantern, led the watchman to the middle of the track and said, "Now you have three choices, old man: being run over, stopping the train, or stopping a bullet."

No wonder Chateau made industrious use of the signal. The train actually rolled to within twenty-five feet of the watchman, who dared not jump off the track for fear of being shot, before it came to a grinding halt. One of the robbers laughed when he saw that the train cow-catcher had actually touched the pile of railroad ties.

As pistol shots began to ring out in the dark, the old man saw his chance to run for safety, after removing the blindfold. One can imagine his reactions when he saw the steaming engine almost within reach of his position on the tracks. Chateau took off like a gazelle into the darkness. It was later remarked that it seemed odd that the engineer did not notice the blindfold on the old man as he waved the red lantern. Engineer John Standthorpe probably saw the red light in the darkness and swung his throttle, long before he could make out the details of the terrified old man on the tracks. Besides, locomotive headlights in those days did not have the range like those of today.

The Missouri-Pacific train had left Kansas City at 4:45 P.M. with several coaches, two of the new Pullman sleeping cars, a smoker, and a combination express and baggage car. At Sedalia it took on an M.K.&T. express car, locked, and without any special express messenger aboard. John B. Bushnell, in charge of two safes, occupied the Missouri-Pacific baggage and express car. Bushnell was a United States express messenger, in charge mainly of the express company's own safe. The other safe belonged to the Adams Express Company. With Bushnell was Louis P. Conklin of St. Louis, baggage master for the railroad company.

The engineer, knowing he was approaching a bridge, and not having any reason to be suspicious, saw the lantern, applied his brakes, and brought the metal monster to a halt. The moment he did so the robbers piled up an obstruction behind the train so that it could not be backed away. It has been said that the robbers sent a man back to the bridge to halt an oncoming freight train, but no record can be found of this or if, in fact, any freight train was expected. In any event, the robbers had plenty of time to do their work.

Pete Conklin, the baggage master, had been sitting peacefully in a chair by the open door of the baggage car, watching the moonlight flick the scenery as the train moved on, and trying to catch some cool breeze at the same time. Suddenly a shot interrupted his meditations, and a bullet struck the door near his chair. Three men, with bandannas over their faces, climbed in through the open side door. Bushnell, farther back in the car, quickly realized that something was amiss. Instantly he slipped through the rear door, ran through the train, and handed the key to his express safe to the brakeman. He then tried to lose himself among the passengers while the brakeman tucked the key into his shoe.

Pete Conklin always believed that the man just outside the car was Frank James and that two of those who came into his car were Jesse and Cole Younger. Soon the engineer and fireman were brought to the baggage car, pushed in, and lined up against the wall with Conklin. When the robbers found the safe key missing, they marched Conklin back through the coaches with them and he was forced to point out Bushnell, who, in turn, was forced to point out the brakeman. No one dared to offer resistance, and the key was turned over to the bandits. A young newsboy, Lou Bales, who sold magazines on the train, had a small firearm which made more noise than damage, and he appeared to be the coolest of the passengers. He fired two shots from the window at one of the bandits standing near the coach.

They all got a big laugh out of that. One of the passengers took charge of Bales so that no harm would befall him.

The proceedings were enlivened by Clergyman J. S. Holmes, of Bedford, New York. He prayed loudly that all might be spared, and that if any must be killed, the unfortunate ones might repent in time to be saved. Then he sang church hymns. Perhaps Jesse would have liked to join in the singing, for he was familiar with church songs. He had sung them many times when he was a Baptist in good standing. However, right now, the songs failed to strike a responsive chord in him.

The robbers returned to the express car. The United States express safe was opened easily with the key, and the cash removed and placed in a wheat sack by one of the outlaws. Then the apparent leader of the group turned to the Adams Express safe. He asked Bushnell the whereabouts of the key and was informed that this was a through safe with no key given to him for it. Blue and blinky eyes flashed above the mask which covered the face of this outlaw who was probably Jesse James. Convinced that there was no key to this safe, Bob Younger went to the engine tender, where he obtained a pick, and brought it back to the express car. He tried to break the hinges of the door with the pick, to no avial. Several sharp blows to the door of the sheet-iron safe also failed to open it.

The biggest of the bandits, no doubt Cole Younger, seized the pick and dealt several smashing blows to the safe. He hit a series of blows in a circle shape and finally was able to knock out a piece of the metal. However, the opening was too small for the man's large hand. Another of the robbers, a small man wearing skin-tight silk gloves, managed to get his hand inside. Feeling a leather money pouch, he seized a knife, cut open the bag and removed the currency in small handfuls. This was tossed into the grain sack with the other currency. From the description of the small man he no doubt was Jesse James.

Not content with the express car haul, the robbers went through the passenger cars, which were occupied to capacity. One man held the grain sack open, and the passengers were ordered to drop into the sack whatever money or valuables they possessed. This demand was emphasized by Jesse James, walking behind the bagman with pistols drawn and ready. Some passengers managed to hide their valuables. One man hid his money and jewelry on the roof of the car by passing them through a ventilation opening. When he went to retrieve them after the car began to move, he found that the night breeze had scattered them.

A comic relief incident occurred when a lanky Hoosier tried to hide under a seat, but his feet stuck out in the aisle. Jesse James, not seeing the obstruction, stumbled to the floor. The poor man under the seat was terrified. He uttered pleas of apology and for mercy. The bandit just got up, merely laughed, and passed on.

For what seemed an eternity to the frightened passengers and crew, the train, with its lights blazing, was held in the open countryside.

Concerning the Missouri Pacific express robbery, Miss Peabody, an ex-Jefferson City lady, and schoolteacher at Denver City, who was on the train, gave the following statement to the Jefferson City *Tribune* reporter:

> After leaving Otterville [said Miss Peabody,] I was dozing in a reclining chair—probably fast falling asleep. Suddenly the train was brought to a halt, and a moment later a man rushed hurriedly through the car. I believe he was the express messenger. Someone asked him what was the matter. "The train is being robbed, that's the matter," he hurriedly replied, and kept

on. Then all was commotion and confusion. Including myself there were three ladies in the car. I confess that I was terribly frightened and thought I should faint, but I saw that there was no one handy to catch or care for a person in a faint, and concluded to omit this part of the programme. Meanwhile, shots were being fired on the outside, and we could hear numbers of men cursing and swearing. I suppose the shots were fired for the purpose of intimidation. I believe our car was next to the smoking car. Directly the door was thrown open, and in stalked two of the robbers. The leader put his hand on the shoulder of a brakeman and said, 'Here, I want you,' and hustled him out. We thought they were going to shoot him, but I suppose now they wanted him to identify the express messenger. It was rare fun—I mean it is amusing to look back at it now, nothing funny in it then—to see the passengers concealing their valuables. Here you would see a man with his boots off, cramming his greenbacks in his socks; several—Mr. Marshall, of Fulton, among the rest—tossed their cash, watches, etc., into a coal-box; others were up on the back of seats hunting holes for their pocketbooks. Wherever any thing could be concealed, something was sure to find its way.

The conductor, excited and nervous, hurriedly passed through, and told all who had valuables to take care of them. The most ludicrous incident I can now recall was when a sanctimonious-looking individual, evidently scared almost out of his wits, broke forth with the old familiar song, "I'm going home to die no more." His quavering, doleful voice echoed through the car with lugubrious effect. Some of the male passengers were ungallant enough to interrupt him with the remark that he had better be getting his money out of the way instead of starting a camp meeting.

Having finished the hymn, he said he had been a follower of the Lord for ever so many years—that he was a true and consistent member of the Church—that he had never wronged a fellow-being, but that if he was doomed to be murdered, he wanted his remains forwarded to his family in New York, and to write them that he had died true to the faith and in the hope of a glorious resurrection.

The tumult outside continued. We could distinctly hear them

pounding away at the Adams Express safe, and their coarse oaths and imprecations at being delayed. Occasionally shots were fired. The leader of the robbers, a tall fine-looking man, accompanied by one of his comrades, passed through the car. "You need not be hiding your money," said the leader, "we do not intend to disturb you." He wore a red handkerchief over his face, with holes cut for his eyes and mouth. Below the handkerchief appeared his beard, very long, but probably false. His companion was a smaller and rougher looking man. His mask was simply a white handkerchief tied over the lower portion of his face. The upper part was plainly visible. He remarked that we must consider them an awful set of reprobates. The inquiry for arms showed three pistols in our car. One of these was owned by a lady. Throughout the whole affair she remained perfectly cool and collected—and refused to accommodate a gentleman with the loan of her pistol. When some one said this was the work of the James boys, she laughingly remarked that her name was James, but she hoped none of her relatives were engaged in such disreputable business.

The newsboy had a pistol and made his way to the front platform. Looking up the bluff, he descried the figure of a man and fired. In an instant the shot was returned. The ball passed between the plucky newsboy and a gentleman who was also on the platform, and both of them sought shelter without ceremony. Thinking that the robbers might fire through the windows, I got off the chair and took a position on the floor. The sanctimonious New Yorker who was going away to die no more, thinking, doubtless, that I was engaged in prayer, softly approached and asked if I was prepared to die? I was not in a humor to enlighten him on the subject.

We were detained about an hour, when, the robbers having accomplished their purpose, gave us permission to proceed. It was one of the episodes of my life I shall never forget.

Somewhere in the darkness was Chateau, probably still running for his life. The outlaws had taken their time, well knowing that it was impossible to raise an effective alarm in that sparsely settled part of Missouri.

When the train reached Tipton, Missouri, Conductor Tebbets wired the news to St. Louis, Sedalia, and Kansas City. Posses rushed to central Missouri, but the robbers had already split the loot and scattered. Before doing this, though, they had ridden over twenty miles to a secluded spot. A total of $17,000 had been taken from the two safes; the amount taken from the passengers was never ascertained.

Hobbs Kerry, a stupid, boastful fellow, was given $1,200 for his part in the Rocky Cut robbery. He hid his saddle in the brush and turned his mount loose near Montrose. He then boarded an M.K.&T. train and went to Fort Scott, Kansas. There he outfitted himself with new clothes, after which he boldly entered a hotel, ate supper, then took a train for Parsons, where he stayed overnight, and then went to Vinita, then to Granby, Missouri, a lead-mining center; from there to Joplin, Missouri, reaching that point on July 18. Kerry then proceeded to Eufala, Indian Territory, where he made the foolish mistake of displaying too much money.

Several weeks after the robbery, Detective Sergeant Morgan Boland, of the St. Louis Police Department, asked permission of Chief James McDonough to do a little quiet investigating in southwestern Missouri. Making friends with the lead miners at Grandy, Boland soon learned of Hobbs Kerry and his high living. Kerry had returned to Missouri by that time, so Boland located him and made friends with him. The simple-minded Kerry, impressed with his greatness as a bandit, boasted of having taken part in the train holdup with the great Jesse James.

Hobbs Kerry was arrested and taken to Boonville, Cooper County, where he made a full confession, telling the whole story and naming the participants as far as he knew them. For thus having turned state's evidence, Kerry got off with a two-year sentence in the penitentiary.

Once more Jesse James was careful about public relations. A

few days after Kerry's arrest, a stranger rode up to a *Kansas City Times* reporter and handed him a letter, dated August 14, 1876, Oak Grove, Kansas. The following is what the letter contained, an alibi offered by Jesse James, the most famous outlaw of all times:

Oak Grove, Kansas
August 14, 1876

Dear Sir:

You have published Hobbs Kerry's confession, which makes it appear that the Jameses and the Youngers were the Rocky Cut robbers. If there was only one side to be told, it would probably be believed by a good many people that Kerry told the truth. But his so-called confession is a well-built pack of lies from beginning to end. I never heard of Hobbs Kerry, Charlie Pitts, or William Chadwell until Kerry's arrest. I can prove my innocence by eight good, well-known men of Jackson County, and show conclusively that I was not at the train robbery. But at present I will give only the names of two of these gentlemen to whom I will refer for proof.

Early on the morning after the train robbery east of Sedalia, I saw the Hon. D. Gregg, of Jackson County, and talked with him for thirty or forty minutes. I also saw and talked to Thomas Pitcher, of Jackson County, the morning after the robbery. Those men's oaths cannot be impeached, so I refer the grand jury of Cooper County, Mo., and Gov. Hardin to those men before they act so rashly on the oath of a liar, thief, and robber.

Kerry knows that the Jameses and Youngers can't be taken alive, and that is why he has put it on us. I have referred to Messrs. Pitcher and Gregg because they are prominent men, and they know I am innocent, and their word can't be disputed. I will write a long article to you for the *Times,* and send it to you in a few days, showing fully how Hobbs Kerry had lied. Hoping the *Times* will give me a chance for a fair hearing and to vindicate myself through its columns, I will close.

Respectfully,
J. James

As he promised, Jesse did write another letter to the editor of the *Kansas City Times* a few days later, written apparently from a James hideout in Texas.

Safe Retreat, August 18, 1876

Dear Sir:

I have written a great many letters vindicating myself of the false charges that have been brought against me. Detectives have been trying for years to get positive proof against me for some criminal offense, so that they could get a large reward offered for me, dead or alive; and the same of Frank James and the Younger boys, but they have been foiled on every turn, and they are fully convinced that we will never be taken alive, and now they have fell on the deep-laid scheme to get Hobbs Kerry to tell a pack of base lies. But, thank God, I am yet a free man, and have got the power to defend myself against the charge brought against me by Kerry, a notorious liar and poltroon. I will give a full statement and prove his confessions false.

Lie No. 1. He said a plot was laid by the Jameses and Youngers to rob the Granby bank. I am reliably informed that there never was a bank at Granby.

Lie No. 2. He said he met with Cole Younger and me at Mr. Tyler's. If there is a man in Jackson County by that name, I am sure that I am not acquainted with him.

Lie No. 3. He said Frank James was at Butler's, in Cass County. I and Frank James don't know any man in Cass County by that name. I can prove my innocence by eight good citizens of Jackson County, Mo., but I do not propose to give all their names at present. If I did, those cutthroat detectives would find out where I am.

My opinion is that Bacon Montgomery, the scoundrel who murdered Capt. A. J. Clements, December 13, 1866, is the instigator of all this Missouri Pacific affair. I believe he planned the robbery and got his share of the money, and when he went out to look for the robbers he led the pursuers off the robbers' trail. If the truth was half told about Montgomery, it would make the world believe that midnight assassins who murdered my poor, helpless and innocent eight-year-old brother, and shot my mother's arm off; and I am of the opinion he had a hand in that dirty, cowardly work. The detectives are a brave lot of boys . . . charge houses, break down doors and make the grey hairs stand up on the heads of unarmed victims. Why don't President Grant have the soldiers called and send the detectives out on a special train after the hostile Indians? A. M. Pinkerton's force, with hand-grenades, and they will kill all the women and children, and as soon as the women and children are killed it will stop the breed, and the warriors will die out in a few years. I believe the railroad robbers will yet be sifted down on someone at St. Louis or Sedalia putting up the job and they trying to have it put on innocent men, as Kerry has done.

Hoping the *Times* will publish just as I have written, I will close.

Jesse James

At one time Jesse James told the papers it was his intention to write sketches of his life for publication, but this apparently was never carried out.

The sheer impudence of Jesse's letters was amusing to the general public; but to the law-enforcement officers it was a different matter as the robberies kept on and on.

CHAPTER 11

The Northfield
Bank Raid

THE SEPTEMBER SUN ROSE SLOWLY, ITS SOFT RAYS PROB-
ing through the heavy mist which covered the countryside. It
was a silent morning, the stillness broken only by the steady
dripping of the heavy dew as it fell like bucket-flung diamonds
from the dense brush and trees. Suddenly another sound began
its rhythmic beat through the damp underbrush. It was the
steady sloshing of horses' hoofs. Soon, eight riders rode into a
small clearing in the forest, several hundred feet from where the
tilled fields met the woods, their linen dusters pulled snugly
around their necks, their hats drawn down over their foreheads.

It was a group of cautious, moody men who dismounted and
looked around, apparently some hours too early for what their
mission called for.

One of the riders, a tall, broad-shouldered young man, peered
toward the morning sun and remarked, "Well, fellows, there's
Mankato. If all goes well we can hit the bank there and the
other one later."

"Right, Cole, but we'd best get a little cold breakfast first, as we have plenty time," replied a tall, slender man of about thirty-two, with a hawklike face and long slim hands.

Several hours passed. The fog lifted with an incoming breeze, bringing into plain view of the eight men the little town of Mankato, Minnesota.

It was September 2, 1876, when the eight robbers rode into town, where they visited the saloons and played cards. Their horses were excellent mounts, and the riders carried bundles behind their saddles and looked like cattle buyers. Two of the group stopped at the Gates Hotel on Sunday, and two at the Washington House, nearly opposite the Gates. It is known that two of the robbers stayed at the home of George Capps at Kasota, five miles south on Mankato on Sunday night. No record appears available as to the activities of the other two for that time. Both parties staying at the hotels refused to register.

At the Washington House one Charles Robinson, employed by Mr. Edward O'Leary, proprietor of the hotel, saw and recognized one of the two men as the noted bandit, Jesse James. Robinson saw the outlaw on Monday morning, just as the visitor was mounting his horse. He called Jesse James by name and asked him what he was doing in that part of the country. The stranger made no reply, glanced at Robinson, then rode away, on Main Street.

Robinson told O'Leary that he was positive the man was Jesse James. He stated he had known him in Mexico, Missouri, where he had played cards with him. Robinson described the visitor as wearing a heavy black mustache and black beard, which had not been prominent when he was in Missouri. Edward O'Leary notified the officials of the several banks in Mankato, as well as the police department.

On Monday morning, September 4, after the First National Bank opened, a large powerful man came into the bank and asked to have a twenty-dollar bill changed. The assistant cashier gave him the change in fives, which the man deliberately counted one by one. At the same time his eyes were directed at the vault in a general survey of the bank. Cashier Hall observed this as the stranger gave him a searching look and left the bank.

The bank was a frame building, the rear of which had been temporarily boarded up, and workmen were engaged in building a substantial addition to the building. Another of the party visited the Citizens' Bank, but nothing unusual was observed. The bank officials had posted temporary guards as a precautionary measure, while the strangers were placed under secret observation by the local guardians of the law. The casual surveillance was kept up; but so innocent were the actions of the group that the police were not impressed.

Another man, whose name is unknown, also stated he had recognized Jesse James as one of the visiting strangers in Mankato. His story also seemed so unreal that little attention was paid to it. The police remarked that it was impossible that Jesse James would pay their small town a visit.

At noon on Monday the entire force of eight robbers rode up in front of the First National Bank and created no excitement. A group of idle citizens, watching the construction work in progress next to the bank, noted and admired the excellent horses the men were riding. Jesse motioned the band to move on, but later in the afternoon they returned. The same "sidewalk superintendents" were still on hand. Evidently believing their purpose was suspected, the eight outlaws rode out of Mankato. In leaving the town, the bandits rode up Main Street, and at the Catholic church two of them rode up Fifth Street, past the Normal School, passing down the steep hill to the pottery road. The outlaws had remounted and were starting toward town, but the group of citizens standing near the bank discouraged them. They believed that in some way an alarm had been given.

They thus abandoned their raid on the Mankato bank. It was then decided to ride in pairs toward Northfield, the scene of their next planned operation. The stage set for today was on a much larger scale than any of the other bank robberies in which Jesse and Frank James and the Youngers were said to have taken part. The gang was to be thoroughly shot up, and several members were to be captured and locked behind prison bars.

A bridge in the center of Northfield connected the east and west parts of the town and led east into Bridge Square. On the corner of Davison Street and Bridge Square was a two-story building called the Scriver Block. The First National Bank stood at the south end of the block, near an alley back of two hardware stores operated by J. S. Allen and A. R. Manning, respectively. Opposite the Scriver Block was a group of stores and a hotel, the Dampier House. There, the young Wheeler boy, home on vacation from his medical studies at Michigan University, was passing the time of day when the robbery got under way.

Early on the morning of September 7, the robbers rode along in pairs so as to avoid suspicion, and met in a wooded area near the town. Then, with their usual bravado, they boldly rode into town and ate at a restaurant on the west side of the bridge. This also was a reconnaissance visit. All the men wore long linen dusters, the style of that time, so as to hide their heavy revolvers and ammunition. They were: Cole, Jim and Bob Younger, Clell Miller, Bill Chadwell (alias William Stiles), Charlie Pitts (whose real name was Sam Wells), and Jesse and Frank James.

Their plan was for Bob Younger, Charlie Pitts, and Frank James to wait in the square until the second detachment arrived. The timing was poor from the start. Bob Younger had tipped the bottle too long and was a bit fuzzy in his reactions. Frank James, too, had been drinking. Although he could handle his liquor better than Bob Younger, on this day Frank was inclined to be a bit trigger-happy and belligerent. Bill Chadwell, who had once lived in Rice County, Minnesota, was elected to lead the bandits safely out of that state after the robbery.

Jesse James had his misgivings about their plans, but Cole Younger is credited with having fostered the idea. Cole contended that Northfield should be struck hard on account of General Butler, who was hated in the deep South as a Union general. He had inflicted widespread suffering and humiliation on the vanquished from his headquarters in Louisiana, after the defeat of the South. He was also prominently connected with the Northfield Bank.

General Butler was the only one ever to use the dreaded Gatling gun during the Civil War, with devastating results at the Battle of Petersburg. And don't you ever forget that!

Accordingly, the first group of three waited in the square, posing as loafers; and when they saw the others ride into view they entered the bank. But the advance guard's entrance was not according to schedule, for they were supposed to wait until Cole and Clell Miller joined them to complete the inside party. When Cole and Miller hurried into the bank, in the wake of the trio already inside, they found the door open. Telling Miller to close the door, Cole dismounted and pretended to adjust the saddle girth of his horse. These actions aroused the suspicion of J. S. Allen, one of the hardware store proprietors. Allen then started for the bank to see what was going on. Miller ordered him away from the building, and Allen left.

But as he fled around the corner, he shouted, "Get your guns, boys! They're robbing the bank!"

Young Wheeler, who was standing on the east side of Division Street, assisted in giving the alarm by yelling, "Robbery! Robbery!"

Just at that time Cole called to Wheeler to get inside. He also fired a shot into the air, the prearranged signal for the three outlaws at the bridge to know they had been discovered. The three came forward with such noise that it was thought a detachment of soldiers was approaching. At the same time a shot sounded inside the bank, followed by a fusillade of shooting. Chadwell, Jim Younger, and one of the Jameses rode up, firing their revolvers and yelling at the people to stay inside the buildings. One pedestrian was a Swedish immigrant who did not understand English. Bewildered, he stood where he was, and was shot down and died a few days later. Later a useless argument raged as to whether one of the robbers shot him or whether he was a victim of a stray bullet from a citizen.

One citizen, Elias Stacy, fired a shotgun blast at Clell Miller just as that bandit was mounting his horse. Birdshot peppered Miller's face, but he got away. Another townsman, A. R. Manning, shot at Charlie Pitts with a breech-loading rifle, but succeeded only in killing the bandit's horse.

Cole Younger was ready to call off the robbery. He yelled to his fellow robbers in the bank to come out for a getaway. Cole's commands were interrupted by a blast from Mr. Manning's breech-loader which wounded Cole in the thigh. Manning backed away to reload and saw the outlaw Bill Chadwell waiting on his horse about eighty yards away. He took another shot, and Chadwell fell to the ground dead, a bullet through his heart.

After young Wheeler had aroused the town he hastened to the drugstore where he usually kept a gun. However, remembering that he had left it at his home, he raced through the store to get a weapon from a neighbor. He then ran toward the hotel where he had seen a gun. But when he found the weapon, it was an empty army carbine. The owner of the hotel, Mr. Dampier, found three cartridges in another room, and in quick order Wheeler was stationed at a second-story window of the hotel, just as the battle began.

Jim Younger was riding by at that instant and Wheeler took a quick shot at him. His aim was too high, however, and the bullet missed. In vain Jim looked around for the sharpshooter, who by then had picked another target, Clell Miller. The bullet passed through Miller's body, severing the great artery and killing him almost instantly. Wheeler's third cartridge had fallen to the floor, breaking the paper wadding and rendering it useless. But Dampier arrived with a fresh supply of ammunition, and another shot by the young man hit Bob Younger in the right elbow as he ran from the bank. Bob quickly executed the "border shift" by throwing his revolver into his left hand, ready for instant use.

There ensued a brief lull in the fighting as each side waited for the other to show itself. The robbers took advantage of the lull, and Bob Younger raced up Division Street where he mounted behind Cole. What was left of the band of outlaws fled the town. The defenders rushed to the scene of the attempted bank robbery to find out what had happened inside the bank. They learned that the three robbers had entered and quickly placed under their guns the teller, A. E. Bunker, F. J. Wilcox, the assistant bookkeeper, and J. L. Heywood, the head bookkeeper who was acting as cashier at that particular time. Heywood told the bandits that the safe had a time lock and could not be opened. An ironic twist was that the safe door was closed and the bolts thrown, but the combination dial had not been twirled. All the bandits would have had to do to open it was turn the handle!

Seeing a chance to escape, Bunker dashed behind the vault and raced for an exit door. Pitts took several shots at him, the second shot entering his shoulder. Meanwhile, Cole's order to abandon the holdup was heard, and the three bandits hurriedly left the bank. The last bandit out turned, and deliberately shot and killed Heywood.

Frank Wilcox, the bank clerk, gave the following account of what happened inside the bank.

"Mr. Heywood occupied the cashier's seat at the desk at the end of the counter. Mr. Bunker and myself occupied the seats at the desk, Mr. Bunker being nearest the opening at the corner. The first thing we knew the three men were upon or over the counter, with revolvers presented at our heads, one of them exclaiming, 'Throw up your hands, for we intend to rob the bank, and if you halloo we will blow your god-damned brains out,' and we could do no otherwise than comply.

"They then asked which was the cashier, to which Mr. Heywood replied, 'He is not in.' They then sprang over the counter and demanded the safe be opened. Addressing each in turn they said, 'You are the cashier,' which each denied. Seeing Heywood seated at the cashier's desk, one of the ruffians went up to him with his long narrow barreled pistol and said, 'You are the cashier; now open the safe, you son-of-a-bitch.' Mr. Heywood said, 'It is a time lock and cannot be opened now.' One of the men then went into the vault, the door being open, also the outer door of the safe. Heywood at once sprang forward and closed the door of the vault, shutting the robber in, when another of the men seized Heywood by the collar and dragged him away from the door and released the incarcerated robber.

"The man who came out of the vault, a slim, dark-complexioned man with a black mustache, then called to the other to seize the silver which was lying loose, about fifteen dollars, and put it in the sack. They did not do this, but seized about twelve dollars in scrip and put it into a two-bushel flour sack which they had with them. The dark-complexioned man, who appeared to be the leader of the three, then again attacked Heywood, insisting upon his opening the safe, threatening to cut his throat if he did not, and actually drawing a big knife across his throat. The heroic and faithful teller, however, was not to be deterred from his duty, and would rather sacrifice his life than betray his trust. Some few moments, it seemed ages to the bewildered and terror-stricken lookers on, were spent in Heywood's staggering to break from the murderous villain and gain his liberty. At length he broke away, and regaining his feet ran toward the door, crying, 'Murder! Murder!'

"The man at once struck him with a pistol and knocked him down, and dragging him to the safe door commanded him to open it. But the intrepid clerk stolidly refused, when the villain shot at him but did not hit him. Evidently the shot was intended to intimidate rather than injure, but the scoundrel had reckoned without his host, for the effect was lost upon Heywood. But upon the discharge of the pistol Bunker made a start for the bank door and ran for his dear life. One of the outlaws [said to have been Pitts] pursued him and shot him in the shoulder. Bunker, however, reached the street and ran to Dr. Coon's office.

"During the whole of the time four or five men were riding up and down Water Street, shooting in every direction and keeping up an incessant fusillade. One of the men outside came riding up furiously and called for the men to leave the bank, 'The game is up, and we are beaten,' he yelled . . . this probably was Cole Younger.

"Almost immediately they took the alarm and somehow jumped over the counter, making their exits. The taller man was the last to go. He mounted a desk at the front, and as he turned to go, fired and shot at Heywood, which I do not think is the one that took effect. Heywood dodged behind his desk and sank into his chair, and as the robber made over the desk railing he turned, and placing his revolver to Heywood's head, fired, shooting him dead.

"He staggered forward and fell behind the counter. The robber made out of the door. I do not remember much more that followed. I was unable to get out of the bank or see how bad Heywood was hurt as a bandit stood over me all the time with a pistol pointed at my head.

"The position of Mr. Heywood in the bank was that of bookkeeper, but he was competent and qualified for almost any position. The cashier, George M. Phillips, left on the previous Monday, Heywood acting in his stead.

"I understand that on the person of one of the dead bandits was a newspaper clipping describing the new burglar-proof safe with its chronometer lock and new vault doors just put in the bank. I suppose the bandits concluded their share of daring and bold method of attacking the bank would do the job for them. Heywood told them a lie when he said the safe could not be opened. The safe was actually unlocked; the door happened to be closed and the bolts were in place, but the combination dial had not been turned. The door could have been pulled open by turning the handle."

The six outlaws galloped out of town on the Dundas Road, riding three abreast and forcing everybody they met off the road. The men of Northfield were in pursuit, and the state capital was also asked for aid. Governor John S. Pillsbury of Minnesota offered $1,000 reward for the capture of the surviving bandits. He later raised the reward money to $1,000 each, dead or alive. The bank and various corporations also offered cash rewards.

Grief over Heywood's untimely death was widespread. Heywood was a man greatly liked and respected, and was a member of the board of Carleton College. He was buried in the Northfield Cemetery on Sunday, September 10, but two other bodies were buried there in the dead of night, the bodies of the dead bandits, with no mourners and no rites. At least, two rough pine boxes were buried there, but it was common belief that the two corpses were spirited away to a medical college to further anatomical science. For many years the skeleton of one of them hung in the office closet of Wheeler, after he became a doctor in Northfield, until finally the building was destroyed by fire. Several years after the raid, an indignant relative of "the skeleton" came to Northfield and got into a heated discussion with Wheeler. But the kinsman left, and the skeleton remained in the doctor's possession.

Without their guide, who had been killed in the gun battle, the outlaws traveled only fifty miles in five days. Some miles beyond Mankato they rested in a deserted farmhouse. The pursuit had been temporarily abandoned, but on receiving a tip that the desperados had been seen in the vicinity of Mankato, patrols and search parties were soon on their trail. But again the fugitives escaped. Some of them crossed Blue Earth River, and two of them, riding a single horse, passed near Lake Crystal.

The trail of blood from Jim Younger's wound was easily followed by a posse. Several miles from Dundas, the bandits stopped to administer to Jim, but it only aggravated matters. He was so weak from loss of blood that Cole and Bob were compelled to ride beside him to keep him from falling out of the saddle. Naturally this retarded their flight.

On September 13, while the harassed party was hobbling through swamps and mire, Jesse turned to Cole and remarked, "Cole, we are in a bad fix, and there is only one way out as I see it. Our trail is as plain as day. What I propose is a horrible thought, but we have been through horrible experiences. Jim cannot live. We cannot successfully retreat carrying him along; we cannot hide; if he remains with us we shall all perish one way or another. I suggest that we dispose of him here and now— he cannot live anyway. With him gone we could travel faster and escape."

The rest of the group looked at each other. They seemed hardly able to believe their ears. Here was Jesse James, their supposed leader, whose life had been saved a number of times during the war by valiant efforts on the part of his guerrilla companions, now proposing to kill one of his own men so that they could speed their flight.

"Damn you, Jesse James," said Cole. "You are indeed a

cold-hearted devil. If any or all of you have such an idea, go take your own paths, and I hope we never meet again. To kill my own brother! I'll stay with him and fight until the very end, and then carry him on my shoulders until I myself fall."

This incident has been vouched for by several who knew the facts of the Northfield escape but were reluctant to speak at the time. Frank, of course, never entertained such an idea. He and Cole remained firm friends, but it was agreed that Frank should accompany his brother; and so the Youngers and Charlie Pitts parted company with the James brothers near Mankato.

On September 21 a farm boy named Sorbel dashed into the small town of Madelia with the news that he had been accosted by two of the robbers. He had been allowed to go free but had been threatened with death if he revealed their presence. The boy's real name was kept secret for many years, so great was the fear that some of the outlaws' friends would seek him out to avenge the capture of the Youngers. The brave lad's warning made it possible to organize a new posse. Thus the robbers were surrounded in a swamp near Madelia. They proved to be the three Youngers and Charlie Pitts.

On hearing that the bandits were near town, Captain W. W. Murphy called for volunteers to go into the swamp and rout out the hungry and hopeless men hiding there. The sheriff and five others responded. There was a violent gun battle, but it was of short duration. Pitts was killed. Jim Younger received five wounds; one bullet shattered his upper jaw and lodged just beneath the brain. Three years later, in prison, a surgeon made an effort to remove the bullet by making an incision in the roof of Jim's mouth and trying to pry loose the leaden pellet. His efforts were futile, but some days later, Jim Younger pleaded with a hospital intern, who made a careful investigation and finally dislodged the bullet.

Cole Younger was also badly shot up in the fight in the swamp, receiving eleven wounds. Bob Younger had a slug in the right lung. As they rode into town, the gallant Cole, despite his wounds, managed to stand up in the wagon and bow to the ladies. They were treated, under heavy guard, in the Flanders House in Madelia, Minnesota. The guard was there partly to protect the wounded robbers from a lynching; but the mob that milled around the hotel was merely curious, not threatening.

When the bandits were recovered sufficiently to be moved, they were taken to the jail in Faribault, Minnesota, to await trial. Four indictments were brought against them. Their attorney advised them to plead guilty and thus escape capital punishment for the death of the bank teller and the innocent bystander.

The Youngers were always on their guard when asked who the two men were who had escaped. One day a man went to Cole and told him word had just been received that their two comrades, the James boys, had been overtaken, one killed and the other wounded and captured.

"How do you know they were the James boys?" Cole asked.

"The wounded man confessed."

"Which one was killed?"

"Frank."

"Which one, the tall one or the little one?"

"The big one."

"Did they say anything about us?"

"No."

"Good boy to the last!" exclaimed Cole, and that was all they could get out of him.

At first the Youngers gave false names and also refused to identify the three dead bandits. However, those three were subsequently identified as Clell Miller, Bill Chadwell, and Sam Wells (alias Pitts).

This conversation confirms the fact that it shows Frank as a tall man and Jesse a short man. Frank was six foot one, and this fact has been attested to by many who knew him, including my grandmother.

There has always been some mystery about why most descriptions of the man killed at St. Joe was given as five feet eleven when Jesse was about five feet eight.

Apparently some reporters used five feet eleven, while some accounts say five-eight; one must remember that descriptions in those days were loosely given. Even from the witness stand Bob Ford said he was five feet eleven and a half when he was no more than five feet eight or nine at most—yet no one contested his statement either.

All three of the Youngers pleaded guilty. Judge Lord sentenced them to life imprisonment in the state penitentiary at Stillwater. Many people believed that they had "cheated the gallows," and it was not long before the law demanded capital punishment in the case of murder.

Bob Younger was slowly dying of consumption during his thirteen years in prison. But during all this time he was a docile prisoner, performing his work carefully under the surveillance of the prison authorities. He won the good will of the warden, who was at hand during his last moments, as did his two brothers who had stood beside him in the heat of battle. They had plotted with him in silence against their fellow men, had shared hunger and privation, prosperity, glorious victory, and bitter defeat. They tried to cheer him with what words of comfort they could muster. A sister, Henrietta, was there to close his eyes after their last look upon a world which he and his brothers had wronged so grievously.

Those thirteen years had proved, to the credit of the dying Bob Younger, a wonderful contrast to the years of violence that had gone to make up the record of his outside life. During seven years of that time he had devoted much of his leisure to the study of medicine, which he took up thoroughly and systematically, reading textbooks and subscribing to periodicals.

A year before his death Bob's health began to fail more noticeably and a listlessness that had been foreign to him ensued. It was not long before it became evident that he had tuberculosis, which had also claimed the life of his mother.

In July of 1901, Cole and Jim were released from prison as a result of persistent lobbying by friends of the Younger family. A law had been passed whereby life-timers could be released after serving twenty-five years, and at last Cole and Jim were back in circulation.

On October 19, 1902, in the Reardon Hotel in St. Paul, Jim Younger committed suicide. The reason for his taking his life, relatives said, was that the parole board had refused him permission to marry. Another reason, however, was that the young woman who had visited him in prison now refused to marry him. He was laid to rest near the grave of his brother Bob. After Cole's death on March 21, 1916, he too was buried there.

Were Jesse and Frank James at Northfield? At Lake Crystal, the two men mounted on one horse were believed to have been the Jameses. A picket fired at them and caused the horse to bolt, and the riders were thrown to the ground. They escaped in the darkness, however, and stole a pair of horses and got away. They took a course due west, crossed into the Dakotas, where they got medical aid from Dr. Sidney Mosher, Sr., a Sioux City, Iowa, physician. He dressed the wound in Frank's leg and a superficial flesh wound which Jesse had suffered in Northfield. After this they took the doctor's horses and also his clothes and made their way into Kentucky and on to Texas and Mexico.

Another controversial aftermath hinged on the question which of the outlaws killed the bookkeeper in the bank? Was it Jesse James, temporarily bereft of calm judgment? Some said it was Pitts; others said Jesse James. This accusation against Jesse, however, was not voiced until after his death, and then the blame might have been placed against him to protect his brother Frank, who was at that time in custody of the law and being tried on several charges.

Cole Younger, who had quarreled with Jesse James after the Northfield fiasco, implied to officers later that Jesse had held the pistol against Heywood's head. However, in 1916, Cole Younger made a deathbed statement to Jesse Edwards James, Jesse's son, and to Harry Hoffman, a close friend, that Jesse had nothing to do with the murder at Northfield. Cole would not identify the real killer, but he rather cryptically said that the man who had perpetrated that crime was "the man who rode the dun-colored horse."

This statement from the dying Cole Younger started some research, and with good results. It was learned that Patterson Stewart of Kansas City, who owned some fine horses, had an employee who kept a dun horse in the Stewart barn. This horse was a fine animal, and was stolen from the barn. The dun-colored horse had a reputation for being a splendid long-range saddle animal. On August 18, Pitts's brother-in-law, Charles Turner, rowed the outlaw party bound for Minnesota across the Missouri River near Parkville, and he stated that it was Frank James who rode the dun horse.

During the post-Northfield trial of the Youngers, the prosecuting attorney's question was, "Who rode the dun horse?" And during parole board hearings in after years, this same question was repeated again and again. No one has ever been positively placed in the saddle of the dun horse except an outlaw who was temporarily using the name of "Howard."

Jesse James also used the name of "David Howard" as is shown in the reports from Walter Kelly, whose boyhood years were spent in Ray County, Missouri, and who had known a tall man down in Kentucky who used that name. It is not odd that Jesse should have used the name "David," since his family always called him "Dave." Kelly said that the Howard he knew was a "blinker"—meaning he was always batting his eyelids, and did so several times a minute when he was awake. Jesse had this habit, due to a granulated eyelid condition which he had suffered as a boy. Also, Kelley stated that this "Mr. Howard" was never without his black kid gloves. His constant wearing of the gloves was principally to hide a missing fingertip on his left hand. Kelly told how Howard was nearly always laughing, and that he never forgot a funny story. These characteristics fit those of Jesse James.

Further information definitely proves that the James brothers were at Northfield and that Jesse expressed a desire to be rid of the wounded outlaw. This is what Cole Younger said in reply to questions asked him by one of his relatives, with the strict promise that anything he said would not be revealed while either he or Frank James was alive:

QUESTION: "Cole, were the James boys in with you at the Northfield raid?"

ANSWER: "Yes, they were. They were using the names of Howard and Woods."

QUESTION: "Why then did you say they were not and that Howard and Woods were the real names of two of the men?"

ANSWER: "Simply to protect Frank James. If it had been thought for a minute that Jesse didn't do the killing of the cashier Heywood, Yankee Bligh and several detectives from St. Louis would have swoped down on Frank, and he would have been tried for that killing. But as long as everyone believed Jesse did it, and as Jesse was dead, it was left to rest that way."

QUESTION: "Who, then, did kill Heywood?"

ANSWER: "It was Frank James, and it was he who rode the dun horse at Northfield. It was stolen from a man named Stewart or something like that, in Kansas City, I believe. This horse was known to be a sprinter, and we always got the best and fastest horseflesh we could. It saved our lives many a time."

QUESTION: "Is it true that Jesse wanted to kill your wounded brother in order to make escape a sure thing?"

ANSWER: "Yes, and I believe he would have carried it out had he been permitted to do so. Frank would never have thought of such a callous thing. Frank and I were very close, but not so with Jesse and me. He and I got along, but it went no farther than that. Both of us were good inside men, and as long as the gang was placed in different categories, we all managed to get along together."

QUESTION: "What do you mean by 'inside men'?"

ANSWER: "The inside men were picked to handle the bank robberies from inside the building, and took care of that part of it. Others were called street men, those who lingered outside the building to protect the men inside. Jim and Bob Younger were good men at that, as was Clell Miller. Frank and Jesse and I took turns doing this. Such fellows as Tucker Bassham and Hobbs Kerry were used only to hold the horses or to frighten citizens away from the locality of the robbery. They never were trusted with any important positions."

QUESTION: "Was Jesse James killed at St. Joe, as claimed?"

ANSWER: "He certainly was. We Youngers were shown photographs of the dead man, and we knew it was Jesse, but we couldn't speak out at that time, as it would have linked us with him and probably would have destroyed our excellent prison record. But one of my sisters—I'll not mention her name— secretly went to St. Joseph and viewed the body to make sure, and she relayed the word to us that it was Jesse. [This was Henrietta, or Rhetta, Younger.] Although we had no doubt of it, for the sands in the hourglass of time just ran out on him."

QUESTION: "Cole, don't you think that a large number of robberies laid at your door were committed by someone else?"

ANSWER: "There's no question of that. We were accused of several holdups after we were in prison.' [At this point Cole waved his hand.] That is all I have to say. Maybe I've already talked too much."

As far as all available records can be checked, this conversation with one of his trusted kinsmen is about the most Cole ever related to anyone in regard to his outlaw career, except for a talk with an old-timer of the St. Louis Police Department, Captain Elias Hoagland. This officer told me of his visit in Springfield, Illinois, to see the famous Cole Younger–Frank

James Wild West Show, several years after Cole's release from prison. Captain Hoagland learned that Cole had been arrested on a drunk charge and was about to be lodged in the city jail. The young officer realized this would ruin Cole, and although he did not know him at the time, Hoagland talked with police officers and succeeded in persuading them to let Cole Younger go. Promising to see that he was cared for that night, he took Cole to his hotel room and put him to bed.

Some days after this incident, Cole contacted the officer and gave him one of his revolvers as a keepsake. Cole confided in his new found friend things he had never told anyone. The Northfield question was still in the minds of numerous people, and for that reason Hoagland asked Cole Younger about Northfield. For the sake of the records it is lucky that he did so, for it substantiates what the Younger relatives had to say about it. It also proves conclusively that Frank and Jesse James were there when the ill-starred attempt was made to rob the bank, and that it was Frank James who killed the cashier.

Other biographers of the Jameses and Youngers have traced their trail from Northfield as far as the capture of Dr. Sidney Mosher, and then supposed the fleeing robbers made their way back to Missouri via the Dakotas or another route. In a personal statement to Cole Younger, of which I have a full record, Frank replied to a question by Cole: "What happened to you and Jesse after we parted at Mankato?"—with this answer: "Not much to speak of. Jesse and I were pretty well beaten, so we laid up in the Dakota Territory for several days after some doctor gave us treatment. After that we went to Wood Hite's home. His father was my uncle, as you know, down in Adair County, Kentucky, and we hid out there for a spell."

However, Dr. Sidney Mosher rushed into Sioux City with the exciting story of having been accosted by two grim-looking men and forced to give them medical treatment near Kingsley. He said they took his clothes and also his horses. This had happened on September 17, and the next day the doctor told his story to the editor of the *Sioux City Democrat*. The editor's sympathies were with the hunted men, and he took advantage of his close friendship with the officers to learn of their plans for the pursuit of the bandits. Then the editor, G. W. Hunt, thwarted the plan of one ambitious citizen to patrol the Missouri River in small boats, as it was thought the Jameses would resort to water travel in their attempted escape from that region. The editor's next move was to overtake the posse of the sheriff and his deputies, which was making good progress on the right trail, and to use a little strategy in turning the posse off in another direction. Later, near the town of Woodbury, the editor and his friend met Jesse and Frank James riding leisurely toward them.

The editor explained his scheme to the outlaws. In return for his help, the James boys were to reveal unknown facts to him concerning their lives and escapades. Frank and Jesse at first thought it was just a joke and got a big laugh out of it. But since they did not know the topography of the land through which they were making their hazardous way, they accepted the editor's offer of assistance.

The editor and the man with him were well known throughout that part of the state, and, of course, the two bandits who were riding with them excited no suspicion. One of the outlaws rode in the editor's wagon with his horse tied behind, while the other outlaw rode his horse alongside the wagon. In due time the strange party reached the confluence of the Missouri and the Little Sioux rivers, where it was decided the James brothers would take a skiff down the Missouri. Near a small cabin they found a skiff which the editor helped them steal, and the Jameses made a safe trip to St. Joseph, Missouri, which they reached after eight days. The editor later stated that the greatest thrill of his entire life was to sleep one night lying between Frank and Jesse James.

To law-abiding people such a rash act on the part of a respected citizen seems very queer, to say the least. In Missouri, however, such actions were nothing new. But in Iowa and Minnesota, such conduct was indeed a rarity. The aftermath—if there was an aftermath to the overzealous admiration of the Jameses on the part of the Iowa editor—was never brought to light. Perhaps his role in connection with the fleeing outlaws was never determined. But his amazing experience was published in his own paper after a few years, with no byline, of course! His readers were left guessing who the anonymous contributor was. It can well be imagined how astonished and enraged the sheriff was on reading that account, as he was a good law officer and accustomed to getting his man.

CHAPTER 12

The James Boys Escape From Northfield

WITH ONE HORSE BETWEEN THEM, JESSE AND FRANK WERE in alien country. On Thursday night, September 14, the Jameses rode close to Lake Crystal. It was raining. Just ahead of them stood a young man named Richard Roberts, who had been posted with several others to guard the road. Tired of standing on the roadside, Richard and his several companions sought shelter from the rain. The boy tried to persuade the others to keep awake.

"Those outlaws will never come this way, Dick," one of them said. "Even if they did, what would you do?"

But the boy was determined to remain at his post, regardless. Late that night, Richard Roberts heard the sloshing of hoofs in the muddy road. A short distance from where he stood the young man saw the outline of a horse on the road, and on the horse was a man . . . no, two. When the riders drew closer to him, the boy noted that one of them had a white bandage around his right leg. This was Frank James, who had received a flesh wound in the thigh.

"Halt! Who goes there?"

Richard covered one of the men with his rifle but they did not stop. The riders tried to urge some speed from the tired animal, but it was useless. The boy pulled the trigger of his rifle. The horse bolted, throwing both riders to the ground, but it was dark and they managed to escape into the muddy field.

Richard rushed to the spot where the two men had been. In the muddy road he found an old hat, a bullet hole smack through it.

"Golly!" he cried. "Maybe I hit one of the outlaws."

But his sleepy companions were not impressed. When the boy reported this encounter to his father, it was determined that the boy probably had been right, especially when four men had walked across the railroad bridge spanning Blue Earth River the previous night . . . the Youngers and Pitts.

Subsequent facts prove that the James boys had been at Northfield and had made a remarkable escape from the area.

It was my good fortune to know Dr. S. P. Mosher of Sioux City, Iowa, the son of the doctor who was kidnapped by the James brothers after the Northfield raid. Dr. Sidney Mosher, the victim, at that time maintained his offices at 407 Jackson Street, near the high school. But other events preceded the abduction of Dr. Mosher.

Early one September morning farmer John Rolph walked to his cabin after finishing his morning chores at his homestead near Luverne, Minnesota. He was about to enter his cabin after washing his face and hands at the outdoor washstand when two dusty, bearded, shabby-looking men rode up. They dismounted and approached the homesteader.

"We want some breakfast and will pay you. We are officers in search of members of the James gang who escaped from Northfield some days ago."

"You are most welcome. Mother, set two more plates."

The meal finished, the two men tossed a silver dollar each upon the table, telling Rolph not to mention their presence so as not to tip off the bandits.

Mr. and Mrs. Rolph were excited by this news, but did not have time to regain their composure before seven or eight men galloped up to their cabin, inquiring if anyone had stopped there in the past few hours.

"Well, yes, sir," said Rolph. "We had two officers here searching for outlaws."

"They wanted to get to Sioux Falls," added his wife.

"Mister, those two were Jesse and Frank James. They and three of the Younger brothers shot up Northfield, killed a couple of men and tried to rob the bank. We killed three of them. Wounded all three of the Youngers and took them to jail."

Rolph gulped as he indicated the direction the two outlaws had taken.

While many accounts differ as what next happened to the James brothers, it is almost certain that from the Rolph farm at Luverne they crossed into Dakota Territory, near Valley Springs, seeking the isolation of the Big Woods country. There they forced Andy Nelson to exchange horses with them, in their haste not realizing that the animals were blind.

The two outlaws rode on. Once they inquired directions to Sioux Falls, South Dakota, also inquiring if there was a telegraph office there.

"We want to report the movements of the outlaws we are chasing," they told the farmer.

The two appeared disappointed when they were told that there was no telegraph office at Sioux Falls. All this time, the posse from the Rolph farm were hot on their trail. The fugitives made for Devil's Gulch in the Split Rock River near Garretson, South Dakota. One account stated that a fight ensued and Frank was wounded in the arm. One posseman later told newspaper reporters that Jesse then spurred his mount to the limit, and with his old battle cry, leaped across the rocky gorge, a distance of fifteen feet. While the dumfounded posse watched, Frank dismounted and made his way down the Devil's Stairway. It was too late in the day for the posse to pick up the trail among the steep cliffs and treacherous rocks.

No one seems to know what happened next. Today visitors are shown a cave and ledge in the Palisades near Garretson where the James boys hid. Most people agree that if they did hide there it was but for a few hours rest . . . they needed rest, as did their horses. No one could escape from such an area without horses to ride.

Riding to Shindler, the Jameses traded their mounts, between Worthing and Canton, for two horses owned by Pete Wahl and Andrew Shuelson. No doubt cash was turned over. They then rode due south.

At Canton, O. A. Rudolph, a banker, quickly gathered a posse and the outlaws found themselves hard pressed. However, once more a posse failed to run down the elusive outlaws. Near Gayville, at the Wadsworth home, a young man had identified himself as Jesse James and bought some supplies from the family. Apparently Frank was hiding in the background, perhaps because of his leg wound.

The following circumstances led up to the confrontation between the James brothers and Dr. Sidney P. Mosher.

On Wednesday morning, September 25, 1876, Dr. Mosher received a call to attend Mrs. Robert Mann, who was seriously ill and in need of a goiter operation at the family home about twenty miles northeast of Sioux City, Iowa. Dr. Mosher went to the Broadbent livery stable at noon to secure a horse for his journey. At the stables a group of men were discussing recent events, especially the raid on the Northfield bank and the pursuit of the outlaws. He listened for a while, then mounted his bay mare and set out for the Mann home.

Dr. Mosher rode all day and about four o'clock he was in the vicinity of Kingsley. The doctor did not know the exact location of the Mann home, and on seeing two horsemen on a nearby ridge, he called to them as he approached. When he was within a few yards of the two men he found himself looking into the barrels of their weapons.

"Hands up!" they commanded.

Dr. Mosher was puzzled by their behavior. The face of the shorter man quivered with emotion and the doctor thought these men must have been looking for the outlaws and had mistaken him for one of them.

"What do you want with me? I'm Dr. Mosher on a sick call to the Mann home."

"We know who you are. You are a detective from St. Paul. I think I will have to shoot you. I am Jesse James," said the smaller man. "I think you have a posse out there in the woods ready to pounce on us."

Dr. Mosher, sitting on his horse with his hands in the air above his head, had to do some fast thinking.

"Why don't you search me to see if I am armed?" he suggested.

He was ordered off his horse and searched. Dr. Mosher was wearing a new suit and he had neglected to transfer some of his more personal things from his old suit to the new one. All he carried was a small box containing a scalpel.

"I still think that I will shoot you. There is nothing here to prove you are who you claim to be."

"Ride back to the next farmhouse and ask them to describe Dr. Mosher of Sioux City. Ask them if there is not a Mrs. Robert Mann who is very ill and if Dr. Mosher is not on his way to treat her."

The plan seemed to find favor with Jesse. Mounting Dr. Mosher's horse, Jesse rode away. In a short while he returned, grinning. The doctor said it was the first and only time he had seen Jesse grin; all the while he was sullen and morose.

"All right, Doc. I guess you are who you say you are. We will have to keep you with us for a while. We don't want to shoot you, but we will kill you quick if you try to give us the slip or if you don't obey orders. You will ride between us and you are to speak only when you are spoken to."

Jesse was riding Dr. Mosher's horse. He told the doctor to mount the one he had been riding. Both horses of the Jameses gave signs of having been hard ridden. They had no saddles but were using grain sacks filled with straw. Jesse rode the fresh horse on ahead, then Dr. Mosher on the little sorrel and Frank James brought up the rear. It was about two o'clock in the afternoon. As they rode along, Jesse was silent, but Frank engaged the doctor in conversation, asking what he had heard of the James boys in Sioux City, laughing at some of the reports, and describing how they had eluded the Yankton posse. At one time, in response to a question by Frank James, Mosher made a remark about the Civil War. Jesse turned and said, "Damn you, Doc. I'll kill you yet!"

Later in the afternoon Frank James handed Dr. Mosher a piece of paper, saying, "Read that. That is what almost cost you your life."

It was a letter from a woman telling him to be on the lookout for a St. Paul detective who was on their trail. It told them to watch for a man whose description fit Dr. Mosher almost exactly.

At suppertime, around six o'clock, they stopped at a farmhouse and Jesse told farmer Wright that Dr. Mosher of Sioux City had had a breakdown and wanted to borrow a saddle. The farmer knew about Mrs. Mann. He brought out his best saddle. Dr. Mosher had to take it, well knowing Wright would never see it again. They also got some food at the farmhouse, eating it after they had ridden some distance into the brush.

It was not until evening that Dr. Mosher discovered that

Frank James had been shot. They came to a halt and were all dismounting when Frank admitted that he could not get off his horse without help. Jesse and Dr. Mosher lifted him from his horse. Dr. Mosher saw then that he had been shot through the fleshy part of the thigh.

"Hadn't you better let Doc look at your wound?" asked Jesse.

The question went unanswered. Dr. Mosher made no comment, for he had been told to keep quiet until spoken to; besides, the wound was clean and would heal with no trouble.

As they stood there, Jesse ordered the doctor to strip. Frank James also began to remove his clothes. Dr. Mosher was given Frank's clothing and told to put them on. Frank was taller than Dr. Mosher and the trouser legs had to be turned up. Frank's coat was a fine one, but the tail had been peppered by buckshot. When they had effected the change of clothing Jesse James pointed to a light some distance away and said, "See that light, Doc? That is where Mrs. Mann is. That is where you are going. When we say go, you head straight for that light and don't look back or we'll shoot you dead. You are to stay in that house all night. Don't any of you come out or try to follow us."

With that, Jesse turned Dr. Mosher toward the light and with his back to the James boys. Dr. Mosher knew this was not the Mann house but he started walking toward the light, knowing that at the least wrong move he would be shot. As he stumbled across the uneven ground in the dusk he heard the click of a revolver and felt sure he was going to be shot. His knees shook so that he could hardly walk. The outlaws did not shoot; however, the doctor came near losing his life by an entirely different means a few minutes later.

On and on he went, running as best as he could. Frank's shoes were too large, and with his trousers too long, his coat flapping in the wind, what a spectacle the poor doctor must have made. As he entered the farmyard the dogs began barking.

He dashed for the door, slammed his body against it, and practically fell into the room.

A woman seated near the fireplace cried out, "The robbers! the robbers!"

The menfolk had just returned from LeMars and were unhitching the horses in the barn. In town, they, too, had learned of that the James gang were in the vicinity. When the woman screamed they grabbed their guns from the wagon and ran toward the house. One man aimed his rifle at Dr. Mosher, trigger finger nervous with excitement. Just when the doctor thought his earthly days were over, a boy who had been awakened by the noise raced toward the doctor and cried, "Father, don't shoot! That is Dr. Mosher from Sioux City!"

After the doctor had explained his presence he offered to go with the men to try and catch the James boys. The farmer said it would be foolish to try such a thing. The next morning Dr. Mosher was taken to Sioux City in a wagon.

After the matter had been well discussed at the livery stable, Dr. Mosher went home and changed clothes. He then rode out to the Mann home and performed a successful goiter operation on Mrs. Mann.

Frank James's trousers were a treasured memento in the Mosher family for many years but ultimately they disappeared.

Dr. Mosher was shortly interviewed by the editor of the *Sioux City Democrat,* probably G. W. Hunt, who had a great admiration for the James brothers. The reporter figured out the probable trail of the hunted men by taking advantage of his friendship with Deputy Sheriff Dan McDonald, who let him see dispatches concerning the freshness of the outlaws' trail.

Dr. Mosher had described the two men to Hunt, so this also helped. Dr. Mosher gave the following descriptions:

"The smaller man, Jesse James, was about thirty, I should say, with full-face whiskers of a dark brown color, worn short at that time. He had snappy blue eyes. His face was roundish, with a stubby nose. He was not a large man, medium height and weight. Appeared nice-looking and evidently hot-tempered.

"The second man was tall, apparently a few years older than the other, his brother. Had blue eyes also, face was angular, and he was rather thin. He wore a beard with sideburn cut, smooth chin, needing a shave at that time. Sandy color hair and moustache. No resemblance between the two."

Hunt feared the overzealous officers might get to the James boys first. He successfully discouraged a scheme of James Wall to capture the Jameses. Wall planned to patrol the Missouri with four skiffs, held close enough to discover any other skiff that might attempt to glide through by night. The editor feared Wall's plan might work, for he knew that Frank James was wounded, and that the outlaws might steal a skiff to float down the river to Missouri. That's exactly what they did do, a little later, and a little farther south down the Missouri in a skiff the editor himself helped steal.

Next he took care of Sheriff John McDonald's posse. He described his adventures for his astounded readers by using the editorial "we" in referring to himself, with no byline.

By the time we discovered that Sheriff McDonald and a well-armed party were on the fresh and well defined scent of the James and must capture them if not thwarted. Hitching up our team, we started out after the sheriff's party, soon overtaking them, and a little strategy succeeded in turning them off in another direction.

Within one hour from that time, and within four miles of the village of Woodbury, on the Sioux City & Pacific Railroad, we espied two men leisurely riding toward us. When within a couple of hundred yards of the advancing horsemen, we stopped our team in the road and awaited their coming.

They first saluted us and then eyed us keenly, intently but apparently casually examining us and our outfit. This being done, we said, "Gentlemen, we know you; have been looking for you; but don't seek your capture."

We then briefly stated to them our business as a newspaper man, satisfied them we were unarmed, and that under certain circumstances we could be trusted. We told them we wanted an account of the plan by which they undertook to rob the Northfield bank, their adventures since, the biographies of all their associates who had participated in the Northfield raid, and such other items as would be interesting to the readers of the newspaper which we were at the time representative, and in return that we would facilitate their escape from the country.

The proposition at that moment seemed so novel, and at the same time so ludicrous to them, that both of the brothers indulged in a hearty laugh. By mutual or tacit acquiescence we seemed to understand each other.

Fearing that we might happen to meet some of the numerous parties scouring the country for our then companions, at our request one of them tied his horse behind our wagon and took a seat beside us, while the other rode alongside.

Driving to a small body of timber a short distance below the village of Woodbury, and adjacent to the Missouri River, their horses were turned loose with some other stock found grazing there, the saddles, bridles and blankets placed in a hiding place, the two men took seats beside us, and we drove for a few minutes in the direction of Sioux City, when suddenly the elder of the James, espying some men on horseback in the distance requested us to turn our ponies in a southern direction; he gave us a reason that the farther we went north the more the country was woke up against them, and that they desired to get out of that section of the country by the shortest and quickest possible way.

That night we camped at a point adjacent to the Missouri River, nearly opposite the village of Sloan, not desiring to risk the chances of stopping at a house. During the night they proposed and we acceded to an oath of pledge that we would not under certain circumstances reveal what facts they gave us until their safe arrival among friends, of which fact they could acquaint us either by telegraph or letter, and in addition, under certain other circumstances pending on the arrest and trial of the Younger brothers, we would not disclose certain other information given us.

That night we all slept together in a bed made of prairie grass, we being favored with the honored position in the middle of our two celebrated companions. After a sound night's sleep, at daybreak, we hitched up our team and kept on down the Missouri Valley in the direction of Council Bluffs, Iowa.

Having resided on the upper Missouri for nearly twenty years, the greater part of which have been engaged in public life, we were known personally to nearly every resident in the section of country in which we were driving with our two companions, and of course the fact of their riding with us disarmed all suspicion as to who they were.

Reaching the Little Sioux River, we drove along its banks to about where it empties into the Missouri River. That evening it was decided by the James brothers to secure a skiff, which, fortunately for them, happened to be moored to a stake by a small cabin.

We were appointed a committee of one to visit a neighboring house to purchase several dozens of eggs, some pounds of butter, and such bread, potatoes, etc., as we could obtain. Having the previous evening purchased some tea, sugar, coffee, crackers, etc., in the store of Ed Haakinson at Sloan, the boys were well prepared for a journey.

The arrangements for traveling were, that they should float along at night, and during the day pull their skiff into some timbered or unfrequented nook in the river; that after reaching Nebraska City they would float down the river in the daytime, as the interest in their capture was not yet awakened so far south.

Having fulfilled our part of the contract, we are pleased to say that the James brothers did theirs by imparting to us facts, which events since transpired has rendered it impossible at the present to give to the public without violating our pledge.

The James boys had a safe retreat down the Missouri and reached St. Joseph, Missouri, in just eight days from the time we parted with them. At the latter place they were cared for by friends.

There is one ennobling feature about the once powerful but now dismembered banditti, that for years have been the terror of railroad, express, and bank corporations. They never take, only in self defense, a human life. They have never appropriated a dollar from others than corporations who could afford it. They have, within the past two years, distributed and spent among friends, many of them poor, upwards of a quarter of a million dollars, and not one of them has ever been known to contract an obligation of whatever character that has not been complied with.

The editor of the *Sioux City Democrat,* carried away by his misplaced admiration of the James brothers, failed to justify his opinion of them with the Northfield bank raid, in which several persons had been killed. Whether or not this editor saw fit to divulge the secrets given him by the outlaws, and the reactions of Sheriff McDonald on learning that he had been tricked, are facts that have been lost to history. But we know that this story, as incredible as it seems, is a true, eye-witness story of the James brothers' escape from Northfield.

The Jesse James Cafe, Northfield, Minnesota (Carl W. Breihan Collection).

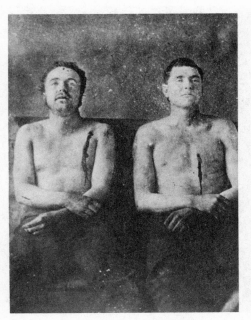

Left: Clell Miller; Right: Bill Chadwell (alias William Stiles). These two members of the James-Younger Gang were left dead in the streets of Northfield after the abortive bank raid (Carl W. Breihan Collection).

This marker depicts an historic event: the first train robbery west of the Mississippi River, near Adair, Iowa (Carl W. Breihan Collection).

Allan Pinkerton gave Jesse a merry chase (Pinkerton's National Detective Agency, Inc.).

Governor T.T. Crittenden was in cahoots with Sheriff Timberlake and Police Commissioner Craig to do in Jesse James (Carl W. Breihan Collection).

Captain Hy. H. Craig, Police Commissioner, Kansas City, Missouri (Carl W. Breihan Collection).

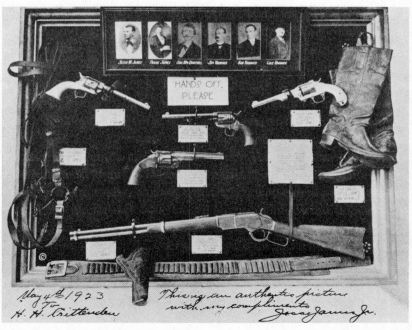

Display of outlaw guns and other possessions belonging to Frank and Jesse James and Cole Younger (Carl W. Breihan Collection).

Frank James, age 54 (Carl W. Breihan Collection).

Left: Mary James; Right: Jesse Edwards James (Carl W. Breihan Collection).

Mary James (St. Louis Art Co.).

Jesse Edwards James, age 19 (Carl W. Breihan Collection).

This stone building was called the Scriver block. The First National Bank occupied quarters at the southern end of the building, the front entrance being on Division Street (Carl W. Breihan Collection).

The last known photo of Frank James, standing between Mr. and Mrs. Pool (Carl W. Breihan Collection).

A very rare photo of Frank James, date unknown (Carl W. Breihan Collection)

(Carl W. Breihan Collection)

Dear friend "Isaac Hilton"
you have always been so faithful.
For all your goodness I give you my thanks forever
The horses were among the best. never were deserters.

I hope the best of luck will be yours. and
that someday everything can be restored to you

I will always remember our wardays together.
Faithfully we fought for a cause. fought for
the rights of many of our good People up and down
the country.
Some of us have begun life anew
Some of us were never officially Surrendered
Some of us have been outlawed
Only God can know our hearts.
Again I give to you my many thanks
Most Sincerely
Jesse W. James

A very rare copy of the only known letter written by Jesse James (Charles Rosamond Collection).

This envelope, personally addressed by Jesse James in 1880, is the only known to exist (Charles Rosamond Collection).

BOB FORD
Slayer of Jesse James

(Carl W. Breihan Collection)

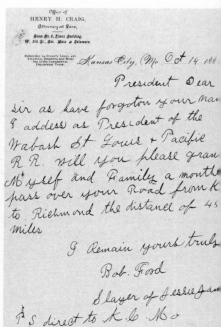

Evidently Bob Ford, murderer of Jesse James, thought he was entitled to a free pass on the railroad for his part in the plot (Missouri Historical Society).

Jesse James in his coffin (Carl W. Breihan Collection).

This picture was taken at the time of the inquest, after Jesse James was shot by his house guest, Bob Ford, who had arranged with Governor Crittenden for his own immunity (Carl W. Breihan Collection).

James' home at the time of the slaying of Jesse, photographed from a cut in the
ɔseph, Missouri *News-Press,* Sunday, November 19, 1919 (Carl W. Breihan Collec-

Jesse Edwards James at the grave of his father, when it was still in the yard of the
homestead at Kearney, Missouri (Carl W. Breihan Collection).

The center stone marks the grave of Jesse James at Kearney, Missouri. The original
marker was over six feet tall, but was chipped away by morbid souvenir hunters. Today
a ground-level marker replaces the remains of the original stone (Carl W. Breihan
Collection).

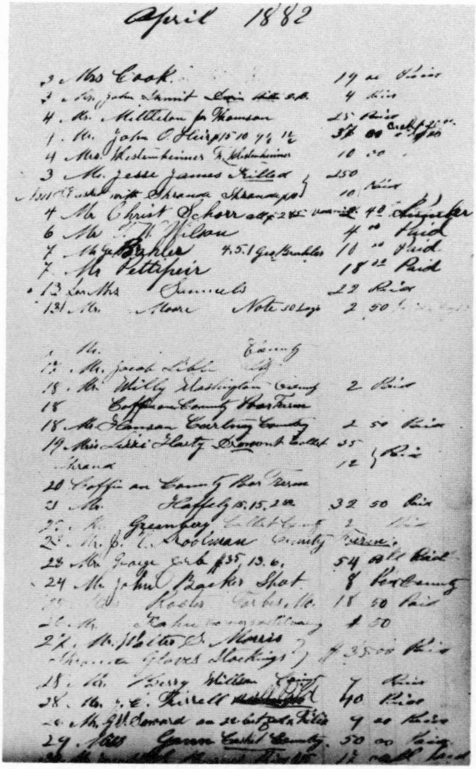

April 1882

3 Mrs Cook 19 00 Paid
3 Mr Jesse James Killed 250
13 Mrs Samuels 22 Paid

Ledger sheet showing payment of Jesse James' casket and shroud, Sidenfaden Funeral Home, St. Joseph, Missouri (R. L. Mack Collection).

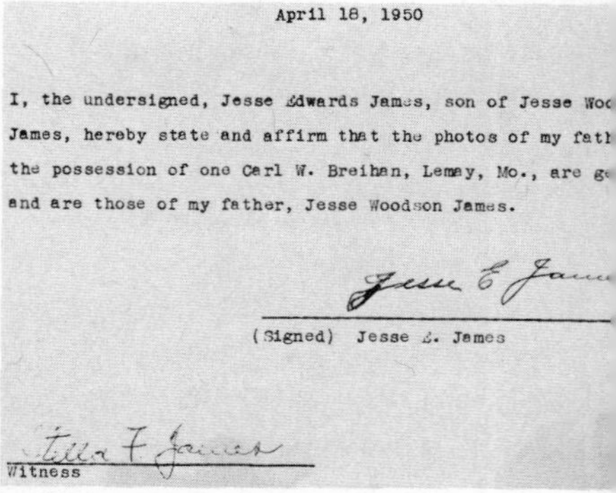

April 18, 1950

I, the undersigned, Jesse Edwards James, son of Jesse Woo[dson] James, hereby state and affirm that the photos of my fath[er in] the possession of one Carl W. Breihan, Lemay, Mo., are ge[nuine] and are those of my father, Jesse Woodson James.

Jesse E. James

(Signed) Jesse E. James

Stella F. James
Witness

Statement from Jesse James' son (Carl W. Breihan Collection).

This hearse was used to carry the body of Jesse James from the undertaking parlor at St. Joseph to the train depot; property of Julio Zamagni (Carl W. Breihan Collection).

CHAPTER 13

Jesse James

in Mexico

THE ABORTIVE RAID ON THE NORTHFIELD, MINNESOTA, bank by the combined outlaw forces of the James and Younger brothers was over. Jesse and Frank were in flight to Missouri, and the Younger boys had been captured and lodged behind prison bars.

With the help of a Sioux City newspaper editor named Hunt the James boys managed to elude the Minnesota posses and escape to their home state. Even there, however, they deemed it unwise to linger within the borders of Missouri, even though they knew every trail and hideaway, and could depend upon countless friends. It was too risky. They made their way to their hideout in Texas where, in the rugged foothills, they had established a place called the Rest Ranch.

To the west of their hideout rose mountains which defied man. Far to the south was the little outpost of Fort Lancaster, and toward the northeast were the dreaded Staked Plains and the Great Salt Plains, areas seldom traveled. Human beings rarely passed this spot—except for a raiding party of Comanches or a band of Mexican border bandits.

The James brothers were restless by nature. After a brief stay at the ranch, they dared the dangers of the border, plunged through thick chaparral, scaled the mountains, and eventually rode down the western slopes of the sand plains along the Rio Grande River. On their way they passed through Santa Rosa, through the desert lands, and through dangerous mountain passes. Obstacles which would have stopped ordinary men were easily conquered by the daring Missourians.

Into the land of Mexico rode the James brothers, finally reaching Matamoras, where they learned that a fandango had been announced to celebrate the season. This was something new to the boys, so they decided to stay in town to watch that.

That evening the dance hall was filled with olive-eyed young Mexican beauties, willing and anxious to trip the light fantastic. Jesse and Frank greatly enjoyed the smooth-gliding dances, and decided it was worth a try to mingle with the dancers themselves. No doubt they looked clumsy compared with the young ladies, especially in their rough border garb. At first the onlookers were amused, but they soon broke out in loud laughter and open ridicule.

It would have been better for the Mexican young men to take a pot shot at the James boys rather than laugh at them. No one had ever done that and gotten away with it. Frank lashed out with his fist, and down went one of the loudest harassers in the group. At the same time a large Mexican struck Frank a blow on the cheek, which sent him spinning headlong into the laps of the two Mexican girls. Jesse did not stand idle; he fired a bullet into the head of the man who had struck Frank.

This started a free-for-all. Frank and Jesse thought flight was the better part of valor, and they made for the door, but their path was blocked by the furious hidalgos. Stilettos glittered in the faint light. Frank and Jesse were struck and stabbed, but the weapons of the Mexicans were poor substitutes for the revolvers of the Jameses. Directing their aim at the doorway, the two bandits fired, killing four Mexicans and wounding six others. As they raced through the cleared doorway, another Mexican raised his arm to strike Frank a blow in the chest with a knife. Jesse fired, and the bullet struck the man in the chest and knocked him to the floor. The Jameses raced to their horses and rode toward the Rio Grande and to safety.

In 1877 Jesse and Frank were living quietly in the little village of Carmen, in the northern part of the State of Chihuahua, Mexico. It might have seemed odd that they had selected such an out-of-the-way place to spend time, but they had their reasons. Carmen was on the road traveled by Mexican merchants and traders with their costly wares. The Jameses had seen samples of the Mexican silver and had made plans to relieve the mine owners of some of their precious cargo. They were joined by three other men. All five were well-behaved and always made a favorable impression on the people of the town. In many instances they displayed their uncanny marksmanship by shooting a pig or a chicken from a great distance. Before the owner of the animal or the fowl could complain, he was paid in cash many times the value of the carcass. In this manner the outlaws gained new friends.

One morning in May, six pack mules, each guided by a separate muleteer and each mule bearing 150 pounds of silver, moved out of the city of Chihuahua. Eighteen men rode with the caravan to guard the metal. All went well until they reached Carmen, where two Americans, apparently not too bright, sought out the guards and talked with them about their own harrowing experiences with Indians and wild animals and how anxious they were to return to the United States. The chief of the guards was asked if these five men could accompany the mule train across the perilous border; of course, they agreed to assist in any fighting if need be, to protect the pack mules at all costs.

The chief consented, and next day the procession of mules and the silver and the guards set out from Carmen with the five simple-looking Americans, who said they were mine inspectors. The suspicions of the guards had been allayed by the favorable comments of Carmen's inhabitants.

For several days they were watched, however, until suspicion was gone and a feeling of confidence prevailed. On the fifth day, the mules were relieved of the loads so that they could graze at a spring and the men got some relaxation. Soon all but two of the guards were enjoying their siesta in the shade. The guns of the party had been stacked against a tree, and the two guards were holding their weapons in a careless and negligent manner.

Jesse gave the signal to attack. The two guards posted at the stack of rifles were killed, and the outlaws commandeered all the weapons. The owners of the train, the mule tenders, and the guards were forced to surrender. Jesse's men departed with the silver, leaving the personnel of the pack train stranded at a place since called La Temido, the place of fear. The robbers rode into Texas, divided the spoils, and congratulated each other on the success of the mission.

After a brief rest at their ranch, the James boys rode into Piedras Negras, a known meeting place of thieves and killers. They were riding just outside of town, near a small village, when a number of Mexican bandits saw them and thought they would be an easy prey for robbery. It was not long before Jesse and Frank learned they were being pursued by a dozen or more Mexicans bent on robbery and slaughter. They tried to impress two riders by shooting off their pistols into the air and yelling at the top of their voices. To their dismay, their plan did not work. Finally Jesse and Frank turned and fired into the group, sprawling four of them on the ground, then raced in pursuit, shooting as they rode. The Mexicans fled back into the village and went into hiding.

That night Jesse and Frank were ambushed by a number of men as they crossed a small stream. Jesse received a slight wound in the shoulder. The brothers charged the hiding place of the would-be assassins and flushed them into flight, but not before one of them lay dead on the ground.

At Monclova, a large town in Coahuila, Jesse and Frank were surprised to find an ex-Quantrillian living there. He had married a Mexican girl and settled down to a peaceful life. As was the custom of the land, the strangers were given a fandango. Jesse and Frank agreed to attend but also made their host promise no one would laugh at their clumsiness.

All went well at the dance until Jesse noticed a young Mexican army lieutenant giving a high sign to an American tourist from Matehuala. Jesse observed them talking in low tones and at times casting suspicious glances at him and Frank. Jesse relayed his suspicions to Frank, but his older brother was intent on pleasing the ladies and informed Jesse not to allow his imagination to play tricks on him. Jesse thought such must be the case until the two men departed hurriedly, and he was sure now that trouble was brewing. He was not wrong. Both men had recognized Jesse and Frank James.

The Mexican army officer and his friend went to the encampment of a Mexican brigade near the town. Here they enlisted the assistance of the commanding officer in an attempt to capture the notorious brothers. They stressed that large rewards were still posted for them in the States, and that fame and renown would be the prize for this night's work. A detachment of eighty men was mustered, and soon the place of the dance was completely surrounded. When the festivities were at their height, the doors were unceremoniously thrown open and an officer strode into the room, followed by a military guard.

The men and women at the dance were astounded by this

rude interruption, to say the least. The only two calm people there were the Jameses.

The officer marched up to Frank and Jesse and demanded their surrender, in the name of the Mexican government. Jesse and Frank broke out in laughter.

"Let the ladies retire," said Jesse, "and we can talk over a proposition."

"You cannot escape—the house is surrounded," said the officer. "But I suppose it is all right to let the ladies retire; no sense in their getting injured."

The room was soon cleared of the women and the officer demanded that Jesse and Frank surrender their weapons.

Their answer was swift and sure. Shots rang out in rapid succession, and four men lay dead on the floor. The demoralized guard fled in panic. The soldiers guarding the house fired in wild confusion, but their bullets had little effect. The darkness was dense and favored the fugitives. Frank and Jesse reached their horses and raced away, to find safety at their Rest Ranch. Oddly enough, many of the people of Monclova denounced the officials for their invasion of the fandango, and actually sympathized with the Missouri bandits. Such was their way with people.

The ranch was well stocked with cattle, and defending the herd against thieves sometimes led to gunplay. A locally noted bandit in Nueva Leon, Juan Fernando Palaciois, decided upon a raid of the James herd, as well as the herds of several other ranchers in the area. Palaciois and his men swept down the Pecos Valley, driving the cattle before them to the banks of the Rio Grande.

As soon as Jesse and Frank learned of the rustling, they followed the outlaws. It was learned that the rustlers had driven the stolen cattle across the river into the United States and were camped in the mountains near El Paso. Believing themselves safe from attack, the outlaws had not posted a guard. It was easy for Frank and Jesse to advance on their camp, fire round after round of ammunition, and make themselves sound like an attacking force of many men. Panic and fear seized the rustlers and they fled, leaving ten of their men dead on the ground.

Palaciois and his chief henchman, Jesus Almonte, had not been at camp when the attack occurred, and they were told that fifty *gringo diablos* had attacked his men and run off with the cattle.

When Palaciois learned that only two men had effected the demoralization of his men, he became furious and decided to follow Jesse and Frank and get back the cattle. He even risked going into Texas, and was close at their heels when the boys turned and sent several of the Mexicans toppling from their saddles.

It would be a losing battle, the two Americans well knew, for the night was the time the Mexicans liked to fight, and anything could happen. Jesse and Frank were in a serious mood when they looked westward and saw some moving objects on the rise.

"What is it, Jess? Comanches, Mexican bandits, or what?"

The moving line of mounted men proved to be United States cavalrymen under the command of Colonel Ranald Mackenzie.

"Soldiers, Frank! Feds at that!" shouted Jesse. "By golly, there were times during the war that I would not have liked meeting such a crowd of them."

It was a strange turn of events for the two Federal-hating James boys, posing as law-abiding Texas ranchers, not only to be rescued by Union troops but also praised as community heroes.

By now, the James boys were recognized by their Pecos Valley neighbors as enterprising traders and cattlemen, they would never have dreamed that such innocent-looking young men could have acquired the world-wide reputation that was theirs. They had acquired considerable property in the valley, and their frequent and prolonged absence from "home" created no suspicion whatever. It was a primitive and restless life, and many of the people in the area made long trips now and then. Among other things, the spirited horses of Jesse and Frank were the talk of the community.

On one occasion, on their return to the valley, Jesse and Frank learned that a Mexican bandit named Bustenado had crossed the Rio Grande and made a night raid among the ranchers. The shocking thing was that the bandits had carried off a girl named Alice Gordon, daughter of Sean Gordon. Jesse and Frank were quick to take up the trail.

On the morning of the third day Frank and Jesse came upon the rustlers. They had to act quickly. They had caught up with the Mexicans while they were eating breakfast and laughing elatedly over their exploits. A little distance from the fire sat Alice Gordon, attended by her Negro servant Joe, whom the outlaws had allowed to come along. The Mexicans numbered at least thirty, and the James boys had mustered only six ranchers to follow them. The odds were greatly against them.

Jesse took command and applied Quantrill guerrilla tactics in his next move. He ordered his men to fire a weapon from each hand and ride pell-mell through the camp. A wild rebel yell from Jesse and Frank, and the eight riders dashed into the midst of the astonished Mexicans. Half the Mexicans were killed in the first foray. The rest, horrified and disbelieving, scurried to horses and raced for their lives. Not more than six of the rustlers escaped. Bustenado himself was brought down with a bullet between his shoulders as he fled from camp.

The cattle were returned to their owners, and Alice Gordon was reunited with her grateful parents. Even to this day some of the older residents of the Pecos Valley area recount the noble exploits of Jesse and Frank James, little caring that they were the noted Missouri outlaws.

As in many other instances, there were people who claimed that Jesse and Frank James never visited Mexico, just as there were some who stated the outlaw brothers never visited Utah, Wyoming, or Montana. I am indebted to the late William Stigers of St. Joseph, Missouri, for the following data which had been misplaced for many years.

During rare moments Frank James talked about his legendary escapades to his friend, Cole Younger, and a young St. Louis doctor who once befriended Frank by getting him a job as a ticket-taker at the Old Standard Theatre in St. Louis, at the northeast corner of Sixth and Walnut streets. Below is the material furnished by William Stigers, from information he received from the doctor.

I have just returned from a pleasant visit to Lee's Summit, Missouri, where I visited Cole Younger and Frank James, the latter having come up from Kearney to see Cole, and it was my good fortune to see both of them together by chance. We had just returned from the Younger cemetery lot, where Cole pointed out the graves of his family members buried there, including John, who had been killed at Osceola, Missouri, in a fight with police officers. We had a very pleasant time, with Cole puffing away at his fancy long pipe, and Frank nipping the bottle occasionally. Although I visited with them the entire day, there was little said about their outlaw career. However, there was about a half hour's talk about some of Frank's life, and I wish to jot it down before it escapes my memory. Frank talked as if in a trance, and sometimes I believe he hardly knew I was present. At any rate, here is what transpired:

Frank said, "Cole, you know we both would have done different if we had been given the chance. You know that Jesse said many times to Mom, 'I would gladly wear duck clothing the rest of my life if I could but be a free man.' I felt the same way at the time and took a chance at the trial and came out free. Once, before Jess died, I had another chance to do this. It was after our trip to Mexico. You know, we made several trips down there, but Jess would not stand for me changing my life.

[At that moment Cole cut in with an inquiry as to what happened to them after the Northfield affair.]

Not much happened to speak of. Jess and I were both pretty well beaten, so we laid up in the Dakotas for several days after some doctor gave us a bit of treatment. After that we went to Wood Hite's home—his father was my uncle—down in Adairville, Kentucky, and hid out for a spell. But we were still too close to home and the detectives. So right after Christmas of that year, we headed for Mexico, with main intentions of hiding out at the ranch. But it was too lonely for Jess, although I did not mind as I had many books to read down there, but they did not interest Jess. We then took several trips to some Mexican towns right over the border, and got into several scrapes with Mexican soldiers and robbers. Jess even got himself shot one time when we ran away, but it was nothing serious. One time we got saved by our own soldiers by mere luck and got a good laugh out of it, as when we were with Quantrill the sight of the bluecoats made our blood boil.

Well, after Mexico, we came back to Missouri, saw Mom, and then went down to Tennessee, and I got into some lumber business. We liked it fine, me and Ann, and my consumption was not acting up much when I worked outside and took it lightly. We got into debt but some of our fine neighbors agreed to help us, and Dr. Eve wanted to settle the whole thing for us. Dr. Eve was quite fond of Jesse. But Jesse was restless again and wanted us to go back on the road after several years of the first peace we actually had known, and the world might have forgotten about us, if that drunken Ryan hadn't gone crazy and got himself arrested right close to my home. I knew he would talk if given the chance, even though Jess accepted him as a good and trusted friend. So we had to run again. You know the rest. It was not too long afterward that Jesse was killed by Ford and I surrendered to Crittenden.

It was getting late and I could see that the two old fellows wanted to retire, so I made a suggestion they do so. In a few minutes they were fast asleep as though they never had a care or a scare in the wide world.

But such was the making of men like the Jameses and the Youngers. They had come from proud and aristocratic people, and those remaining tried to live down and forget the name they had spread across the United States, nay, the world.

I have checked the records regarding the young doctor, whose name was Wolfort, the man who had furnished Bill Stigers with this information. He is Dr. Louis J. Wolfort, as shown in the 1900 St. Louis directory and medical records.

Intense and lengthy research into the authenticity of this statement by Frank James shows that Dr. Wolfort was a brother of Dave Wolfort, the St. Louis horse trader, who supposedly bought the horses once used by the James-Younger band. I suppose he was as surprised as anyone to learn who had once owned the animals.

Dr. Wolfort lived on Dillon Ave., St. Louis, not far from Frank James's residence and that of Colonel Butler, a political leader in that city at the time. It seems that it was through the doctor's appeal to Butler that Frank James was given the job at the Standard Theatre.

It is also interesting to learn that afterward the Cella family of St. Louis, owners of the Fairgrounds Race Track of the time, gave Frank a job there as assistant race starter. A. B. Dade was the chief starter for the races. Frank would use a long black bullwhip, and crack it as the starting signal. Also, research reveals that Jesse James entered several horses in the races at the old Cote Brilliante Track at the southwest corner of Easton and North Kingshighway in St. Louis, years before, using the name of Howard, as he was known elsewhere. Al Spink, dean of the sports writers in the 1870's, verifies this in his published work.

During the course of this work, it also was learned that Cole Younger carried on his show, "Hell on the Border," with the D. B. Murphy Shows, under the management of Lester (Pete) Brophy and Tom Kearney of St. Louis, who controlled the concessions. Cole had wax figures of all the noted outlaws of the time, with accounts of how they died, and made them more realistic by using fake blood and posing them in the manner of their death. It also was learned that Cole stated that draw poker was first used by the guerrillas during the Civil War, in Missouri, and that Frank James was a master of the art. It was also in St. Louis where the Jameses and the Youngers had their boots made.

To further clarify the connection between Frank James and Dr. Wolfort, I might mention that Dr. Wolfort was the house doctor for the American Hotel at the time. This was the property of the Cella family, and where Frank James lived for a long time.

CHAPTER 14

The Glendale
Train Robbery

THE NEWS SPREAD LIKE WILDFIRE THROUGH KEARNEY AND Liberty, Missouri, and threw every man, woman, and child into a state of excitement. The butcher boy almost dropped his basket of eggs when he heard the local postmaster tell the news.

"Have you heard the news? The James boys are back!"

"What? Where? When? How?"

"Here, Silas, read it yourself," the newsbearer said, as he tossed a newspaper to the storekeeper.

There it was. The headlines blared out the news under date of October 8, 1879, announcing another terrible railway raid which had been successfully carried out by an armed band. Again it appeared that the hosts of terror had taken over from the forces of law and order.

Since the abortive days of the Northfield raid, and the absence of Jesse and Frank James from their home State of Missouri, nothing much had occurred to whet the appetites of the ex-Quantrillians. The 1876 fiasco in Minnesota had placed the

Younger brothers behind prison bars at Stillwater and had caused the western borders of Missouri to be free of the dreaded James brothers.

For three years Jesse and Frank had pursued devious ways in the wilds of Texas and Mexico and had later taken up residence in Tennessee with their families. Many Missourians had hoped that their exile would be permanent; others had been waiting for something exciting to happen.

It seemed only natural that these ex-guerrillas should come back to their old haunts to execute their plans of crime. The eastern part of Jackson County, the western part of Lafayette, and southward through Cass County constituted the very center of the field of operations chosen by the old guerrilla leaders, Quantrill, Todd, Anderson, Pool, Clements, and others during the Civil War. The Sni Hills and the heavy timberland bordering the Big and Little Blue Rivers afforded them excellent hiding places when pursued by Federal forces, and from their retreats in the hills they had made concentrated forays upon the towns of Independence, Pleasant Hill, Lexington, Kansas City, and others.

Besides, the outlaws had known every pathway over the hills and every crossing place along the streams. Since the war, nature had hardly changed the forest-crowned hills and the deep, tangled underbrush or the sparkling rivers and streams. Another factor of safety for the outlaws was that around this area were the farms and dwellings of their friends and sympathizers. People who assisted the Jameses and their friends said little about it in those hectic days, but later generations brag that "Jesse slept here or there" or even exhibit some memento the outlaw had given them.

October 7, 1879, was a beautiful, sunny, warm day. The woods had not yet taken on their majestic burst of color, but nature was lovely in the ripeness of the summer's close. While the majority of Missouri's citizens went about their business of farming, clerking, or similar pursuits, others planned the crime that would throw the tiny hamlet of Glendale into national prominence.

Glendale was a lonely wayside station in the western part of Lafayette County, Missouri, on the Kansas City branch of the Chicago & Alton Railroad. It was some twenty miles from Kansas City and wedged in between rugged and beautiful hills, in the midst of a region where bloody deeds had been committed during the war by both Confederate and Union guerrilla forces. The name of Glendale itself was probably suggested by the lofty dark hills, torn into clefts and glens and dales, and such an area provided an excellent place of concealment for men and horses. The outlaws had picked the best opportunity existing on the line between Kansas City and Chicago for their bold robbery.

Glendale, known for its lovely surroundings, had no more than a half dozen male inhabitants at the time. Besides the station house, the business in Glendale consisted of a post office and a general store kept by the postmaster, Mr. Anderson, a genial Scot. There was also a small blacksmith shop or saloon.

It was a pleasant evening, and when night fell the store was lighted. The postmaster and four other men gathered in front of it to discuss current events, leaving the sixth male inhabitant, Mr. McIntire, the station master, to mind the depot. Suddenly a stranger joined the circle, tapping Mr. Anderson on the shoulder.

"I want you."

"What do you mean?" the astonished postmaster asked.

The stranger did not reply, but stepped aside and said, "Here, boys."

In a minute half a dozen rough-looking men, muffled and masked, stood by the stranger's side, pistols in their hands.

"Now take care. Make tracks out of this," said the leader.

"Where are we to go?" asked one of the prisoners.

"To the depot," was the brief reply, as the little company of amazed citizens filed away to the station. In the depot were the operator-agent, Mr. McIntire, and W. E. Bridges, assistant auditor of the Chicago & Alton line, who was having coffee with the agent's mother in a room above the depot.

The leader of the masked men told McIntire that he wanted to send a message to Chicago.

"All right."

But before the agent knew what was happening, a heavy hand was placed on his shoulder, and he was told that he was a prisoner. At the same time another bandit tore the telegraph instrument from its moorings and threw it into the brush.

"Now," said the leader, "I want you to lower that green light."

"But," stammered the agent, "the train will stop if I do that."

"That's the idea, precisely what we want it to do, my buck, and the sooner you obey the better. I will give you a minute to lower the light," said the leader, thrusting a pistol into the agent's face.

McIntire looked up into the face of the man holding the gun. He saw a cold, fixed stare that told him that if necessary the man would carry out his threat without compunction. The order was obeyed, and the light lowered, a sign which would cause the engineer of the oncoming train to stop. To make doubly sure, the robbers placed a heap of railroad ties across the tracks.

"All right, now, what's in the room above us?" asked the outlaw.

"My mother and Mr. Bridges, auditor for the road," said McIntire.

One of the robbers mounted the stairs and relieved Bridges of his money and his watch. Mrs. McIntire was assured nothing would happen to her son if he obeyed orders, and the bandit returned to the platform with Mr. Bridges in tow.

It was a little after seven o'clock. The band of robbers had now been in Glendale an hour, anxiously awaiting the arrival of the train. The prisoners in the station house were wondering what would happen next, especially to them. They did not appreciate the fact that they were about to witness an epic event.

Then the distant rumbling of the train was heard; louder and louder it fell upon the ears of the listeners. The engineer sounded the whistle and ordered the brakes applied. The train stood still on the track, with the engine at the water tank. Two of the masked men rushed to the cab and demanded the coal hammer.

"What do you want with it?" asked the engineer.

"Damn you, hand it over quick or you'll never run another train!"

The man handed the outlaw a heavy sledge hammer used for breaking coal. At this time, the conductor, John Greenman, came to the platform, ready for his new orders, as he expected on account of the lowered green signal. One of the robbers rushed up to him with a cocked revolver. He was joined by another bandit. Both were masked. The conductor was powerless to resist, and with mingled feelings of alarm and disgust he was compelled to await the pleasure of these holdup men.

The whole group, with the long-bearded man at their head, gathered at the door of the express car. The one with the sledge hammer started to break down the door which had been locked from the inside by the messenger, William Grimes, at the first sign of danger. He had also taken the money from the safe and put it his satchel. He had swung the safe door closed and was making for another door, but it was too late.

"Damn you, give me the key to the safe!" demanded one of the men.

"Take it if you want it," replied the courageous messenger.

In a moment the faithful Grimes lay senseless on the floor,

struck down with the revolver butt. The safe was ransacked, the money in the satchel was taken, and the great train robbery at Glendale was over. The bandits had netted between $35,000 and $40,000 in a robbery which had not taken ten minutes. The train was then ordered to proceed after the prisoners had been released.

Before leaving, the leader of the gang gave Bridges a dispatch to send to the *Kansas City Journal* from the next station. It was dated Blue Springs, Missouri, and read: "We are the boys who are hard to handle, and we will make it hot for the boys who try to take us." The message carried the names of Frank and Jesse James, Jack Bishop, Jim Connors, Cool Carter, and three others.

What the worth of the dispatch was, no one could tell, but everyone was sure that Frank and Jesse James were members of the band. It was never denied that where Frank was excellent in planning, Jesse was equally excellent in execution. Many sources stated the following six men were involved in the Glendale affair: Jesse James, Edward Miller, Robert Woodson Hite, William Ryan, James Andrew Liddil, and Daniel Tucker Bassham. Others included the name of Jim Cummins. Those "in the know" emphatically claimed that Frank James was in Tennessee when the Glendale robbery occurred. There is ample evidence from various sources to show that Frank tried hard to persuade Jesse not to return to Missouri or to engage in outlawry after three years of comparative peace.

Tucker Bassham, the simple lad of Jackson County, soon appeared to have too much money for one in his circumstances, for Jesse had given him a thousand dollars for holding the getaway horses. This money Bassham buried near his home. Major James Liggett, marshal of Kansas City, suspected that Bassham had taken part in the holdup, but he deferred action in the hope that Bassham might lead him to other members of the band. When it seemed that this hope would not materialize,

Deputy Marshals Keshlaer and Langhorne arrested Bassham on June 30, 1880, and lodged him in the Kansas City jail. He was brought to trial on November 6 and pleaded guilty. He was convicted and sentenced to ten years in the Missouri State Penitentiary at Jefferson City, but later was pardoned for giving testimony against Bill Ryan.

Tucker Bassham's confession appeared in the November 7, 1880, issue of the *Kansas City Journal.*

On Monday night preceding the robbery, two neighbors of mine came to me and said they had put up a job to rob a train, and wanted me to go along with them. I told them I didn't want nothing to do with robbing no train, and wouldn't have nothing to do with it nohow; but they kept on persuading and finally went away, saying they would come back in the morning and that I must go with them. They said a very rich train was coming down on the C. & A. and that we could make a big haul, perhaps $100,000. Well, that kinda persuaded me, but still I didn't like to go. They finally told me that Jesse James was arranging the things and it was sure to be a success.

Well, then they left. My wife kept pestering me to know what was going on and what they wanted, but I didn't let on to her. I kept thinking about it all night. Of course, I'd often heard of Jesse James, and kinda had confidence in him. Then I was pretty poor. There wasn't much crops on my place and winter coming on, and I tell you it looked pretty nice to get a little money just then, no matter where it came from. I thought to myself, if I don't go it'll be done just the same anyhow. They'll be down on me and ten to one I'll be more likely to get arrested if I ain't there than if I am.

Well, I kept thinking it over and in the morning they came to the house early and ate breakfast, and then went out and loafed around the timber and in the cornfield all day so nobody would see them. In the evening they came in and we ate supper and they gave me a pistol, and we all got on our horses and rode off together. We soon met another man on the road, and when we got to Seaver's schoolhouse, about a mile and a half from my house, they give a kind of a whistle for a signal, and two men came out of the timber and rode up. One of them was introduced to me as Jesse James. This was the first time I had ever seen Jesse James in my life. The other was Ed Miller of Clay County.

Bassham said that Jesse James then gave him a shotgun and furnished each man with a mask, and that they all rode on in silence toward Glendale. No instructions were given. When they arrived at Glendale, they noticed a light in the store, and Bassham was ordered by Jesse James to go in and capture the inmates and bring them over to the station. On looking in the windows he found the usual group of loiterers had left the store and sauntered over to the depot to await the incoming train. The people in the waiting room were being guarded by one of the men. Jesse James then told him to walk up and down the platform, as the train approached, and fire off his shotgun in the air as fast as he could. The telegraph operator was forced at the point of a pistol to lower the green light and thus signal the train to stop. Jesse James then asked him if there were any loose ties to lay across the tracks. He said he didn't know of any. The men went out and found some and laid them across the tracks to halt the train if it failed to stop for the green light. Meanwhile the train approached; Bassham walked up and down the platform firing off his gun; Jesse James and one of the men jumped into the express car, and Miller jumped on the engine in the manner familiar to all.

When it was over, Jesse James fired his pistol, which was the signal for all to leave, whereupon they jumped on their horses and rode rapidly for about half a mile till they came to a deserted log cabin. They alighted and entered. Someone produced a small pocket lantern, and somebody else struck a match. Jesse James threw the booty down on a rude table in the middle of the room, divided it up, and shoved a pile to each as they stood around the table. Bassham's share was about a thousand dollars.

Jesse then said, "Now, each of you fellows go home and stay there. Go to work in the morning and keep your mouths shut, and nobody will ever be the wiser. In the morning this country will be full of men hunting for you and me."

Major Liggett was more than ever determined to catch the outlaws. Keeping Bassham under watch told him he could not accomplish his purpose by straightforward means, so he resolved to employ strategy. The major decided that the man who could help him was George Shepherd, former guerrilla, former bank robber, and former friend of Jesse James. He knew that Shepherd was working at Jesse Noland's dry goods store in Kansas City, so he sent for him and made him a proposition.

Shepherd liked the idea of helping capture Jesse James. He was promised a false newspaper item saying that he was suspected of being connected with the Glendale robbery and therefore was wanted by the police. He was supposed to use this clipping as a means of gaining Jesse's confidence. Then, when the opportunity presented itself, he was to kill Jesse James. For this he would be given half the reward money, as well as $50 a month until the job was done.

Several weeks after the Glendale affair Shepherd set out on this mission. The circulated reports that the James family was at odds with him seemed false, for the certainly was received warmly at the Samuel place in Kearney. Shepherd told Dr. Samuel and his wife that he was suspected of complicity in the Glendale holdup and, while he had no part in it, he was forced to flee on account of his previous record. He confided that he wanted to join Jesse and his gang. They believed him, and Dr. Samuel directed him to a point on the main highway where he met Jesse and some of his men.

Shepherd repeated his story to Jesse, and Jesse said he was glad to see him. The outlaws returned to the Samuel home and spent the night there. The next day they went to the home of Benjamin Marr, some twenty miles from Kansas City. There, plans were laid to rob the Empire City Bank. Shepherd had only a small weapon and a very poor horse, so he excused himself and said he wanted to get better equipment. Jesse agreed it was the wise thing to do and told him to meet the band on the third night following, at a spot in Jackson County known as Six Mile.

Shepherd hurried back to Kansas City, where he imparted this information to Major Liggett. The major provided Shepherd with a good horse and several Smith & Wesson revolvers of heavy calibre. Shepherd reached the Six Mile area and was informed by Benjamin Marr that Jesse and his men had gone to Rogue's Island and expected him to be there. At the outlaw camp he found Jesse James, Jim Cummins, Ed Miller, and another man.

On November 1, 1879, the outlaws rode to the vicinity of Empire City, all set for the robbery. Late in the afternoon it was agreed that Shepherd should ride into town to get the lay of the land and the exact location of the bank building. It was after dark when Shepherd got there, and he was astonished to see lights burning in the bank. A dozen men inside were waiting, all armed with double-barreled shotguns. Apparently Major Liggett had telegraphed a warning to the bank officials.

Shepherd remained in town all night, as Jesse James had instructed him to do. He returned at nine in the morning to find the camp deserted. Familiar signs told him that the outlaws had moved on, so he followed the trail several miles down the road, where the men were hidden in the brush, slightly drunk. Shepherd became alarmed, for he knew that they had not had any liquor when he left them. He supposed some of them must have gone into town for it. To add to his fears that his plot may have been discovered, Cummins remarked that the bank they were to attack was heavily guarded and he wondered who had betrayed them. Shepherd began to sweat, but then Jesse James said casually that Cummins had gone into Galena to get whiskey, and had heard rumors there of the impending raid.

Shepherd suggested that the best thing for them to do was to get out of there.

They all agreed, and rode south, Ed Miller about a hundred yards to the right, Cummins and the other man the same distance to the left, Jesse James and Shepherd in the center. Thirteen miles south of Galena, near Short Creek, Shepherd drew rein, allowing Jesse to advance several yards. Instantly Shepherd drew one of the heavy revolvers and fired one shot. Jesse James pitched from the saddle to the ground and lay as if dead.

As he reported it later, Shepherd viewed the body for a brief instant but did not fire again, since the outlaw did not move. Jim Cummins and another man rushed at Shepherd, Shepherd's animal was a splendid one, and he soon outdistanced the men—all, but Cummins. They kept firing at each other, and Shepherd received a slight wound in the left leg below the knee. He then wheeled his horse, took deliberate aim, and brought Cummins to a halt. Shepherd rode into Galena, where he was placed under the care of a doctor for about three weeks. He told Major Liggett that he was certain he had killed Jesse James and badly wounded Cummins.

Jim Cummins later stated that Shepherd never fired a shot at Short Creek, especially not at Jesse James. According to him, when Shepherd returned from Empire City he was slightly under the influence of liquor, and since Cummins had already ascertained that the bank was guarded, he and Miller distrusted Shepherd and planned to kill him. They fired at him as he was riding into camp, and he escaped.

Other reports claimed that Cummins had received a serious wound in the right side. Bits of clothing, driven into the wound, arrested the flow of blood from the artery, or else the wound might have been fatal. The surgeon who furnished these facts stated that he had performed the operation on Cummins, placing a ligature on the artery.

It seems almost impossible that Shepherd, if he fired at Jesse

James, would have missed his target. Shepherd had been a guerrilla through the war and a bank robber afterward, and he was a crack shot. He stated that his bullet struck Jesse on the side of his left ear. Jesse's mother stated that she believed him dead, or pretended to believe so, to put people off the track. In later years she said that the wound had been an ugly one and that her son had been disabled for a long time because of it. It will also be remembered that Jesse was not heard from for almost a full year; subsequent facts clearly disproved Shepherd's claim that he had killed the outlaw.

Yet another story appeared in connection with the Shepherd affair. On March 6, 1882, the following item appeared in a Kansas City newspaper:

> A sensation was created here among the police and county officials by the fact that George Shepherd, the ex-guerrilla and bank robber, who claimed to have shot Jesse James, the notorious outlaw, at Joplin, Missouri, just after the Glendale train robbery of 1879, had proved a traitor through that trouble. He now admits that his wound in the leg and the account of the killing was all a put-up job with the James brothers for the purpose of procuring the large rewards offered. The plan to get the reward money having failed after long perseverance and much swearing, he now says that he would no more shoot Jesse James than he would his own brother.

This is just another of those puzzles which probably will never be solved. Naturally, the friends of Jesse had to admit that he had been shot to keep Shepherd in the good graces of the authorities. On the other hand, Jesse's nature being what it was, it is doubtful that Shepherd would have lived very long after the affair if the story had been true.

CHAPTER 15

The Glasgow
Stage Holdup

THE GLASGOW STAGECOACH WAS HELD UP ON SEPTEMBER 3, 1880, as Sam McCoy was driving his team from Mammoth Cave to Cave City, Kentucky. As the stage reached a desolate spot along the way, two mounted men emerged from cover, and with leveled guns ordered McCoy to pull up his team.

The passengers on the stage were Judge R. H. Rountree and his daughter, Elizabeth, of Lebanon, Kentucky; P. S. Rountree, his nephew, from Fairmount, Minnesota; J. E. Craig of Lawrenceville, Georgia; S. M. Shelton from Chattanooga, Tennessee; and several others.

After the bandits had taken the passengers' valuables, one of them passed a bottle of whiskey around and insisted that each victim take a drink. This sounded like the typical trick of Bill Ryan, a member of the James gang and a known whiskeyhead. The other robber, because of his pleasant, flattering speech to the ladies, sounded like Jesse James. After a few minutes conversation, the bandits lifted their hats courteously and allowed the passengers to proceed.

The two outlaws then galloped off in the direction of Cave City and robbed another coach that had just left for Mammoth Cave. The only occupants of this vehicle were a Negro preacher and the driver. When the first stage reached Cave City, a posse was organized and a diligent search was made of the territory, with the usual negative result.

Lieut.-Governor James E. Cantrill issued a proclamation offering $500 reward for the arrest of the robbers. Of course, the reward money was an incentive for all the amateur sleuths in the area. G. W. Bunger, a deputy sheriff of Ohio County, appeared in Cave City with a suspect, one T. J. Hunt, who was an ex-guerrilla known as "Guerrilla Tom." His trial was held on November 20, 1880, and he was bound over for the Barren County Grand Jury, which indicted him in April, 1881. The case did not come up for trial until March 31, 1882, when a verdict of guilty was found, and Hunt was sentenced to three years in the penitentiary at Frankfort, Kentucky, in spite of his pleas that he was innocent.

Oddly enough, at the very time of Hunt's trial, Jesse James was shot and killed by Bob Ford. Jesse's picture was carried in all the newspapers throughout the country, and Judge Rountree instantly saw that a terrible mistake had been made in the identification of Hunt as the stage robber. Thereafter, the judge used his utmost efforts to correct his mistake by working for Hunt's release. At the time of Jesse James's death, the outlaw was wearing Judge Rountree's watch and Mrs. James was wearing Miss Rountree's diamond ring. (This also contradicts stories that Frank James and Jim Cummins were the two bandits who robbed the Mammoth Cave Stage.)

Judge Rountree's efforts in behalf of Hunt were successful, and he was granted a new trial. Affidavits were obtained from Charles and Bob Ford, who stated that Jesse James and Bill

Ryan were the two who had robbed the stages. Dick Liddil also made an affidavit to the same effect, and another was obtained from Bill Ryan himself, who was then serving a term in the Missouri State Prison for his implication in the Glendale train robbery. Governor Blackburn of Kentucky granted Hunt a full pardon on May 1, 1882. The state legislature passed a bill awarding Hunt $1,500 for his stay in prison.

While some writers have called Bill Ryan an asset to the James gang, a thorough study of this man's life, foolish arrest, and cause of death leads one to believe he was a liability, just as Frank James always asserted. A drunk cannot do any job well. Such was the case with Ryan. It was his love of whiskey that caused his arrest and ultimate confinement in the Missouri State Prison. Perhaps Ryan had fed Jesse's vanity. Frank, on the other hand, always predicted that the boozer would cause trouble for the gang and that it would be best to get rid of him.

It was near White's Creek, not far from Nashville, Tennessee, that Frank and Jesse had a discussion with regard to Ryan. Frank lived at the Felix Smith place and assumed the name of Ben Woodson, and appeared to be engaged in hauling lumber for the Indiana Lumber Company. Jesse lived some distance away, using the name Howard, and he and Ryan were frequent visitors to Frank's house. Frank tried to persuade Jesse to drop Ryan then and there for, as usual, he was dead drunk. Jesse, however, took the attitude that Frank did not like the man because Jesse had taken him "under his wing."

"Jesse, I wish you wouldn't bring that damned drunken Irishman to my house any more. You better keep an eye on him pretty close. His big mouth and loose tongue will get us into trouble when he's full of whiskey someday."

"Oh, you just don't like Bill, but he's all right," Jesse assured his brother. "Yeah, I'll admit he does drink a bit, but he's all right; so stop worrying."

In March, 1881, the Jameses were in Selma, Alabama, living

incognito at the St. James Hotel on Water Street. Jesse was still suffering from his lung wounds, and it is said that he wanted to consult a specialist there. In Selma the bandit brothers also visited the home of John Norris, a boyhood friend from Clay County, Missouri. At the hotel they registered as the "Williams" brothers, using separate rooms as a precaution.

On Friday, March 11, at three P.M., U.S. Army Paymaster Alexander G. Smith rode leisurely along the towpath that paralleled Muscle Shoals Canal, several miles from Florence, Alabama, carrying payroll money for the engineers' camp at Bluewater. Three masked men dashed up and made the startled paymaster a prisoner and confiscated $5,200. They forced Smith to travel with them almost all that night, releasing him many miles from the point of the holdup, during a heavy rainstorm.

The robbers had removed their masks prior to that and had chatted with Smith in a friendly manner. Smith said one of them, apparently the oldest of the three, was always quoting Shakespeare and acted more like a preacher than an outlaw. The second was a loud-mouthed braggart who smelled of whiskey; the third, apparently the leader, was younger than his companions, talkative and polite, but always on the alert. The descriptions fitted the combination of Frank James, Bill Ryan, and Jesse James.

But, as Frank had predicted, Bill Ryan was to get them into serious trouble. On March 26, 1881, Ryan rode into White's Creek and stopped in front of W. Earthman's general store. Loudly he stomped into the saloon section of the store and demanded the best liquor in the house.

"Gimme me some raw oysters an' some of that raw whiskey on the back bar!"

A bottle of the best whiskey was put before Ryan as he put a gold coin on the bar. Before long, Ryan was drunk, and began to brag about who he was, and to create a disturbance. Maddox, the bartender, appreciated Ryan's free spending, but soon became disgusted with the man's vile manners and tried to calm him down. Unsuccessful in this, alone, he called the owner, W. Earthman, to assist him.

Ryan jumped up and looked suspiciously around the room. "Stand back, stand back!" he yelled. "There ain't nobody in this place can tell me what I can do and what I can't do. Stand back, 'fore someone gets hurt. Know who I am? I'm a rough and tough desperado, that's what; a killer, that's who I be, an' my name's Tom Hill."

Ryan started to jerk out his guns, but Earthman jumped behind him and held his arms to his sides and tried to talk some sense into him. At this point someone called for the blacksmith, whose shop was next door. He was a powerful Negro, and he and another man who had come into the store assisted in disarming Ryan and searching him. They found $1,300 in gold on his person. This, in connection with Ryan's boast about being an outlaw led them to believe him. There was no identification on him, however, so Ryan was turned over to the Nashville police for investigation. It was not long before photographs of the talkative Ryan were being sent around.

The Kansas City Police were quick to see that "Tom Hill" was Bill Ryan, a much-wanted member of the infamous Jesse James band. They took their information to William H. Wallace, prosecuting Attorney of Jackson County, Missouri, who declared that the photo was that of Ryan.

Wallace had run on the platform that he would rid Missouri of the James outlaw band, and here was his opportunity to prove himself. Ryan was sent to Missouri, indicted and tried for his part in the 1879 Glendale train robbery. The case against him depended on the testimony of Tucker Bassham.

The case came to trial at Independence, Missouri, about five months later. It was beyond doubt the most exciting contest in any court in Missouri or in the West. After fifteen years of unchecked robbery and bloodshed, it was the test case between the law and the bandit. Many of Wallace's friends advised him to dismiss the case and let it go. They said it was not worth a man's life to conduct the prosecution, and in the end would only result in acquittal. But Wallace told them he would rather be shot than show the white feather.

Ryan felt that his old friends would rally to his defense in spite of the foolish circumstances of his arrest. The old guerrillas did rally, and Jesse James and his followers rode up from Nashville, ready to act at the first opportune moment. The rumor was spread that the Jameses were intent on freeing Ryan, and excitement ran high in Independence, especially at night when rockets were seen exploding in the wooded section around the town. No doubt they were meant to tell Ryan that his friends were standing by.

The trial began on schedule. The defendant was apparently provided with means, for his counsel consisted of eminent men and gifted lawyers, R. L. Yeager, an ex-prosecuting attorney of Jackson County; Blake L. Woodson, an experienced criminal lawyer, and B. J. Franklin, a former congressman.

Ryan's friends crowded the small courtroom, armed to the teeth. Many of them slept in the courthouse so that they could get the best seats. People said that they had not seen so much clamor in Independence since General Jo Shelby chased the Federal troops through the town just before the Battle of Westport during the Civil War.

Tucker Bassham, the state's principal witness, was brought from Jefferson City by A. Hays, brother of Colonel Upton Hays, formerly of Shelby's command. Captain M. M. Langhorne had been appointed special guard for Ryan, not only in the courtroom but even escorting him from the jail to the courthouse. The captain was a brave man and would die before shirking his duty. He too had been a member of Jo Shelby's Iron Brigade during the war.

Tucker Bassham was under the constant guard of Amazon Hays, a deputy marshal of Jackson County, to protect him from the outlaw's friends. When they heard that Governor Crittenden had given Bassham a full pardon for his participation in the Glendale robbery so that he would testify against Ryan, they set fire to his house in the Cracker Neck Region, forcing his family to flee to Independence. The governor even sent two large cases of rifles to Independence in case of emergency, but they were never opened. However, this action resulted in a motion for a new trial, Ryan's attorneys contending that the jury had been tampered with by the suggestion that they arm themselves with rifles.

No doubt there were many men just waiting for Jesse or Frank James to give the signal to attack Independence in an attempt to rescue Ryan. For years it was general gossip in the locality as to why Jesse did not attack the town. Did he fear Captain Langhorne?

It was later learned from one Walter Kelly that Jesse's reason for not attacking Independence had been a sound one, and we now learn how Kelly became aware of that. Kelly had lived in Ray County, Missouri, as a boy, having come from Kentucky, where he had known a man named David Howard, a quiet man with a small family and several spirited horses. He also stated that Howard was never without kid gloves and that he was constantly blinking his eyes. Kelly's father and their neighbor, a Mr. Stone, had been Confederate soldiers and both appeared to know Mr. Howard very well, although they spoke little of him. Several incidents burned into the brain of young Kelly, especially the occasion one night when he peeped into the kitchen and saw his mother feeding Howard and heard Howard asking for a fresh horse. The next morning they found a fagged-out animal in their barn.

Of course, as with all of us, time shapes various conditions in the path of life, and so, with the death of his father, young

Kelly moved to Missouri to live with an uncle. It was also about this time that Ryan was brought to trial, and Kelly and his uncle went to town to witness it. One morning William Gregg asked the boy's uncle if he might have the lad deliver a message for him. Thus, young Kelly took a letter to a man waiting at the old bridge across the Blue River. It was an easy matter for the boy to locate the spot. Shortly thereafter, two men rode up. He at once recognized one of them as David Howard, whom he had seen in Kentucky.

"Well, what do you know, of all people!" grinned the outlaw. "What brings you here, and how is your good mother?"

"The man in town told me to deliver a message to some fellow here.

"I am that man, son. Let me have it."

Later Kelly became curious, as naturally he would, and we can well imagine his amazement when he learned that David Howard was Jesse James and that the message he brought to the outlaw was addressed to "Maurice Langhorne." From all appearances, then, Jesse James refused to attack the town in an effort to rescue Ryan because Langhorne was his guard, and Jesse and Langhorne had been Confederate soldiers and also were close friends.

Prosecuting Attorney Wallace still had trouble on his hands. He needed the affidavit of some well-known citizen of Independence on the motion for a new trial, to the effect that there was no sort of intimidation of the jury. It was thought he would have trouble finding a private citizen with sufficient courage to make it. Wallace appealed to Colonel J.E. Payne, an ex-Confederate soldier, and without a moment's hesitation he went into open court with Wallace and signed the affidavit.

The air was full of threats of assassination, especially against Prosecutor Wallace and the witness, Tucker Bassham. Bassham told Wallace that he had been assured they both were on the death list, and Bassham tried to persuade Wallace to leave the country with him. Friends of the bandits were coming into Independence at night and galloping their horses up and down in front of the place where Bassham lived, and making threats to take his life. Tucker Bassham took to his heels, and Wallace stated that was the last he ever saw of the man.

So, in spite of the threats against Wallace's life during the trial, he refused to be intimidated; he was the first to succeed in trying a member of the James gang and getting a conviction.

The conviction of Ryan broke the backbone of the James band. A jury had done what it was supposed no Missouri jury would ever dare to do. Courage sprang up in hundreds of breasts. Witnesses began to talk. Squads of men, headed by Captain M. M. Langhorne, Whig Keshlaer or Amazon Hays or Cornelius Murphy or Police Commissioner H. H. Craig or Sheriff Timberlake of Clay County, all Southerners, began to scour the country in search of the James boys. It was the beginning of the end.

Some writers have declared that William Ryan was a member of the James band who robbed the train in September of 1881, at Blue Cut, not far from Glendale. It would have been impossible for this to be so. At that time he was being held in jail awaiting trial for the Glendale robbery. Prosecutor Wallace stated later that in separate interviews with Dick Liddil, Clarence Hite, and Charley Ford. They all agreed that the outlaws involved in the Blue Cut affair had been Frank and Jesse James, Wood and Clarence Hite, Dick Liddil, and Charley Ford.

The official records show that Ryan was convicted by jury for robbery in the first degree in Jackson County, at Independence, Missouri, on October 15, 1881, after being arrested early in 1881. Ryan was sentenced to twenty-five years, August Term of Court, 1881, under Cause No. 1954. Ryan was received at the State Prison in Jefferson City on October 16, 1881, as convict No. 2677. Sentence was later commuted to ten years after Ryan claimed to be dying of consumption, with benefit of 3/4

Law on January 4, 1889, by Governor Moorehouse, and he was discharged on April 15, 1889.

Ryan returned to the Independence area and stayed with an uncle, John McClosky. He did not die of consumption, however. Soon after his release he began hitting the bottle again. One day he went into town and began drinking heavily at the Mahan & McCarthy saloon on Main Street. His whiskey-clouded mind brought back memories of his old war comrades, and he wanted to go to Blue Springs, where a number of them could always be found. He borrowed a fast mare from Tommy McMahan and was soon on his way. Riding like the Headless Horseman of Washington Irving fame, he galloped headlong on the road to Blue Springs. A section of the road ran through some heavy timber. The next morning the horse trotted home alone, and when friends went to investigate, they found Ryan dead, his head smashed. He had either been thrown from the dashing horse or had struck his head on a low-hanging limb.

CHAPTER 16

The Muscle Shoals
Robbery

SILAS JONES SHIFTED IN HIS CAPTAIN'S CHAIR, JUST ENOUGH to give his aching backbone a little relief. He had become so engrossed in listening to the old-timers cracker-barrel discussion of world events for the past few years that he had stiffened up somewhat. With eyes half-closed and munching on a cracker and cheese, he continued to listen. These sessions around Ike Smith's pot-bellied stove were always interesting and sometimes were punctuated by friendly arguments.

One of the subjects being discussed was the Custer fight at the Little Big Horn. They all agreed finally that Custer had been foolhardy in his attempt to crush the Sioux Nation all by himself. They also agreed that Custer was to have commanded one of the three army divisions operating against the Indians under Sitting Bull and Crazy Horse in the Black Hills country. Unfortunately he was called to Washington and angered President Grant by giving distasteful testimony before a Congressional committee engaged in investigating charges against Secretary

Belknap, reflecting upon Grant's brother Orville, a frontier post-trader. Displaced as head of the division, Custer secured a modification of the presidential order, and on June 25, 1876, led his Seventh Cavalry to death, not a man surviving.

These Missouri farmers talked about the coming of the telephone and Edison's invention of the incandescent lamp in October of 1879, as well as the lack of rainfall in Clay County. Then they talked about the assassination of President James Garfield, which occurred July 2, 1881. The President, a graduate of Williams College, was on his way to attend his class reunion when he was shot. He was removed from Washington to Elberon, New Jersey, and died there September 19, 1881. The assassin, Charles J. Guiteau, was hanged in the jail at Washington on June 30, 1882.

The abortive raid on the Northfield, Minnesota, bank was next discussed at length. Few of the men seated in the store were not in sympathy with the Jameses and the Youngers, but they felt that silence at this point was the wiser courage. These ex-Confederates became very excited as they spoke of how Cole Younger and his brothers, Bob and Jim, had been severely wounded and captured after Northfield. Three of the bandits had been slain by the citizens, and the Younger brothers had been sentenced to life imprisonment in the Stillwater Penitentiary. There was speculation as to whether or not Jesse and Frank James had been members of the band of Minnesota robbers; most of the men agreed that they had been but they admittedly were pleased to know they had escaped.

These arm-chair historians, for some reason or another, did not discuss the robbery that had taken place at Muscle Shoals, Alabama, on March 11, 1881. Perhaps they felt that the ensuing complications, resulting in the arrest and imprisonment of Bill Ryan, did not give them much room to hang their pro-James opinions upon, therefore the less said the better. Especially since the majority of those present felt reasonably sure that

Jesse and Frank James, with Bill Ryan, had pulled off that caper.

However, other robberies occurred prior to that which kept the old-timers supplied with conversation for a long while. One was the daring holdup of the Chicago, Alton, & St. Louis train at Glendale in 1879; the other the holdup of the Glasgow, Kentucky, stage near Cave City.

Several years previously the Jameses had decided to move to Nashville, Tennessee, in an effort to live peacefully as well as to escape the long arm of the law. One dark night two covered wagons left Liberty, Missouri, one driven by Tyler Burns, the other driven by John T. Samuel, half-brother of Jesse and Frank. Riding behind the wagons came the noted Missouri outlaws, mounted upon the finest horseflesh obtainable. In the wagons rode Zee and little Jesse and Annie Ralston James, wife of Frank.

The latter part of August, 1877, found the travelers in Humphreys County, Tennessee, near Waverly. Jesse rented a farm from a man named Link, and it was there that his twins were born and within a week or so died. The stone markers erected over the graves can still be found, stones which Jesse, in his grief, carved by hand to mark the graves. The boys had been named Gould and Montgomery after the doctors who attended Zee James. Jesse liked Tennessee. His son had been born in Nashville in 1875; now he and Frank thought that state might offer sanctuary to two weary outlaws.

No one suspected who "Mr. Howard" was; all his neighbors said he was a good farmer, and a man who knew his horses. He had a racing mare named Red Fox, an animal which he often entered in the local racing events, always winning. After nearly two years of farming and cattle raising Jesse decided to pull up stakes and visit his brother in Nashville.

To allay suspicion of the local folks Frank had gone on to Nashville while Jesse remained at Waverly. Using the name of

B. J. Woodson, Frank James lived at the home of Ben Drake for a time, and then moved to the house of Drake's sister. His health improved, he moved to the Josiah Walton place in White's Creek, several miles from Nashville. People may have thought it odd that Woodson always carried two heavy pistols, but they never mentioned it.

During the off season Frank drove a team for the Indiana Lumber Company; later he made cedar buckets for the Prewitt-Spurr Lumber Company. Frank and Annie lived in a small log cabin at the time, and it was there that thier only child, a son, was born and was named Robert Franklin James. The child's parents dressed him as a girl and called him Mary Woodson, believing that perhaps one day an identity change might come in handy for the father.

In Frank's final move in Tennessee he rented the Felix Smith farm on White's Creek. His health and financial status improved, but one day Jesse brought his family to Nashville to live with Frank's family, and the older brother was disturbed about that. When Jesse rode off to engineer the Glendale affair and the Glasgow Stage robbery, Frank remained at home. He wanted no part of it.

But upon Jesse's return to Nashville his influence on Frank began to take its effect. It is believed that if Jesse had never returned Frank would have lived out his life in peace in Tennessee, with no one the wiser. Even with Jesse on the road again, Frank continued his peaceful existence in Tennessee. Word reached the Woodson home regarding the Glendale and Mammoth Cave stage holdups and Frank knew that Jesse and some of his men had become active again. He just shook his head and made no comment. While Jesse was away, on July 17, 1879, Zee gave birth to a daughter named Mary at the Felix Smith farm.

Many followers of the James legend seem to agree that the holdup of the paymaster at Muscle Shoals, Alabama, was a spur-of-the-moment proposition; that the boys had not gone there for the purpose of a robbery. However, inasmuch as Bill Ryan accompanied them, this leaves some doubt in the minds of others for Frank James hated Ryan, while Jesse tolerated him. Jesse always seemed partial to men who placed themselves on a lower plane than his own.

However, others claimed that Jesse, still suffering from his lung wounds, wanted to consult a specialist in Selma, Alabama. But there appears another background to this visit to Selma. The farm adjoining that of the Jameses in Clay County, Missouri, was the property of Frank Silas Norris and his wife, Sarah. Being neighbors and both families having migrated from Kentucky to the Show-Me State, the Norris family and the Jameses became close friends. The Norris family had a son named John, who became very close to the James boys, plowing the fields and providing the family table with wild fowl and other meat.

When the Civil War broke out, John Green Norris and his friend Frank James joined the Confederate Army under General Sterling Price. The Norris daughter married Robert Woodson Hite, favorite first cousin of Jesse James, near Adairville, Kentucky. Major George T. Hite, the father of "Wood" Hite as he was called, had married Nancy James, a sister of the Reverend Robert S. James, father of the outlaws. It was at the Hite home that Jesse James tried to commit suicide in 1870 when he learned that his sister Susan planned to marry Allen Parmer, an ex-guerrilla. After the war, John Green Norris returned to Missouri, then moved to Selma, Alabama, where he later married Mollie Graddick, daughter of a locally distinguished physician. The newly married couple built a home on the corner of Jeff Davis Avenue and Washington Street, and later Norris became one of the leading contractors in Dallas County.

According to the Norris family, Jesse's visit to their city was a peaceful mission, merely a trip to visit with a boyhood friend and playmate. The Norris family has in their possession an original photograph of Jesse James taken at New Orleans about that time, as well as a pair of stiff shirt cuffs inscribed: "To John Norris from Jesse James."

While in Selma, Jesse and Frank refused to stay at the Norris home, but resided incognito at the St. James Hotel. The manager of the hotel, James Dedham, later said that both men were polished gentlemen and he never once had reason to doubt they were what they represented themselves to be.

On Friday, March 11, 1881, U.S. Army Paymaster Alexander G. Smith walked out of the Campbell & Coat Banking Company, Florence, Alabama, swung a heavily laden saddlebag over the back of his horse, mounted the animal and rode down the muddy street toward the engineers' camp at Bluewater. The camp was situated on the Tennessee River several miles downstream, toward Tuscumbia.

As Smith rode leisurely along the towpath that paralleled Muscle Shoals Canal, several miles from Florence, three masked horsemen with pistols drawn sprang out of the brush, disarmed him, grabbed the saddlebag, and tied his hands behind his back. They took his watch and $221 from his pocket; then, strangely enough, they returned the watch and $21 to the victim. They extracted $5,000 from the saddlebag, making the total haul $5,200.

Thus the Missouri outlaws, whose names were to become a household word, had successfully accomplished their only robbery in the deep South. Their partner in crime at Muscle Shoals was Bill Ryan, a fearless braggart whose liking for whiskey sometimes made him an ally not worth having, as Frank James had said many times.

The three outlaws then forced Smith through the dense forest, generally northward toward the Tennessee border. The four of them rode through the wild forest, a wilderness unbroken save by the work camps of United States Engineers at intervals of several miles along the Muscle Shoals Canal. At dusk the robbers removed their masks and became very talkative. They said they were Texans; that they had been scouting the area for more than a week, plotting to rob the paymaster. They bragged that they were not strangers to the region, having passed through the canal zone more than once on missions into Alabama. Smith later declared that the noisy man wanted to shoot him, but the second man, obviously the leader, and smaller than the other two men, replied that they were not killers and that he would permit no harm to come to the prisoner.

As they rode on hour after hour, past Bull's Mill and Center Star and on into the darkness of the forest, the robbers questioned Smith about current events. Paymaster Smith later stated that he was fearful most of the time, yet could not help marvel at the good-natured attitude of his captors. One, he said, appeared almost to be a preacher as he quoted from the Bible.

About twenty miles from the scene of the holdup the men stopped in a dense, deeply secluded spot. The bandits dismounted, squatted on the ground, and carefully divided the $5,200 equally between them. They then untied the arms of their victim and remounted their horses. As they sped away in the darkness, one of them threw Smith his overcoat, shouting, "Pass the night comfortably, Mr. Smith."

The bewildered paymaster wandered all through the thick, black, unfamiliar forest. Toward dawn a terrible thunderstorm struck the area, causing the lost man more discomfort. Finally on Saturday Smith stumbled into Bluewater Camp, weary and ill. He was informed that several parties had gone to search for him, but with the coming of the storm, had given up, believing him dead.

Throughout the night the bandits stretched their tired horses across North Alabama into South Tennessee. There, in the

Nashville-Waverly area, where they had been living under the names of B. J. Woodson and J. D. Howard, they felt themselves comparatively safe.

On March 16, 1881, Ryan was arrested while on a drunken spree in a saloon at White's Creek. His photo was sent to various cities, and in Kansas City he was recognized as Bill Ryan. He subsequently was tried, convicted of being involved in the Glendale train robbery, and sent to the penitentiary.

What would happen to the Jameses in Tennessee now that Ryan was in the hands of the police? Shortly after Ryan's arrest Mr. Woodson rode the short distance over to Mr. Howard's farm to see him about a "mule." Their main concern—would Ryan talk?

The James boys could take no chances, even if Ryan did not divulge their presence in Tennessee, the detectives might guess it since Ryan was arrested there. They would have to send their wives and children into safe seclusion and then hit the outlaw trail again. The morning after Ryan's arrest Jesse and Frank James met at a prearranged place near Nashville. There they shook hands, and then the two rode off in opposite directions.

Time was running out for Jesse, but before this happened two more exciting robberies occurred. One was the holdup of the Chicago, Rock Island and Pacific train on July 15, 1881, wherein the conductor of the train and an employee were killed. The last daring robbery placed on the doorstep of the Jameses was the bold robbery of the Chicago and Alton train near Blue Cut, Missouri, on September 7, 1881.

The Blue Cut affair was the last for Jesse. Things began to happen fast after that; Bob Ford had killed Wood Hite and was anxious to see Jesse out of the way because he feared retaliation for having killed Wood. Jesse was now living in St. Joseph, Missouri, with Bob and Charley Ford likely prospects for a new gang. However, Bob Ford was in secret collusion with Governor T. T. Crittenden of Missouri and Sheriff Timberlake of Clay

County and Police Commissioner Craig of Kansas City to betray Jesse James. The end came on April 3, 1882, when Bob Ford fired the shot which ended the earthly career of Jesse James.

What would Frank do? Would he avenge the death of his brother? The death of Jesse James, accompanied by the treachery of several gang members, unnerved Frank James to such an extent that he at once considered surrendering to Governor Crittenden, with the understanding that he would be granted a fair trial. On Thursday evening, October 5, Frank James quietly walked up the steps of the capitol building, accompanied by Major John Newman Edwards. There he handed over his weapons to Governor Crittenden and gave himself up to the authorities. It was decided by the prosecution to try Frank for the murder of Cashier Sheets during the Gallatin bank robbery, for they felt this was their strongest case against him, other than the Winston train robbery for which he would also be tried. Colonel A. H. Powell of Lee's Summit and Bob Hudspeth of Jackson County posted $100,000 bond to assure the authorities that Frank "would not skip the country."

At noon on September 6, 1883, Prosecutor Wallace completed the state's argument with a speech which would have done credit to any orator. The courtroom (Gallatin Opera House) fairly trembled with applause after Mr. Wallace's speech but quickly hushed as the baliffs were directed to administer the oath to the jurors.

It was nearly four o'clock when the bailiff was notified that the jury had reached a verdict. The courtroom was breathless as Foreman William T. Richardson read: "State of Missouri vs. Frank James; charge, murder. We, the jury in the above entitled, find the defendant NOT GUILTY as charged in the indictment."

But six hundred miles away there was an old score to settle. Alabama had not forgotten the Muscle Shoals matter. Although freed in Missouri, Frank James was refused bail by United States Judge Judy Krekel and in February, 1884, the unhappy bandit was hustled aboard a train and under guard taken to Huntsville, Alabama.

After languishing in the custody of the Madison County authorities for two months, Frank James finally heard the indictment against him brought before the United States Circuit Court. On April 17 he heard the testimony of some twenty government witnesses who recalled seeing three mysterious horsemen in the area in 1881. Yet, most of them were not too sure about their testimony of "recalled" descriptions of the men; after all, three years had elapsed since the robbery.

Paymaster Smith was the next witness. He told, with theatrical gestures, how he was held up by three men and forced to ride twenty miles with them before they turned him loose. He dwelled at length on the subject of his faithful service to the government, and how he owed his life to the one robber who refused to allow a companion to shoot him. But when Judge Harry Bruce pointedly asked Smith if he could identify Frank James as one of the men, Smith replied that he was "not positive."

District Attorney Day then produced his star witness, James Andrew (Dick) Liddil, one-time member of the James gang, and who had promised Governor Crittenden to turn state's evidence against Jesse James if such a time ever occurred. Liddil droned from the witness stand that he had followed Jesse and Frank and Bill Ryan from Missouri to Nashville, and had actually overheard them plotting the Alabama holdup. He also said that he later heard Frank and Jesse declare that they and Ryan had pulled the job.

Liddil's evidence against Frank James, wholly circumstantial, made a bad impression on the jury, and as one reporter put it, "they probably will give little credit to his testimony."

Called next to the stand were Frank Silas Norris and his

daughter, Mrs. Robert Woodson Hite, both of whom testified that Frank James and Dick Liddil had spent several days in the Hite residence at Adairville, Kentucky in March of 1881. It seemed like all the witnesses had a poor memory for none mentioned the shooting of Wood Hite at the Bolton home near Richmond, Missouri, in December of 1881. Seven or eight witnesses who followed Mrs. Hite identified Frank James as one of the three men they had seen in the Muscle Shoals area three years before.

Frank James did not lack expert legal counsel. He had cleverly engaged four of the South's most competent lawyers, men eminently respected throughout North Alabama and South Tennessee, General Leroy Pope Walker, esteemed Confederate military hero and first Confederate Secretary of War, Richard Walker, R. B. Sloan, and James W. Newman. Upon their advice Mrs. Annie Ralston James, Frank's beautiful wife, and their well-mannered six-year-old son, Robert, had been brought from Missouri to attend the trial.

General Walker began the defense by shattering the district attorney's evidence by parading six witnesses before the court, each swearing that on March 11, 1881, he had seen Frank James walking the streets of Nashville, Tennessee. Attorney James W. Newman, recalling Dick Liddil to the stand, had the man admit that he had been brought to Alabama from Missouri to testify against his former friend "under agreement" with Missouri authorities that their influence would be used to relieve him of all offenses charged against him. Attorney R. B. Sloan came next, pointing an accusing finger at Liddil and stating he was a thief and a robber. Liddil admitted several indictments were still pending against him.

At three o'clock, before a packed courtroom, the distinguished General Walker rose calmly and quietly to defend his client, former soldier in the Army of the Confederacy. His strategy was evident. The general knew personally most of the jurors; also knew they were all ex-Confederate soldiers, remembering him best as a general in the field rather than as an attorney. He also knew their love and devotion for the lost cause.

General Walker casually leaned upon the jury-box railing, reminding the twelve men seated there that he was proud to defend Frank James, not only because he once was a Confederate, but also he was a man who would come to the aid of a friend or a cause in the hour of need. He extolled the bravery and courage Frank had displayed at the Battle of Springfield in 1861 and of his subsequent capture by the Federals; of his release and of his services with Quantrill. In low, whispered tones the general electrified the hushed courtroom with cruel details of how Yankees of the Missouri Enrolled Militia had come to the James home, humiliated Mrs. Samuel (James), whipped young Jesse with ropes, and hanged his stepfather, Dr. Samuel, until he nearly died. Although some years out of time (1875) the general also gave a horrifying version of how the Pinkertons bombed the James home at Kearney, crippling Frank's mother and killing his half-brother Archie Samuel.

At six o'clock in the evening of Friday, April 18, 1884, Judge Harry Bruce gave the jury a clear, fair, and impartial charge and the twelve Confederate veterans filed out of the room, one after another, slowly and solemnly. Almost immediately they returned with a NOT GUILTY decision. Judge Bruce rapped his gavel and said, "Defendant is discharged."

Instantly, the crowd loudly applauded and shouts rang out through the courtroom and down the hallways. Frank James gratefully shook General Walker's hand, while admirers patted him on the back and Huntsville ladies gathered sympathetically around Mrs. James and little Robert.

As Frank James left the courtroom he was re-arrested by Sheriff Frank Rogers of Boonville, Missouri, hustled aboard a train and brought back to his home state, once more a prisoner.

But the powerful pendulum of public opinion swung to the support of the noted bandit. Why another trial? Why more state money wasted? Hadn't Frank James stood enough for alleged crimes after the war? Seven prominent Missourians signed Frank's bond and the Boonville indictment yellowed on the record books. In 1885 it was officially forgotten and the famous bandit became a full-fledged citizen and a free man. Minnesota, too, forgot her indictments against Frank for his supposed participation in the Northfield raid.

CHAPTER 17

The Winston
Train Robbery

THE END OF MARCH, 1881, BROUGHT TORRENTIAL RAINS to Missouri, giving the arm-chair historians and cracker-barrel philosophers ample time to discuss the happenings of the day. The favorite topic of the day was the game of guessing who had participated in the holdup of the paymaster at Muscle Shoals, Alabama. Three men had been involved, and it was the general opinion that Jesse and Frank James and Bill Ryan had maneuvered the daring robbery, getting away with $5,200.

It took most Missourians less than a week to guess who the bold robbers had been, but nothing was ever proven against the Jameses, even though Frank later was tried at Huntsville, Alabama, for his alleged part in the crime, only to be acquitted in short order.

Now other things were happening to put a different complexion on the table of conversation. A different kind of crime occurred miles away from Missouri.

America from Cape Cod to the Golden Gate and from the

mountains to the sea was in the throes of a great sorrow. In the midst of general and widespread prosperity, the whole land was suddenly convulsed with horror at the dastardly attempt of Charles Jules Guiteau to take the life of President James A. Garfield. On July 2, this murderer fired three shots at the President. He stated the death of the President was necessary for the good of the country.

Just as relief came in the approaching convalescence of the wounded President, America was again startled by the news of another daring robbery. This occurred on July 11, 1881, at the bank of Davis & Sexton, in Riverton, Iowa, a small town at the extreme southwestern corner of the state. On July 10, two "cattle traders" appeared in the area and called on the Burks & Parsley Farm to examine some thoroughbred horses.

During the night two of the best horses disappeared from the Burks & Parsley stables, and the next morning the cattle traders rode into Riverton on fine animals. After carefully surveying the town and the bank building, the two men rode to the farm of a man named McKissick, where they ate dinner and had their horses attended.

Monday, July 11, was a hot day, business was slow, and Cashier Sexton was sitting alone in the bank when these two cattlemen rode up to the bank. They hitched their horses in the rear of the building and, entering via the front door, one of the two men asked Sexton to change a five-dollar bill. As the cashier turned to comply, he heard a strange noise, and, looking up, found himself staring into the barrel of a wicked-looking Dragoon pistol. Sexton was ordered to throw up his hands, and he did so at once, still clutching the five-dollar bill.

The second robber went behind the counter and swept all the cash he could find into a leather pouch. Then the two bandits walked toward the rear door, forcing Sexton to accompany them, his hands still raised high. Reaching the door, they hastily bade him good afternoon, sprang into their saddles, and with a parting salute from their pistols, rode swiftly away.

Sexton quickly raised an alarm and soon a well-mounted and well-armed band of determined citizens was on the trail of the robbers. Even though the pursuit was an eager one, the possemen never saw anything of the fugitives except their tracks. The two cattle buyers left Riverton with $5,000 of the bank's money, minus the five-dollar bill Sexton retained and kept as a souvenir.

Who were the Riverton robbers? Of course everyone said they were Jesse and Frank James. Yet they were wrong. The two bandits were Missourians—Charles Knox Polk Wells and another whose name is lost to history. The name of Polk Wells, as he was generally called, posed a curious question. It was later found that Polk Wells was arrested for his part in the Riverton robbery and admitted to the Iowa State Penitentiary on April 1, 1882, from Fremont County for grand larceny, to serve a sentence of ten years. He escaped on May 19, 1882, and was returned May 4. He was sentenced on May 19, 1882, from Lee County to serve a life sentence for murder. The murder referred to was the killing of John Elder, age seventy-three, night attendant at the prison hospital, who was chloroformed to death. It is claimed that during an escape Wells also killed a man at Fort Madison, Iowa. Wells was transferred from the Fort Madison State Penitentiary to Anamosa Reformatory on August 26, 1896, aged forty-five. At that time he was insane, and died on September 11, 1896.

Other startling news flashed over the wires was that Billy the Kid had been slain by Pat Garrett, and while that was just beginning to make conversation another event occurred in Missouri which overshadowed even that news.

On Friday evening, July 15, 1881, the Chicago, Rock Island and Pacific train left Kansas City, with its usual complement of passengers but with a lighter treasure than usual, both in freight and bullion. In fact, there was not more than $2,000 in currency and a few bars of silver, which naturally would be too heavy for anyone to carry off in a hurry. The express agent was Charles H. Murray, the conductor was William H. Westfall, Wolcott was the engineer, and Frank Stamper was the baggage-man.

It was said that the chief motive for robbing this train was vengeance on Westfall. It was reported that he was a conductor on the Hannibal & St. Joe line some years before when the James gang attacked a train, and that, when the Pinkerton detectives went in vain pursuit of the robbers, Westfall acted in the capacity of guide for the officers. It was also stated that Westfall had been the conductor who piloted Pinkerton agents to the Samuel home when the murderous bomb was thrown into the Samuel home, killing Jesse's half-brother and maiming his mother. However, it has been denied that Westfall had any connection with that night's work.

The train proceeded as far as Cameron, where four passengers boarded the cars. At 9:30 the train reached Winston, the next station east, where more passengers boarded her, together with several stonemasons, among them Frank McMillan (referred to as John McCulloch in some reports). These stonemasons were in the employ of the railroad, and it was their function to repair and build piers along the creeks and gulleys. It was not unusual for them to board the train at any point for a ride to another location.

It was dark now, and the train had not gone far out of Winston when the murderous work began. The seven men who had boarded the train at the last two stops were well stationed. Three of them rode in the smoking car, two were on the rear platform of the baggage car, the other two on the front platform of the baggage car, where they could keep an eye on the fireman and the engineer. The bell connected to the engine was pulled, presumably by a frightened passenger. The fireman, guessing the trouble, said to the engineer, "Give her hell." The engineer suddenly turned around and became aware of two masked men with drawn revolvers, seemingly rising from the pile of coal in the tender. Suddenly the fireman and the engineer leaped from the train onto the cow-catcher of the engine, where they hung on for dear life as the bandits fired at them. Finally they escaped into the nearby woods.

William Westfall, the conductor, was collecting tickets when a masked man, believed to be Frank James, dressed in a linen duster and wearing a straw hat, followed by two others, came into the car, yelling, "You are my prisoner! You are the man I want!" Westfall was shot in the shoulder, and when he turned, the man fired again but missed. Another robber fired the shot that killed Westfall as he staggered out to the platform and rolled to the ground.

Frank McMillan, the stonemason, was coming to the door of the smoking car at the same time and was shot dead by a stray shot. Some of the passengers said that McMillan was shot deliberately while trying to get out of the baggage car and that his body was pushed off the train.

When Charles Murray, in charge of the express company's safe, heard the shooting he guessed the reason. He hurried to close the door which had been left open for air. But his legs were suddenly grabbed by one of the four masked men who commanded him to come out of the car. Murray was forced to give the outlaws the key to the safe while they held him and Stamper under their guns. They stuffed the money into an old grain sack but grumbled in disappointment at finding only a small sum.

"Is this all you got?" demanded the apparent leader.

"You've got it all except the silver bricks," replied Murray.

"Damn you and your silver bricks!" retorted the bandit, striking Murray a blow with his pistol.

The bandits had not intended to rob the passengers, so the night's work netted them very little. About a mile from Winston the robbers stopped the train, got off, and disappeared into the woods. Then they hastily mounted their horses.

In the underbrush near Sibley's Landing on Big Dog Creek, a short distance from the scene, a crumpled piece of paper was found. This proved to have been dropped by one of the robbers. It read:

Kansas City, July 12, 1881

Charley

I got your letter today, and was glad to hear you had got everything ready in time for the 15th. We will be on hand at the time. Bill will be with me. We will be on the train. Don't fear. We will be in the smoker at Winston. Have the horse and boys in good fix for fast work. We will make this joust on the night of the 16th. All is right here. Frank will meet us at Cameron. Look sharp and be well fixed. Have the horses well gaunted. We may have some running to do. Don't get excited, but keep cool till the right time. Wilcox or Wilcott will be on the train. I think its best to send this to Kidder. Yours till and through death.

Slick

The law officers were able to draw the following descriptions from people who had seen the strangers near Winston about sundown on the day of the robbery, as well as from train passengers.

1. Big bay gelding, heavy mane and tail, about sixteen hands high. (John Samuel, Jesse's half-brother, owned this animal and stated later that Jesse had been riding him that summer.) Rider was tall, heavy, erect, high cheekbones and broad face, darkish whiskers over his face, dark hair, good talker. (Note: Jesse James was not a tall man and far from heavy. Never wore a belt over size 34.)

2. A little bay gelding (the one stolen by Frank James and Dick Liddil in Ray County, Wood Hite's horse). Rider was

about thirty, average height, stoop-shouldered, light-complexioned, solid build, not much whiskers, very slouchy, said little. This sounded like Wood Hite.

3. A sorrel gelding, about 15½ hands high, ordinary mane and tail, collar marks, no blaze in face (Lamartine Hudspeth's horse, ridden by Dick Liddil). Rider was about thirty, dark-complexioned, dark hair, dark whiskers, short and round face, average build and height. Was this Dick Liddil?

4. A tall sorrel, stolen from a man named Matthews, most noticeable of all, blaze face, light mane and tail, white hind feet, sixteen hands high (Clarence Hite's horse). Rider was tall, slender, light-complexioned, about twenty years old, front teeth bold and prominent, fuzzy whiskers. Was this Clarence Hite?

5. A light little bay mare, stolen by Frank James and Liddil in Ray County, shod by blacksmith Potts at Liberty, and identified while in possession of Sheriff Timberlake. Rider described as slender man of thirty-five to forty, light-complexioned, with light burnsides whiskers, intelligent, good talker, neat in dress. Talked about Ingersoll and quoted Shakespeare. Was this Frank James?

The first news of the robbery led to the impression that of course the James boys had been in on this last outrage. The whole affair bore their private trademark. Further evidence provided no other reasonable conclusion.

Marcus A. Lowe, attorney for the railroad, and Sheriff Brown Crosby of Daviess County declared unhesitatingly they had every reason to believe members of the band had been Frank and Jesse James, Polk Wells, Jim Cummins, Allen Parmer, brother-in-law of the James boys, Jim or Ed Miller, a brother of Clell who had been killed at Northfield, and John Samuel, step-brother of the Jameses. Subsequent events, however, tended to show that at least the Jameses, Dick Liddil, and the Hite brothers had been part of the bunch.

William Pinkerton, from his office in Chicago, had this to say:

"The work undoubtedly was done by Jesse and Frank James, who are the only survivors of the James and Younger gang, the remainder being dead or in the penitentiary. Jesse James lives in Clay County, Missouri, and he can gather a party to rob a train in Clay County in about two days' time. He has a thorough knowledge of the country, and if need be will be secreted by the citizens for months so as to avoid arrest."

The voluminous testimony of those who were on board the Rock Island that July night makes it possible to give a more detailed and accurate account of that robbery than of any of the previous raids.

Mr. Frederick Henkel of Chicago had this to say:

"I think it was about twenty minutes past nine o'clock. I had just had my supper, and was enjoying a cigar in the smoking car. I think that the station is Princeton, Mo., where we had our supper, somewhere between Cameron and Winston stations. About the time we arrived there we noticed a crowd of rather hard-looking characters about the station. They were together in groups of twos and threes. When we were through supper they yelled 'All aboard.' The first we knew the train was flying along at a rapid rate, and a man, very large, thick, heavy-set, with a black beard, short but thick, came in, followed by a couple of others. He was dressed, as far as I could notice, in a linen coat and a straw hat, and the other parts of his clothing I don't recollect. The trio came in by way of the front platform of the smoking car, and one of them, the man with the black beard, had a revolver cocked, in his hand. He muttered something and commenced to fire at the conductor. He ran out, and the others crowded up to him."

"Which way did the conductor run?" Henkel was asked.

"He ran toward the rear platform out of the door, where I

heard more shooting. We all ran back to the sleeping cars where we belonged and threw ourselves on the floor. I only saw the gang at the station while they were in knots, and I should suppose that there was at least a dozen of them. I should think that there were four of them who came into the smoking car. After the trouble was over we found the conductor's lantern and his brains on the rear platform."

"Was the train stopped?"

"No, we were on a stop when the bandits got on. The robbers held possession of the train. Three of the gang jumped on the engine, and with cocked revolvers compelled the engineer and fireman to submit. They couldn't do anything else. They were armed, but they couldn't get a chance to use their guns. In the excitement they crept away from their captors and put out the headlight. They also put on the airbrakes so that the speed was slackened. At Winston, to which they ran the train, one of the brakemen jumped off and telegraphed the death of the conductor and the stonemason, McMillan. The jig was up then, and the robbers ran away.

"As soon as the train was in possession of the robbers, the passengers jumped down on the floor. Some of them hid under the seats. You see, it was unhealthy to be upon your feet at that time. It rained lead. There were six ladies in the sleeper, and as soon as they heard the shooting they just dropped on the floor like the other passengers. They were frightened but they showed as much grit as the men. We couldn't show much, for not one of us had a revolver. John McMillan was killed with the conductor. I think that the thieves recognized them and they were put out of the way on that account.

"I think that the express messenger, C. H. Murray, deserves a deal of credit for his pluck. The robbers shouted to him to open the door of his car and pulled him out. They struck him twice over the head with a revolver, but said they would not kill him because of his grit. The robbers only got $900 in money and a $1,000 bond. There was a large amount of bullion in the safe, but it was too heavy for the robbers to carry away. The passengers all endeavored to hide their watches and money. One of them, a Chicago drummer, put his valuables in the water cooler. I wrapped mine in a pocket handkerchief, lifted the cover of a spittoon, laid it in, and put the lid on again. But the passengers were not molested. We found five bullets in the smoker and thirteen in the baggage car."

Another eye-witness, Major Anthony, reported it this way: "I boarded the train at Atchison. When we stopped at Cameron, Mo. (a point eleven miles southwest of Winston), where we had supper, two men got on and took seats in the sleeping car, and soon engaged in an altercation with the conductor on the subject of fare. About eleven miles this side of Cameron (Winston), several more passengers got in, and the conductor made the remark that he was afraid there was going to be trouble. There was something in the manner of the man who made a fuss about the fare, he said, which made him think that mischief was brewing. We had not gone three-quarters of a mile after we left this stopping place when the trouble began. Someone stepped from the platform in front of the smoking car and laid his hand on Conductor Westfall's shoulder, as he was standing in the front part of the car, and said to him, 'You are my prisoner.' The conductor dodged down and ran further into the car. At this time there were already three armed men in the car, and when the one who had spoken to the conductor followed him in there were four. As he did so this one fired at the conductor twice, the first time with the revolver which he held in his right hand. The ball struck the right sleeve of the conductor's coat, tearing it from a little above the wrist to past the elbow, where it entered the arm. The man fired the other revolver, and the conductor turned to leave the car, and when he reached the platform someone else must have shot him in the back, inflicting a wound from which he died in about twenty minutes.

"About the time this happened, the fireman, seeing that something was wrong, said to the engineer, 'Give her hell,' a laconic way of telling him to get up all the speed he could. The engineer started to do so, but at the same moment three men arose from among the coals in the tender and began firing. They did not hit either the engineer or the fireman with their bullets, but one of them struck the fireman on the side of the head with a large chunk of coal. They then left the engine cab and climbed around and took seats on the cow-catcher, while the three robbers to whom they had entrusted the job of capturing the engine took possession of it. But as they did this the gang who had the securing of the express car on their hands attacked it.

"They obtained admission and threatened to kill the messenger, Charley Murray, a slight and lightly built man, weighing perhaps 120 pounds, if he did not give up the keys. He did as they requested and they opened the safe, which was found to contain $900 in money, a $1,000 bond, and a quantity of silver bullion. They were intensely chagrined when they found that the safe contained so little, and asked, 'Where is the rest of the money, damn you?' Murray announced that that was all he had under his charge. They insisted that he must produce more, to which Murray answered, 'You can't draw blood from a turnip.'

"The leader of the seven men engaged in the express safe robbery said savagely, 'Well, damn you, I'll draw blood from you then,' at the same time striking him a blow on the head with his revolver, which laid Murray out senseless.

"I have no doubt that the gang fully intended to go through the whole train. The first man who entered the smoking car and who fired the first shots at the conductor, cried out, 'Hands up' as he advanced. The others seemed taken back at the large number of people they found in the car, and looked from one another and hesitated. The one who had entered the car looked around him after he had shot a couple of times, and seemed to be surprised that he was alone, and then backed out of the car, waving his revolver as he did so to keep the passengers from rising upon him."

"The passengers were considerably scared, weren't they?"

"Yes. I've been in one or two tight places before, and did not feel particularly scared. I was in the sleeper, and I called for every man in the car to get his weapons and prepare to do his duty. Not a soul, however, had one in the car. Then the fun began. It was amusing to see the fellows going down for their watches, and money, and other valuables, and hunting for places to hide them in. One man, who seemed in an agony of despair, called out, 'They can have all the money I own,' at the same time diving under a seat. All sorts of places were utilized as hiding-places for money, etc. Men pulled off their boots and shoved their wads or watches into them. Spittoons were utilized for the same purpose. I popped my money into the pillow, a pretty safe place, I think. The men on the car were terribly frightened, much more so than the women. The idea prevailed that the robbers were shooting through the windows at the passengers, and as many as could find snug refuge under a seat stowed themselves there, and remained there until long after the firing was over. On the other hand, not a woman seemed to be a particle excited. It was wonderful how coolly they took it. They now and then asked for an explanation of what was going on, and for pretty definite information as to when the affair was likely to end; but when, naturally enough, they found their curiosity could not be satisfied, they remained calmly in their seats and awaited future developments.

"There was one great danger which we escaped, as it were, by a miracle. When the car stopped, it did so not two hundred yards in front of a high trestle. When the robbers had command of the locomotive they urged the train along at a tremendous rate of speed. Had this speed been kept up while the train was running along the trestle, it would, so railroad men tell me, have jumped the track to a dead certainty, and have become a total wreck, with a great destruction of life. The brakeman, Cole, however, by his opportune opening of the airbrake, slacked the train up and averted the calamity.

"A great deal has been said concerning this last outrage. The newspapers have made a special point of writing in an amusing vein of the timidity of the passengers, who could be so completely overawed by seven men. Courage in an editorial sanctum is one thing, and courage in front of a loaded Smith & Wesson revolver is another."

Strangely enough, at the time of the Winston robbery, there was not one dollar outstanding in reward money for the James boys or members of their band. During Governor Hardin's administration nearly all the rewards offered by the state were withdrawn, then the private corporations withdrew the incentives they had advertised, after which Governor Phelps wiped out the few offers remaining.

On the July 26, Governor Crittenden met with representatives of the leading railroads at the Southern Hotel in St. Louis. The governor, realizing he was unable to offer a reward large enough to entice men to capture the Jameses, asked the railroad officials to provide the needed assistance. After a four-hour session, it was agreed that the railroads would furnish $55,000 reward for the capture of the seven train robbers, or $5,000 for the arrest and conviction of each member of the gang. The proclamation further stated an additional reward of $5,000 would be paid for each of the James boys, and a further reward of $5,000 each for their conviction.

A diligent search was made. However, not a dollar of the stolen money was recovered, nor any of the robbers caught.

Many people shook their heads in disgust and amazement, muttering that the bandits were still on the loose and that probably more would be heard from them later.

CHAPTER 18

Jesse James'
Last Train Robbery

WHEN CONDUCTOR HAZELBAKER LEFT CHICAGO ON Tuesday morning, September 6, 1881, he little dreamed that in a few short hours his train would be the object of a daring robbery. The train of the Chicago & Alton Road reached St. Louis, where a brief stay-over was effected, and about nine o'clock on the evening of September 7 the train was in the region of Glendale, Missouri, the scene of a recent holdup. Many people on the train were discussing that robbery when suddenly the train was brought to a halt in a deep ravine called Blue Cut, a spot where the Missouri-Pacific line crossed the track of the Chicago & Alton line. The people glanced at each other, wondering what was wrong. Another holdup? Surely not so soon on the heels of the other!

Quickly the cars were boarded by twelve masked men. Engineer L. Foote was first accosted and ordered down from his engine. He and the fireman, John Steading, obeyed in the face of the pointed revolvers. The express messenger, Fox, scented danger the moment the train had stopped and had jumped from his car and hid in the weeds. The leader of the robbers wore a white cloth with eyeholes over his face. He yelled that he would kill Foote and Steading on the spot if Fox did not show up with the vault key. Fearing that the bandits would carry out their threat, Fox came back and at once was knocked unconscious. The leader seemed particularly annoyed when he found only about $2,500 in the safe.

Just prior to the bandits' boarding the train cars, Conductor Hazelbaker and the brakeman, Burton, advised the passengers of what was happening, and many of them had time to hide some of their possessions. It was a brave act on the part of these two men; a braver one when they dared the bandits' guns and walked back along the track to flag down an approaching freight train. Had it been allowed to crash into the passenger train, a number of lives might have been lost. Perhaps Hazelbaker's own story might prove more graphic.

"When I reached the sleeper I told Burton, my brakeman, to flag down the train following. I knew there was a freight train after me, and it would wreck my train, and I knew that that train must be stopped. Burton said he did not like to go but the brave fellow went just the same. We dropped off together, and they began to fire at us. Shots whistled all around us. I think there were probably twenty shots fired at us altogether. We finally succeeded in flagging down the freight train just in time, and I went back and, climbing aboard the sleeper, took a back seat and waited quietly to be robbed."

Hazelbaker further stated that the gang swore a great deal and seemed to center their rage on him. The leader, who said he was Jesse James, put a pistol under the nose of the conductor and said, "Damn you, smell of that. That's the pistol I shot Westfall with at Winston!" The outlaw went on to say, "Now, listen, all you dogs; the next reward that is offered we'll burn your damned train, and don't forget it. We will cut the Pullman loose and save it because Pullman is white, and never offered a reward like you damned railroads and the no-good governor of Missouri, but we'll make a bonfire of your train as sure as you live."

The leader seemed incensed by the fact that recent high rewards had been offered for the arrest or death of the James band.

When Hazelbaker was asked what he thought of their attitude, he replied, "From their talk it appeared that the robbery was a piece of dare-deviltry in revenge for the Winston reward being offered. They constantly shoved pistols under my nose and reminded me of Westfall's fate. After they left we pulled out, and as quick as we could."

"How many were there?" he was asked.

"There were six in the sleeper and four or five outside."

"Did they expose themselves?"

"Not at all. I could see their forms, but absolutely nothing of their features. The leader, supposed to be Jesse James, had on a white muslin cloth with holes cut in it around his head, as if he had made a mask of a handkerchief. The others wore masks of dirty cloth or calico. They were all slender men except the apparent leader, who was taller and well-built."

"Could you identify any of them?"

"No, and there lies the trouble."

"How much money do you suppose they took?"

"I could not tell. They took from each passenger between $1.00 and $300.00, and maybe got a couple thousand. I don't know how much was in the express car."

Apparently the robbers obtained about $2,500 from the express car and $3,000 or $4,000 in money and jewelry from the passengers.

Fox had this to say: "When they robbed the safe of everything, I ran back into the smoking car and hid most of my money. The robbers came in and ordered me, with an oath, to lie down. I did so, and they shoved a gun up to my head and told me to fork over. I said my money was under the cushion. They told me to get it, and I got it in a hurry, you bet. It was somewhere in the neighborhood of fifteen dollars."

Several women fainted during the robbing of the passengers, but the bandits threw water in their faces and told them to hand over their money.

Engineer Foote gave some interesting testimony of the affair which should not be overlooked.

Between three and four miles east of Independence is a deep cut, over which the Missouri-Pacific track crosses the Chicago & Alton, and it was just before entering the deepest part of this cut that I saw a pile of stones, probably five feet high, on the top of which was a stick, to which was attached a red rag, and behind the whole stood the leader of the robbers. Of course I stopped. I was then approached by four of the gang, besides the leader, who said, "Step down off that engine, and do as I tell you, or I will kill you." He then told me to get the coal pick, which I did, after some parleying, but as a revolver was pointed at my head I could not refuse to obey.

Then they marched myself and John Steading, the fireman, to the express car, and ordered me to break the door down, which I did. Messenger Fox had hidden in the weeds by the roadside, but they swore they would kill me if he didn't come out, and so I called for him and he entered the car with two of the robbers, who forced him to open the safe and pour the contents into a sack.

They seemed disappointed in not getting more booty, and knocked Fox down twice with the butt of a Navy revolver, cutting his head in a fearful manner. They then marched us to the coaches, where they kept us covered with revolvers while they robbed the passengers. After the last car was gone through they marched us back to the engine, when the leader said, "Now get back there, we will remove the stones. You have been a bully boy and here is a little present for you," and he handed me two silver dollars. I told them that I would remove the obstructions, and the entire gang skipped over the embankment, and were out of sight in a twinkling.

In going through the passengers, each one was made to hold up his hands, and what was taken from them was put into a two-bushel sack, which was nearly full of watches, money, and other valuables. They didn't take anything from me.

The leader told me to take the $2 and drink to Jesse James or I would be killed. He also warned me to quit this road or I would be killed, and they were out to destroy the Alton & Rock Island roads.

Some accounts state that Fox was killed; however, he was not. Others claim that Whiskeyhead Ryan was a member of the band that night, but this would have been impossible. At the time of this holdup, Ryan was serving time in the Missouri State Penitentiary for his complicity in the Glendale train robbery of 1879, after being arrested in Tennessee.

Descriptions of the bandits fit Jesse and Frank James both. It is believed that this was the first robbery in which Frank participated since 1877. Mrs. Samuel, the mother of the James boys, said that it could not have been Jesse James, for he had been shot by George Shepherd. This was supposedly true, but the wound was not fatal, and Jesse recovered. However, subsequent events prove that the shooting was all a put-up affair and that Jesse had not been shot at all. Also, no sign of a head wound was visible on the corpse of Jesse James after he had been killed. This is such a puzzle, and so many questions need be answered, that it is best to leave the decision to the reader.

Matt Chapman, first to be arrested in connection with the Blue Cut robbery, stated that Jesse and Frank were there. Later, Dick Liddil, also a member of the gang, after surrendering with a promise of pardon, stated that both the James boys were there, together with Jim Cummins, Wood Hite, Clarence Hite, and Charley Ford. Several others of the band were Andy Ryan, Ed Miller, and Matt Chapman.

On March 27, 1882, John Bugler, one of the Cracker Neck region citizens involved in the Blue Cut robbery, was arraigned at Independence, Missouri. In the meanwhile, John Land, who also was under indictment in the same case, made a full confession, and implicated the James boys, Jim Cummins, Dick Liddil, and others as stated.

Land stated that at least ten days before the robbery he had been interviewed by Creed Chapman and John Bugler, who told him that Jesse James and Jim Cummins had put up a job to rob the Chicago & Alton Express train at Blue Cut, and they invited him to take a part. He refused at first, but gave in. He then fled to Clay County, advising the Cracker Neck boys to go about their business and assist the officers in the search, promising to make an equal division of the money and at some convenient time return and pay each party his respective share. This part of the program was never received any part of the money. Land, Bugler, and Chapman were arrested three days after the robbery, but there was insufficient evidence to convict them of their part in the crime, in spite of their confessions.

The Blue Cut train robbery was the last spectacular assignment the James brothers undertook. The division of any haul, as far as is known, was made fairly and promptly, and complaints on that score were not heard from the ever-changing membership of the band. After the Blue Cut robbery, however, harsh words were exchanged between several members of the gang, and this led to the killing of Wood Hite by Bob Ford, who had complained about the division of the spoils. Wood Hite, a cousin of Jesse, was buried in a shallow grave; Jesse never learned of his death. This matter, coupled with the promise of amnesty and the reward money, prompted Ford to murder Jesse James in St. Joseph, Missouri, on April 3, 1882, a bright and warm Monday morning.

CHAPTER 19

What Brought About
Jesse James' Death

ONE OFTEN WONDERS IF ONLY THE REWARD MONEY tempted the Ford brothers to kill Jesse James. Many new incidents have been discovered which might have influenced them. Several of these had their origin at the George Hite mansion in Logan County, Kentucky.

Hite was an uncle of Frank and Jesse James, and his son, Wood Hite, was Jesse's favorite cousin, as well as a later member of his outlaw band. George, against the wishes of the family, had married the pretty widow Peck at Adairville, Kentucky, a circumstance which led to many of the family members leaving the house. But by 1882, the second Mrs. Hite had left her husband, and shortly after Jesse's death, she and George were divorced.

Many claimed that she was in love with Jesse James, and that his liaison with her was the cause of disaffection among the Hites, the Jameses, and other members of the band. However, others said it was Dick Liddil who carried on an secret love affair with Mrs. Hite and that this led to the murder of a colored man named John Tabor.

Tabor, a servant at the Hite place, carried notes to Mrs. Hite's secret lover, and one day Wood Hite caught him and killed him. Wood's stepmother hated him and swore out a warrant accusing him of Tabor's murder. He was taken to Adairville by Marshal Jeter, but escaped easily from the store-jail by means of a hundred-dollar bribe. The guard just seemed to have vanished.

Another incident occurred on the Hite property between Wood and Dick Liddil which brought about further enmity in the group. In the great barn, which stood several hundred feet from the house, Wood had accused of Liddil of stealing from him and Jesse. Liddil denied the charge, with Hite suggesting that they shoot it out.

Strapping on their pistols, they walked alone to the barn to do so. Each man's stand was selected and no firing was to occur until each had reached his station. However, Liddil fired prematurely and missed. Hite immediately put a tree between himself and the would-be assassin. Liddil did the same, firing until his weapon was empty. When Liddil retreated toward the house, Wood began his firing. Neither man was hit in the cowardly escapade, and the matter was smoothed over by family members.

Some months before, Jesse and a man named Miller had had a disagreement at the Hite residence and agreed to fight a duel in a thickly wooded section across the Tennessee line. Several hours later Jesse returned alone. Miller never was heard from again. No one dared question Jesse about it, and the secret died with him in 1882.

The Liddil-Hite incident in Kentucky led to the Hite's death in Missouri and created an incident which caused the Fords to further fear the wrath of Jesse James. In October of 1879, the Chicago & Alton train had been robbed at Glendale, Missouri.

This was Wood Hite's first appearance as an outlaw. Here the robber band consisted of Jesse and Frank James, Wood Hite (alias Robert Gregg), Tucker Bassham, Bill Ryan, Ed Miller, and Dick Liddil, and several others.

In September of 1881, a train was robbed at Blue Cut, Missouri, with Clarence and Wood Hite both being in the James band, as well as Dick Liddil, Jim Cummins, and a few others. On December 4, Wood rode into the yard of the Ford home in Ray County, Missouri. Martha, a sister of Charley Ford, was cooking breakfast in the lean-to kitchen. Wood asked if any of the gang were in the house, telling Martha that he was suspicious of Liddil regarding the division of the Blue Cut robbery money. She replied that Liddil and Bob and Charley Ford were still asleep upstairs. At the news that Dick Liddil was in the house, Wood exploded into profanity. He informed Martha that Dick had a lot of gall to hang around the gang after stealing money from the Blue Cut loot bag before the proceeds could be divided. Besides the outcome of the duel which Wood still brooded over, both he and Liddil were supposedly in love with Martha (Ford) Bolton's fourteen-year-old daughter.

Martha tried to act as peacemaker, but hotheaded Wood Hite was not to be placated. He stamped upstairs into the bedroom where the two Ford boys and Dick Liddil were sleeping. During an angry exchange of words, Wood said to Liddil, "You've got one hell of a nerve speaking to me at all after the damn lies you've been telling!"

That set off the shooting. Hite fired and wounded Liddil in the hip. Liddil returned the fire, the bullet entering Hite's left shoulder. By this time Charley Ford had leaped from a window into the snow and sprained his hip. When the fight was over, Wood was dead, shot through the head. Who had fired the fatal shot, Liddil or Bob Ford?

About two weeks later a group of detectives raided the Hite residence in Kentucky and arrested Clarence Hite for his participation in the Blue Cut robbery. Found guilty, he was sentenced to twenty-five years in the Missouri State Penitentiary. This planted the seed of fear in the hearts of the Ford brothers. They feared the consequences should Jesse believe they had killed Wood Hite. Some people claimed that Jesse never learned of his cousin's death, others stated he did, and that was the reason Liddil turned himself over to the law for protective custody. At any rate, these circumstances led to the early death of the noted outlaw. Liddil took the road he thought best, for he knew his connection with the gang was forever severed with the death of Wood.

Bob Ford feared Jesse for he was not a member of the band. In fact, during 1881 Bob Ford had gone to Kansas City and worked for a detective agency there. Having known the Jameses, Ed Miller, and Dick Liddil, he was hired to track them down. Bob Ford was the one who opened negotiations for the surrender of Dick Liddil to the authorities several weeks after Hite's death.

On February 22, 1882, he had a secret interview with Governor T. T. Crittenden at the St. James Hotel in Kansas City, to formulate plans to capture Jesse James. After Liddil surrendered to Sheriff Timberlake of Clay County, Missouri, he was taken to Kansas City, where he and Bob Ford worked secretly with the officials.

Another incident occurred to strengthen the Fords' hatred and fear of Jesse James. Jim Cummins, often linked with the outlaw band, knew many details of its operation. When Jim got too talkative, Jesse chased him into Arkansas, intent on killing him. This was before Dick Liddil's surrender, and he was Jesse's riding partner at the time.

Jim dodged, however, and backtracked into Missouri, stopping at the home of Bill Ford for several days. One day, for some reason he began to fear that Jesse was close by, so he saddled his horse and rode away. His hunch proved correct, for he had just ridden off when Jesse and Liddil rounded a bend leading to the Ford house. Bill Ford was not at home, but his wife and fourteen-year-old son, Albert, were there. The boy was Cummins's nephew, for Jim's sister, Artella, had married Bill Ford. Jesse inquired about Jim but was told that he had not been there for some time.

Dissatisfied with their story, Jesse and Dick took Albert into the woods and tried to force the truth from him. They were unsuccessful, however, and before Jesse could again catch up with Cummins, that fatal day in St. Joe arrived. This was another reason for the Fords' willingness to destroy Jesse, revenge for the torture of their nephew. The best reason of all of course was the promise of the reward money.

Sheriff Timberlake placed great faith in Bob Ford's willingness to do away with Jesse James. He knew that Bob and Charley both had been with Jesse on several occasions and guessed that Bob was secretly awaiting his chances all along. Apparently Charley knew nothing of the plans until the day of the actual shooting.

On the night of April 1, 1882, Jesse James rode up to the home of Captain Ford in Ray County and called Bob Ford outside. He told him he had work for him to do, and the two rode off. The next day Captain Ford notified Sheriff Timberlake that Bob had gone to St. Joseph with Jesse James, and the sheriff held a posse in readiness to march, with Liddil to act as leader of the sheriff's men.

Jesse told Bob that he planned to rob the Platte City Bank. Upon reaching the suburbs of St. Joe, Jesse became suspicious of Bob Ford for some reason and never allowed him out of his sight for even a moment. He had Ford sleep in the same room with him and even followed him when he went to the barn. Charley Ford also was present, as Jesse had said it would take three men to pull the job.

The outlaw paid no attention to Charley, but kept a careful

watch on Bob so that the latter was unable to communicate with Sheriff Timberlake. Each morning before breakfast Jesse would take Bob with him downtown to get the morning papers. Of course, Bob was ill at ease, for even though the news of Liddil's surrender so far had been kept out of the papers, the sheriff had informed Ford that some of the reporters knew something was afoot and headlines might appear at any moment. In fact, Jesse had questioned Bob about Liddil but had been told that no news had been heard of him for some time.

Ford made it his business to scan the papers as quickly as possible for he well knew what it meant to have Jesse learn of Liddil's surrender. On April 3, Bob and Jesse went downtown for the papers, as usual. It was planned for the outlaws to leave St. Joe that evening for Platte City. The two returned to the James home at Thirteenth and Lafayette Streets about eight o'clock and sat down to examine the papers. Jesse sat in front of Ford, reading the St. Louis *Republican.* Ford hastily scanned the Kansas City *Journal* and saw nothing there, but the headlines of the Kansas City *Times* told of Dick Liddil's surrender.

Unseen by Jesse, Ford placed the paper under a shawl on the chair, but on his way to the kitchen for breakfast, Jesse picked up the shawl and threw it on the bed, and, taking the paper, walked into the other room.

Mrs. James poured coffee and then sat down at one end of the table. Charley was at the other end and the two children sat one on each side of their mother. Jesse spread the paper on the table in front of him and began to read the headlines. We can well imagine Bob Ford's feeling at that time. He later stated that he saw in Jesse's eyes a glare that he had never seen there before.

"Hello. What have we here? The surrender of Dick Liddil."

"That's news to me," gulped Bob Ford.

"Very fishy, if you ask me," said James. "You right here in the vicinity these three weeks and you knew nothing of it? I wonder why they kept it secret so long. I've got an idea."

Bob Ford could stand no more. He pushed back his chair, arose and walked into the front room.

A few moments later Jesse appeared in the room and said with a smile, "Well, Bob, it's all right, anyhow."

Bob Ford knew that he had not fooled the cunning bandit. He knew that plans were being made to waylay him as they rode toward Platte City that very evening. Ford could tell that Jesse was now aware that he was there to betray him. The only reason he was not already dead was that apparently the outlaw did not wish to kill Ford in the presence of his wife and children.

Jesse also appeared willing to risk a test of Bob, for he deliberately unbuckled his belt with its weapon and threw it on the bed. The revolver in the holster was a .45 caliber Smith & Wesson Schofield model, but he also removed a pocket revolver, which was a .45 caliber 2¼-inch barrel derringer type, and also placed that on the bed. Jesse's supposing that Ford would not kill him in his own house was a fatal miscalculation.

The outlaw then busied himself to impress on Ford's mind that he had forgotten the breakfast table incident.

He picked up a feather duster, remarking, "That picture is awful dusty."

Ford later stated there wasn't a spot of dust on the picture, but that Jesse placed a chair beneath it and then got upon it and started to dust the framed motto. Ford stated that up to that time the thought of killing Jesse had never occurred to him, but as the outlaw stood there with his back to him and unarmed, he decided it was now or never.

Without hesitation Bob drew his Smith & Wesson and sent a slug crashing through Jesse's head. This nickel-plated revolver, Serial No. 3766, Model No. 3, was the same weapon Jesse had given Bob as a present some days before. At the sound of the shot Charley Ford ran into the room and right behind him was Mrs. James.

Bob Ford asked a passerby to notify the police that Jesse James had been killed, and in a little while Marshal Craig came to the house and placed them under arrest. At ten o'clock that morning telegrams were sent to Sheriff James R. Timberlake, of Clay County; H. H. Craig, Police Commissioner of Kansas City; and to the executive mansion at Jefferson City, which read, "I have killed Jesse James." They were all signed, "Bob Ford, St. Joseph."

Another version of the killing of James was given in later years by Joe McKee, Bob Ford's bartender at Jimtown, Colorado. In substance his story agrees quite a bit with what has been stated, although no mention was made that Ford was working with the law officers.

If McKee's story is true, then not much credit was given to Bob Ford for ridding Missouri of Jesse. It was well known that no one could have taken the outlaw face to face. No one, of course, condones a cowardly act, but according to McKee's version, Bob Ford was far from being the coward he is supposed to be. This is McKee's story:

It was well known that anyone who incurred Jesse's displeasure went for a ride, and young Bob Ford was not unaware of that term. Jesse and the Fords were not related in any manner as some writers have stated. Bob remained around the St. Joe residence for a few days, posing as a Mr. Johnson, a cousin of Mr. Howard.

It was Bob Ford's duty to go downtown to get Jesse's mail and newspapers, as the outlaw wished to remain completely out of sight. There were no mail deliveries in those days and everyone had to go to the post office to pick up his mail. All papers and mail were received under the name of Thomas Howard. He sent for young Ford to take care of this chore.

There were no secrets between them concerning the reason for Jesse's being holed up, and so all went well. Ford never opened the brown wrapping around the newspapers, so he seldom knew the headlines. Jesse was very jittery around that time, knowing that it was but a matter of time until he would be all through and done. On this particular day when Ford delivered the Kansas City papers, headlines in bold type stated that the Ford brothers were in a deal to capture Jesse, and when Jesse read that, he started to act like a crazy person.

He told Ford that he had received bad news and that they would have to ride out that very night. Ford, being no fool, suspected what that meant, and hoped to beat Jesse to the draw. Jesse usually took his guns off only when going to bed, but in order to throw Ford off, he removed his guns to get upon a chair to dust or straighten a motto picture.

Now the seat of an ordinary chair is but eighteen inches from the floor and in this case there was no need to remove his guns. There was hardly any reason to get upon a chair at all. Any size man could reach such a picture while standing on the floor. Jesse was an ordinary sized man and he could also have done so.

There the Kid, as Jesse called him, took full advantage of the situation and let Jesse have it in the head, killing him instantly.

The reward money was an afterthought, according to McKee, who said Bob gave him this story and swore it was true. In fact, the Fords saw very little of the reward. Ford also told McKee that he never intended to kill Jesse until the outlaw spoke of "going for a ride." The Kid knew what that meant. Yes, the story sounds most logical.

At ten o'clock, the morning of Jesse's death, Assistant Coroner James W. Heddens, M.D., was notified, and Undertaker Sidenfaden was instructed to remove the body to his establishment. (The regular coroner was in Jefferson City on business that morning.) While the body lay in a remote room of the building various comparisons were made by reporters to determine the dead man's identity.

An inspection of the body revealed two large bullet wounds on the right side of the breast within three inches of the nipple, a bullet wound in the leg and the absence of the tip of the middle finger of the left hand. (Jesse lost the first joint of this finger when he was a boy. He was playing with a pistol when it discharged and tore off the first joint.) The lung wounds were received during the Civil War, one at the fight at Flat Rock Ford, August 13, 1864, and the other at Lexington, Missouri, May 15, 1865, when he was shot by Pvt. John L. Jones, 3rd Wisconsin Cavalry, while trying to surrender. The leg wound was the result of a Federal ambush shortly after the Battle of Centralia.

There were three other distinct marks of identification which have never been mentioned before, but were seen on the corpse by those who knew where to look. Jesse had a severe case of granulated eyelids which never completely healed and which caused his eyes never to be at rest. As a young boy, he had an abscess in his right groin; it was lanced in 1862 by the Sallee physician, Dr. Glen E. Bishop, at St. Joe. This left an identifying scar.

The other prominent disfigurement was the result of getting his left foot caught in the stirrup of his saddle shortly after the war ended. The inside ankle bone was pushed inward and never healed properly, leaving a deep impression there instead of the bones' normal position. Was this the injury sustained by the bank robber at Gallatin, Missouri, when his horse threw him and dragged him by his left foot?

Inquest records show that the gun used by Bob Ford was a Smith & Wesson and not a Colt as generally believed. Charley Ford said, "Bob had a Smith & Wesson, and it was easier for him to get it out of his pocket."

Bob Ford admitted, in part, "I could see that it was all over with Jesse when that Smith .44 slug tore through his head."

It is not my intention to give a complete résumé of the coroner's inquest and the testimony given by various persons, as most of this is familiar. After the inquest, however, the two Ford boys were at once committed to jail charged with murder, under a warrant sworn out by Mrs. Jesse James. They pleaded guilty to the killing and, on April 17, 1882, were sentenced to be hanged on May 19, and to be held in the Buchanan County jail until that time.

On the same day, Governor Crittenden issued unconditional pardons to Charles and Robert Ford. But their fame, if such it was, was short-lived, for Charley committed suicide at Richmond, Missouri, just two years later, and Bob Ford was shot to death by Edward O'Kelley, in the Creede, Colorado, mining area in 1892.

The body of Jesse James was given to his widow for interment, and, in accordance with the wishes of his mother, it was arranged for the outlaw to be buried at the old homestead at Kearney. Frank James arrived in St. Joe on Tuesday morning following the shooting, and registered at the World's Hotel. Wednesday morning Frank left St. Joe and went to the homestead at Kearney. He remained there during the last rites. If anyone knew of his presence there, nothing was ever said.

At 4:30 P.M. on the sixth, the funeral cortege arrived at the James-Samuel homestead, where the casket was lowered into the grave. Mrs. Samuel screamed that someone had cut off Jesse's right hand. She made them bring the casket back up and open it. After that, she calmed down, and Jesse was buried.

The fabulous Jesse James had been feared and hated as a robber and a killer, yet to some he came to be revered as an American Robin Hood. Perhaps this is partly due to his devotion to his mother and to the persecution heaped on his family and friends. At any rate, he has gone into folklore as a hero, and his memory is kept alive by the famed murals painted by Thomas Hart Benton for the State Capitol at Jefferson City.

The popular folk song mentioning Jesse has perpetuated this image. As long as the ballads are sung they will continue to denounce Ford as a "dirty little coward" for firing the shot which killed Jesse, not taking time to listen to Bob's side of the story, and caring even less about such an explanation. Most people were overwhelmed by the outlaw's death and the way he died. They continue to consider him a martyr and Ford a yellow-livered coward.

N. Alvarez, *James Boys in Missouri.* Ames Publishing Co., 1906.

Augustus Appler, *Guerrillas of the West.* John Appler, Publisher, St. Louis, 1875.

R. T. Bradley, *Outlaws of the Border.* J. W. Marsh Co., St. Louis, Mo., 1880.

Carl W. Breihan, *The Complete & Authentic Life of Jesse James.* Federick Fell Publishers, Inc., New York N.Y., 1953–1970.

Carl W. Breihan, *The Day Jesse James Was Killed.* Frederick Fell Publishers, Inc., New York, N.Y., 1961.

Carl W. Breihan, *Younger Brothers.* Naylor Co., San Antonio, Texas, 1961.

W. C. Bronaugh, *Youngers' Fight for Freedom.* Stephens Printing Co., Columbia, Mo., 1906.

James W. Buell, *Border Outlaws.* St. Louis Historical Publishing Co., 1881.

James W. Buell, *James and Youngers*. I. & O. Ottenheimer, Baltimore, Md.

John Callison, *Bill Jones of Paradise Valley*, M. A. Donahue Co., Chicago, 1914.

David J. Cook, *Hands Up*. Republican Print, Denver, 1882.

Courtney Riley Cooper, *High Country*. Little, Brown, Boston, 1926.

Henry Huston Crittenden, *Crittenden Memoirs*. G. P. Putnam's Sons, New York, 1936.

Homer Croy, *Jesse James Was My Neighbor*. Duell, Sloane & Pierce, New York, 1949.

Jim Cummins, *Jim Cummins' Book*. Reed Publishing Co., Denver, 1903.

Jos. A. Dacus, *Life & Adventures of Frank & Jesse James*. Thompson & Co., St. Louis, Mo., 1880 & 1882.

Henry Dale, *Adventures of the Younger Brothers*. Street & Smith, N.Y., 1890.

Emmett Dalton, *When the Daltons Rode*. Doubleday, Doran, Garden City, New York, 1931.

Kit Dalton, *Under the Black Flag*. Lockhart Pub. Co., Memphis, Tenn., 1914.

Joe DeBarth, *Life of Frank Grouard*. Combe Printing Co., St. Joseph, Mo., 1894.

J. H. De Wolf, *Pawnee Bill*. Pawnee Bill's Wild West Co., 1902.

Roy F. Dibble, *Strenous Americans*. Boni & Liveright, New York, 1923.

Jay Donald, *Outlaws of the Border*. Coburn & Newman Printing Co., Chicago, 1882.

Katherine C. Doughitt, *Romance & Dim Trails*. Tardy Publishers, Dallas, Tex., 1938.

Thomas Duke, *Celebrated Criminal Cases*. James Barry Co., San Francisco, 1910.

J. P. Earle, *History of Clay County*. Henrietta, Texas, 1900.

John Newman Edwards, *Noted Guerrillas.* J. W. Marsh Co., St. Louis, Mo. 1880.

Clyde Evans, *Adventures of the Great Crime-Busters.* New Power Pub., New York, 1943.

Charles Finger, *The Distant Prize,* D. Appleton-Century Co., New York, 1935.

Darrell Garwood, *Crossroads of America.* W.W. Norton Co., New York, 1948.

Welche Gordon, *Jesse James and His Band of Outlaws.* Laird, Lee Co., Chicago, 1890.

Alvin Harlow, *Old Waybills, Romance of the Express Companies.* D. Appleton-Century Co., New York, 1934.

Harry B. Hawes, *Frank & Jesse James,* Washington, D.C., pamphlet, 1939.

George D. Hendricks, *Bad Man of the West.* Naylor Co., San Antonio, 1941.

J. L. Hill, *End of the Cattle Trail.* Moyle Pub. Co., Long Beach, Cal.

Stewart Holbrook, *Little Annie Oakley.* The Macmillan Co., New York, 1948.

W. Stanley Hoole, *The James Boys Rode South*, 1955.

James Horan, *Desperate Men.* G. P. Putnam's Sons, New York, 1949.

Freeman Hubbard, *Railroad Avenue.* McGraw-Hill, New York, 1945.

Seth K. Humphrey, *Following the Prairie Frontier.* University of Minnesota Press, Minneapolis, 1931.

George Huntington, *Robber & Hero.* Christian Way Co., Northfield, Minn., 1895.

Jesse Edwards James, *Jesse James, My Father.* Sentinental Printing Co., Independence, Mo., 1899.

Robertus Love, *Rise and Fall of Jesse James.* G. P. Putnam's Sons, New York, 1926.

John McCorkle, *Three Years With Quantrill.* Armstrong Herald Print, Armstrong, Mo.

George Miller, Jr., *Trial of Frank James.* E.W. Stephens Press, Columbus, Mo., 1898.

John D. Mitchell, *Lost Mines of the Southwest.* Journal Co., Phoenix, Ariz., 1933.

Alexander W. Neville, *Red River Valley.* Carl Hertzog, El Paso, Tex., 1948.

Northfield News, Sept. 7, 1876, *Northfield Bank Raid.*

James Bradas O'Neal, *They Die But Once.* Knight Publications, New York, 1935.

William A. Pinkerton, *Train Robberies.* International Association Chiefs of Police, Jamestown, Va., 1907.

Wm. MacLeod Raine, *Guns of the Frontier.* Houghton Mifflin, Boston, 1940.

George Rainey, *No Man's Land.* Cooperative Pub. Co., Guthrie, Okla., 1937.

Clarence E. Ray, *The James Boys.* Regan Publ. Co., Chicago.

Ruth T. Robertson, *Famous Bandits.* Washington, D.C., 1928.

Wm. Ross & Victor Edwin, *Reign of Soapy Smith.* Doubleday, Doran, Garden City, New York, 1935.

Jesse Lewis Russell, *Behind These Ozark Hills.* Hobson Press, New York, 1947.

George Scott, *Such Outlaws as Jesse James.* Gerald Swann, Ltd., London.

Wm. A. Settle, Jr., *Jesse James Was His Name,* 1966, Univ. of Mo. Press.

Dolph Shaner, *The Story of Joplin.* Stratford Press, New York, 1948.

St. Joseph Daily Gazette, St. Joseph, Mo., April 9, 1882.

Floyd B. Small, *Autobiography of a Pioneer.* F. B. Small, Seattle, Wash., 1916.

Leonard J. Street, *Abroad at Home.* Century Co., New York, 1914.

Zack T. Surley, *The Last Frontier.* The Macmillan Co., New York.

Fred E. Sutton, *Hands Up,* Bobbs-Merrill Co., Indianapolis, Ind., 1927.

William Targ, *The Great American West.* World Publishing Co., New York, 1946.

Thaddeus Thorndike, *Lives & Exploits of Frank & Jesse James.* Ottenheimer Pub., Baltimore, 1909.

Frank Triplett, *The Life, Times and Death of Jesse James.* J. H. Chambers Co., St. Louis, Mo., 1882.

Stanley Vestal, *The Missouri.* Farrar & Rinehart, New York, 1945.

Western Baptist Pub. Co., *Speeches & Writings of Wm H. Wallace.* Kansas City, Mo., 1914.

Chicago Posse, *Westerners' Brand Book.* 1946.

Dan Winget, *Anecdotes of Buffalo Bill.* Historical Pub. Co., Chicago, 1933.

W.P.A. Writers' Program, *Missouri, Guide to Show-Me State.* Duell, Sloan & Pearce, New York, 1941.

Cole Younger, *Cole Younger.* The Henneberry Co., Chicago, 1903.

Personal Interviews & Correspondence with the following:

Stella James and Jesse Edwards James (son and daughter-in-law of Jesse James).

Robert F. James and Mae James (son and daughter-in-law of Frank James).

Charles Kemper (former historian of Jackson County, Mo., Historical Society), who knew the Jameses and their families.

Harry Younger Hall (nephew of the Younger Brothers).

Harry Hoffman (personal friend of the James-Younger families).

English Westerners Society.

Pinkerton Detective Agency Records.

Union-Pacific Railroad Records.

Missouri-Pacific Railroad Records.

Wells Fargo Files.

Mary Morrow, daughter of Ben Morrow, ex-guerrilla and pall-bearer for Jesse James.

Kerry Ross Boren Files (historian, Daggett County, Utah).

Numerous contemporary newspapers and files of many historical societies.

William Stigers, whose family was very close to the Jameses, St. Joseph, Mo.